State and Local Government

State and Local Government

2011–2012

Edited by
Kevin B. Smith
University of Nebraska–Lincoln

Amanda Balzer
University of Nebraska–Lincoln

Los Angeles | London | New Delhi
Singapore | Washington DC

CQ Press
2300 N Street, NW, Suite 800
Washington, DC 20037

Phone: 202-729-1900; toll-free, 1-866-4CQ-PRESS (1-866-427-7737)

Web: www.cqpress.com

Cover design: Judy Myers, Graphic Design
Composition: C&M Digitals (P) Ltd.

♾ The paper used in this publication exceeds the requirements of the American National Standard for Information Sciences—Permanence of Paper for Printed Library Materials, ANSI Z39.48-1992.

Printed and bound in the United States of America

15 14 13 12 11   1 2 3 4 5

ISBN: 978-1-60871-834-4
ISSN: 0888-8590

Contents

Preface

State and Local Government takes an annual sounding of the most important political trends and policy challenges facing subnational governments. For the third year in a row, the dominant issue for state and local governments is coping with the fallout from the biggest economic recession since the Great Depression of the 1930s. While the recession officially ended in the middle of 2009, the changes it precipitated continue to drive not just policy choices, but the distribution of power within the entire federal system.

For the past couple of years, states became dependent on the federal government to help balance the books, and with that dependence came a shift in power toward Washington, DC. That is all about to change. Short-term bailout funds are drying up, and the 2010 midterm elections swept in Republican majorities in many state legislatures and governor's offices. Fiscal conservatism is the political order of the day, and states find themselves asking tough questions about the nature and responsibilities of government. Do we cut or eliminate services? Do we consolidate to improve efficiency? Do we raise taxes or find other forms of revenue? Should we stop innovating and freeze new programming? Do we de-prioritize all issues not related to solving the budget crisis? The answers are not clear, but it is certain that all states and localities are asking the same basic questions. As the readings in this volume attest, state and local governments are using this opportunity to take on unionized public employees, cut jobs, and create "do-it-yourself" government, as well as tackling gay marriage and immigration—two issues federal officials have buried beneath the dismal economy. With innovation and policy change being tested in the "natural laboratories" of states and localities, the next several years may be a learning experience for all levels of government.

Following the format of previous editions, this book samples the political and policy landscape of states and localities by drawing on the best writing from a wide variety of published sources. These include publications familiar to long-term readers like *Governing* magazine and *State Legislatures*. Building on the precedent established by recent editions, there are now even more selections drawn from academic publications. Where appropriate, we have edited these (mostly by redacting the technical methods sections) to ensure they remain accessible to as broad an audience as possible.

As always, the readings are all new to the current edition and organized by key institutions, processes, and policy areas. All of the introductions have been updated to reflect the content of the new selections and also to account for the political and policy changes that define the dynamic world of state and local politics.

Putting together this volume requires the efforts of many people, and special thanks are owed to the excellent editorial team at CQ Press: Charisse Kiino, Nancy Loh, Melinda Masson, and Elizabeth Kline. We hope that you find what follows informative and thought-provoking.

Federalism and Intergovernmental Relations

Tough economic times can put a strain on relationships. The relationships between employers and employees, banks and lenders, and businesses and investors were all shaken up by the financial nosedive of the past few years. That goes for government relationships, too. The relationship between government and citizens, for example, has been volatile. In 2008, it was "throw the Republican bums out for getting us in this economic mess"; in 2010, it was "throw the Democratic bums out for failing to get us out." Extremely tight budgets have also reset relationships between governments. Federal, state, and local governments are reassessing their partnerships; driven by severe financial stress, they are shaking off old ways of doing business with each other and evolving a new chapter for federalism.

The readings in this chapter assess the changing nature of those intergovernmental relationships. Some of these changes are win-win; rather than compete with each other in a zero-sum fight to attract economic development, some subnational governments are working together to achieve the greater regional good. Some of these changes are not nearly so team-oriented; they are hardball politics, fights over who gains and who loses power. As we shall see, the federal government's deeper pockets have given it an opportunity to assert its policy preferences over states and localities. States and localities are not always happy with this shift. In some cases, states are so upset they are revisiting constitutional questions about state power that many thought were settled by the Civil War.

THE EVOLUTION OF FEDERALISM

Federalism is the central organizational characteristic of the American political system. In federal systems, national and regional governments share powers and are considered independent equals.[1] In other words, states are independent sovereign governments. They must obey the mandates of the U.S. Constitution, but with that caveat, they are free to do as they wish. State governments primarily get their power from their own citizens in the form of their own state constitutions. At least in theory, they are not dependent on the federal government for power, nor do they have any obligation to obey federal requests that are not mandated by the U.S. Constitution.

In practice, the federal system established by the U.S. Constitution left the federal and state governments to figure out for themselves who had to do what, and who had to foot the bill for doing it.[2] Initially, the federal and state governments tried to keep to themselves, pursuing a doctrine of dual federalism, or the idea that federal and state governments have separate and distinct jurisdictions and responsibilities. Dual federalism fell victim to the need to exert centralized economic and social power to fight two world wars and deal with the Great Depression.

These needs, and the general acknowledgement that the state and federal governments had shared and overlapping interests in a wide range of policy areas, gave rise to what became known as cooperative federalism. The core of cooperative federalism is the idea that both levels of government must work together to address social and economic problems, and the basic division of labor that emerged was for the federal government to identify the problem, establish a basic outline of how to respond to the problem, and then turn over the responsibility of implementation to state and local governments along with some or all of the money to fund the programs.

Cooperative federalism defined and described the basic relationship between state and federal governments for much of the 20th century. Critics of this arrangement, though, feared that the transfer of money at the heart of the relationship allowed the federal government to assert primacy over the states. Power centralized in Washington, DC, as the federal government became a primary source of money for programs run by the states. This trend spawned a backlash that coalesced into a sustained political agenda termed New Federalism. The central goal of New Federalism was to reverse the flow of power from the states to the federal government, principally by reducing the flow of federal money to the states and by granting states expanded policy-making powers.

New Federalism made some progress under Presidents Ronald Reagan, George H. W. Bush, and Bill Clinton, but stuttered to a halt with President George W. Bush. Very early during his tenure as president, powerful forces aligned to reverse the trend of decentralization that had emerged during the previous two decades. A recession; the terrorist attacks of September 11, 2001; and drawn-out conflicts in Afghanistan and Iraq all created pressures on the federal government to take the central role over states and localities. It was not simply circumstances driving a centralization of power at the federal level, but also part of a deliberate policy agenda. The Bush administration pushed for federal primacy across a wide range of domestic policy areas (notably education and emergency management) that were traditionally the jurisdiction of state and local governments. State and local governments were often not happy with federal usurpation of their policy turf, but at the end of the Bush presidency, their ability to resist the expanding power of the federal government became severely limited. In 2008, the Great Recession that plunged the nation into the greatest economic crisis since the Great Depression of the 1930s gutted state and local budgets. Rather than pushing for increasing independence from the federal government, states and localities found themselves heavily dependent on federal dollars simply to balance their books.

The administration of President Barack Obama in many ways has been good to states and localities, sending hundreds of billions of dollars to governments that desperately needed to fill empty treasuries. Indeed, on Obama's watch, the federal government, at least for a few years, became the single source of funding for state and local governments. The problem, at least from the state and local perspective, was that the federal government often wanted something for its money. And that something was a focus on federal—not state and local—policy priorities.

The central concern of intergovernmental relations during the era of cooperative federalism—that is, that the federal government would usurp the powers of the states through its purse strings—has returned with a vengeance. Many in state government are not happy with this development, especially as they see the federal government ignoring critical national responsibilities (illegal immigration being the prime example). This fractious relationship has led some states to at least consider refusing some federal grants to avoid the accompanying policy obligations, and some states to go even further by taking on traditional federal responsibilities (e.g., enforcing immigration laws) or even considering ignoring laws passed by Congress (e.g., refusing to enforce, or "nullifying," parts of a massive federal health care law).

This chapter contains a series of essays that highlight a variety of the sometimes cooperative, sometimes fractious intergovernmental relationships that characterize the evolving nature of federalism.

The first essay by Alan Greenblatt provides a general overview of the current relationship between state and federal governments. That relationship, as Greenblatt details, is complicated. Both levels of government are heavily dependent on each other—the states on the feds for money, the feds on the state for actually implementing policy. That reliance, however, does not change the fact that state and federal governments sometimes want to move in opposite directions.

The next reading is by John Lombard and John Morris, two academics who examine *coopertition*, a term that encompasses how subnational governments are learning to cooperate as well as compete across state and local borders. The following essay by Donald Kettl details the sometimes nasty political fights that can break out because of the frictions caused by federalism. Take a controversial topic like the federal government's health care law, throw in a constitutional issue about the limits of state and federal power, garnish with a side of partisanship, and get a recipe not just for friction between governments, but for disagreement within them.

Finally, an essay by Emily Badger takes a look at one of the odder aspects of the federal system: the method by which we elect a president. Presidential candidates compete not for popular votes, but for electoral votes. In essence, they compete for states rather than the popular vote. The Electoral College has struck many over the years as an overly complicated, jerry-rigged means to elect the leader of a democratic nation, especially as once in a while it throws someone into the White House who got fewer popular votes than the other candidate (most recently in 2000, Al Gore won the popular vote; George W. Bush got the most electoral votes). Reforming the Electoral College is a tough issue, though, because the federal system demands the states play a primary role in the constitution of the federal government. As this essay details, some states think they might have solved this conundrum.

NOTES

1. Kevin B. Smith, Alan Greenblatt, and John Buntin, *Governing States & Localities* (Washington, DC: CQ Press, 2004), 26.

2. The U.S. Constitution does lay down a basic set of responsibilities for federal and state governments. See Lee Epstein and Thomas G. Walker, *Constitutional Law for a Changing America: Institutional Powers and Constraints*, 5th ed. (Washington, DC: CQ Press, 2004), 323.

1

Federalism in the Age of Obama

Alan Greenblatt

Relationships between the states and the federal government are changing. States are still thinking creatively—and controversially—about public policy, but states are also broke. The federal government is forging its own policy path as the national debt continues to climb. Federalism in the age of Obama is complicated.

From *State Legislatures,*
July/August 2010.

There's one thing both critics and supporters of the new Arizona immigration law can agree on. The state acted out of frustration at Washington's inability to address the issue. This is a point President Barack Obama stressed during a speech calling on Republican Governor Jan Brewer to veto the measure. It's also a point Brewer made hours later at the signing ceremony for the bill, which calls on local police to check the proof of legal status for anyone they have reason to suspect might be in the country illegally.

"We in Arizona have been more than patient waiting for Washington to act," Brewer said. "But decades of inaction and misguided policy have created a dangerous and unacceptable situation."

In recent years, this has been a frequent complaint of state lawmakers across a whole range of issues. When Washington has been unable to resolve pressing issues, states have rushed to fill the policy void. And it's not just immigration.

During the presidency of George W. Bush, the federal government concentrated primarily on war and terrorism, with relatively little attention paid to domestic matters. That left plenty of running room for states to address a wide range of issues such as stem-cell research, securities regulation and minimum-wage increases.

Under Obama, that balance is starting to shift. He has clearly harbored ambitions of addressing nearly every major domestic issue. In many cases, that has meant calling on the states to implement policies he has pushed, in areas such as education and health care.

Given the continuing financial constraints states are facing, they have turned frequently to Washington for help. Obama has not been shy about exploiting that need, imposing new requirements on states to prod them to pursue his policies.

On other matters, though, the action clearly remains most vibrant in the states— not just on immigration, but on other issues, such as climate change.

> *"States have done an incredible job of working together. While Washington has been on hold, states have made many efforts to reduce energy use."*
> —California Senator Fran Pavley

CHANGING THE RULES

Oklahoma Representative Randy Terrill, sponsor of that state's stringent 2007 immigration law, sees "no greater example of federalism in action of late than on the immigration front. It's always been states that have stepped into policy voids left by the federal government."

Since 2007, when the last major push on immigration failed in the U.S. Senate, states have enacted hundreds of laws, mostly aimed at making life less comfortable for illegal immigrants and those who hire them.

As Terrill suggests, taking ownership of an issue has become a familiar role for state lawmakers. That dynamic is just as evident when it comes to climate change.

The U.S. Senate has frequently served as the undertaker for global warming bills over the past decade. Its most recent effort suffered a near-death experience when the sole Republican co-sponsor pulled his support a couple of days before the bill's scheduled introduction in April.

Its remaining sponsors are forging ahead, and climate change may yet be revived in this Congress (although even its supporters are not optimistic at this point). It's clear, however, that the Senate will not support a cap-and-trade regimen as ambitious as the one passed by the House last year—or the cap-and-trade programs already in place in the Northeast or being planned among other regional consortiums of states.

> *"It's always been states that have stepped into policy voids left by the federal government."*
> —Oklahoma Representative Randy Terrill

"States have done an incredible job of working together," says California Senator Fran Pavley. "While Washington has been on hold, states have made many efforts to reduce energy use."

And even when Washington has acted, states have often provided the model. That's true of the vehicle gas mileage standards Obama imposed this spring, which were largely based on Pavley's pioneering 2002 law regulating greenhouse gas emissions from cars. And it's certainly true of Obama's primary legislative accomplishment, the health care law that was patterned in large degree on earlier efforts in Massachusetts and other states.

So does this mean that even in the age of Obama, states will continue to lead the way toward innovative policymaking? The answer is complicated.

For one thing, states are broke. It's hard to innovate on an empty wallet. You can't even get a pilot program off the ground. Instead, legislators have to expend a great deal more time and energy trying to protect existing programs from drastic cuts than developing new ideas.

States are left relying on Washington for an expanding share of their revenues. Federal money—dominated by Medicaid funds— made up just over 25 percent of state spending as recently as FY 2008 before jumping to 30 percent in FY 2009. The current fiscal year's share is likely to be even higher.

"One of the trends that we see—it's not really new in the Obama administration, but I think it's increased exponentially—is this push toward the carrot and the stick," says Marcia Howard, executive director of Federal Funds Information for States, which tracks federal grant money for NCSL and the National Governors Association.

Most of the spending in last year's federal stimulus law passed through states and localities, helping states fill budget gaps, keep Medicaid patients enrolled and avoid laying off teachers. But as any legislator will tell you, most of that money came with significant strings attached.

States could not change their Medicaid eligibility laws. They had to follow so-called "maintenance of effort" rules on education as well, meaning they couldn't reduce their levels of existing spending once they accepted the federal help. And the entire package, from road construction to weatherization, was predicated on states meeting unprecedented transparency and accountability requirements.

It's arguably in education that the Obama administration has pushed states the hardest. The criteria for its Race to the Top fund—a $4.35 billion pot of grant money left largely to the discretion of U.S. Education Secretary Arne Duncan—led at least 10 states to change their laws in hopes of winning some of the money.

Last November, Obama and Duncan visited Madison to talk about education. Duncan was particularly harsh, calling Wisconsin's laws antiquated, unacceptable and even "ridiculous." Rather than take offense, both chambers of the Legislature the next day passed a package of four bills meant to appease him.

"There's no question those of us in Wisconsin want to have as strong an application as we can to get at the $4.35 billion," Senator John Lehman, who chairs the Education Committee, said during floor debate. "It is true that a big carrot got people thinking."

HUGE ROLE FOR STATES

The health care law was patterned on earlier state efforts, and Washington is relying heavily on states to carry it out. States will have to administer a vast expansion of Medicaid—estimated at 16 million more enrollees—as well as the system of exchanges that are meant to link individuals and small businesses with private insurance plans.

"I'm going through my mourning period of how much

> *"This is an administration that doesn't take the states and locals as it finds them. It has an agenda. The focus will be on national goals."*
> —Paul Posner, George Mason University

work there's going to be," says Alabama Medicaid Commissioner Carol Steckel.

She predicts the new law will bring 400,000 more people into her state's Medicaid system by 2014, doubling its size. That means far greater costs for the state down the road in administration and patient care, despite increased federal subsidies. "I have no idea how my state is going to be able to afford this," Steckel says.

States have been lining up with lawsuits meant to block the health care law, but few legal experts believe they have a chance to succeed. Assuming they don't, that means a huge share of state budgets and administrative efforts will be devoted to federal priorities on health care.

That represents a major shift from recent years, when states were basically able to experiment on the federal dime. The Massachusetts health law, for example, would never have gotten off the ground without a heavy federal subsidy.

A FINANCIAL BARREL

Now states will have a lot less choice about how they spend their health care money— and certainly less choice about limiting their expenditures. Arizona Governor Brewer may have snubbed the president by signing the immigration bill the same day he decried it. But Obama already had played a similar turnaround on her.

In March, Brewer signed a budget reduction package that would have kicked 300,000 adults off the Medicaid rolls and—a first among states—eliminated funding for the Children's Health Insurance Program. That was the plan, at least.

But Obama signed his health care law five days later, which had the effect of voiding Brewer's effort. The federal health law bars states from lowering eligibility requirements for either CHIP or Medicaid over the next several years, at the risk of losing all Medicaid funding. Now, because Arizona's cuts hadn't officially taken effect, state legislators are

> *"It is true that a big carrot got people thinking."*
> —Wisconsin Senator John Lehman

scrambling to find funding to restore their budget reductions. All told, Arizona officials estimate the federal law will cost the state $11.6 billion over the next 10 years, which Brewer calls "financially devastating."

There's not much she can do about it. Losing Medicaid funding altogether would be even more devastating.

Obama understands that he has states over a barrel financially. He has shown a great deal of interest in collaborating with states when he can, and he certainly is willing to federalize ideas that bubble up from them. But he also understands that their budget situations have diminished the ability of states to set their own courses.

The federal spigot may be about to shut off, as this spring's struggles to find extra money for Medicaid and teachers demonstrated. And the White House and a Congress riven by partisanship may leave plenty for states to do on their own. Still, this is not an administration that will support a federalism that provides more money to states to focus on their own plans and initiatives.

"This is an administration that doesn't take the states and locals as it finds them. It has an agenda," says Paul Posner, a federalism expert at George Mason University in Virginia. "The focus will be on national goals. I can see this administration pursuing additional ways to put money down in the state and local sectors but tying it to strong national goals. It's going to have to be a twofer."

The result might be a kind of symbiotic federalism. Washington needs states to carry out its grand visions on the ground, but the administration also fully intends to give them numerous pushes in its preferred direction.

Most federal money goes out to states through set formulas. But the Obama administration is clearly interested in pursuing variations on its Race to the Top model, using competitive grants to get states to dance to its tune.

If the effort at the federal level is successful, it will put a new twist on the old observation from Supreme Court Justice Louis D. Brandeis that states are the laboratories of democracy.

"Rather than states being the laboratories of democracy in and of themselves," says Howard, of Federal Funds Information for States, "some of them will become the federal government's laboratories of democracy."

2

Competing and Cooperating Across State Borders in Economic Development: A Call for "Coopertition"

John R. Lombard and John C. Morris

Reaching across political borders, state and local governments are learning to blend cooperation and competition into a working relationship that benefits everyone.

The quest for successful economic development projects is a task that occupies much of the time of both state and local government officials, both elected and administrative (Rubin 1988). For elected officials, successful economic development provides tangible benefits for constituents. Administrative officials are charged with the tasks to attract new businesses—marketing, structuring incentives, negotiating terms, and arranging and monitoring any government investment in the project. For both kinds of officials, economic development can increase the tax base, create new jobs, enhance the quality of life for citizens, and (perhaps) lead to future economic growth as other new businesses follow. At the heart of this activity is a culture that sees successful economic development as the ability of a government to compete against other governments and prevail, at the clear expense of the "losers."

In recent times the context of competition has changed, moving from local or regional competition to national and international competition. As we continue the trend toward an integrated global economy (Friedman 2005), local governments (or state governments) are no longer competing against only neighboring local governments (or states); they are competing against other nations. This trend has not only altered the ways in which practitioners address economic development but also caused scholars to rethink the ways in which they conceive of economic development theory.

Scholars have devoted a great deal of time and resources to building a comprehensive literature in this area. While much of the early work in the field was largely descriptive in nature, recent work has begun to develop more tangible theoretical underpinnings to apply to economic development studies. An important assumption of

From *State and Local Government Review* April 2010.

8

much of this work follows the same trend as seen in the practitioner culture—that governments must compete with other governments to be successful in their efforts to attract new businesses. The most recent trend is a movement toward the importance of cooperation (or collaboration) in successful economic development. Cooperation is attractive because it means that governments can pool resources with other governments and thus increase their competitiveness. However, as Gordon (2007, 2009) reports, practitioners are often caught in a paradox: they understand the benefits of cooperation, but their prevailing culture still defines economic development in terms of a competition. It thus seems difficult, if not impossible, to reconcile the apparently opposite forces of cooperation and competition.

This essay presents the argument that competition and cooperation are not diametrically opposing forces; rather, both are crucial to successful economic development in the twenty-first century. The environment of economic development is complex and subject to global forces whose impacts reach to regional (Feiock, Moon, and Park 2008) and local levels. No longer do governments compete only regionally, they compete globally. Success in this endeavor requires "coopertition" (Watson and Morris 2008) among actors at the local, state, and regional levels. Coopertition involves a realization by both scholars and academics that successful economic development in a global economy requires changes in both practitioner culture and academic theory. In short, competitive advantage is enhanced when governments cooperate. Any one government participating in a coopertition may not "win" a specific project, but the enhanced competitiveness brought about by coopertition increases the chances of "winning" future projects. Our intent is to illustrate ways in which coopertition can add to both the theory and practice of economic development.

We approach this endeavor from the perspective of federalism. The intergovernmental context of American governance is remarkably flexible, yet successful coopertition in this context requires an understanding of the strengths, as well as limitations, of federalism. In addition, we suggest that scholars can enhance our understanding of economic development by more thoroughly examining the role of a convener in cooperative or collaborative economic development activities. We offer anecdotal evidence of this role in cooperative economic development activities, an emerging concept in studies of administrative collaboration, and suggest that such a role is critical to successful coopertition.

We begin with a brief definition and explanation of coopertition leading into a discussion of economic development in the context of American federalism and present a framework to illustrate the benefits and challenges of cross-border coopertition in this context. We then present a more detailed discussion of coopertition and the role of the convener and offer several exemplars to illustrate these ideas. The essay concludes with some thoughts and observations about directions for future research.

DEFINITION OF COOPERTITION

The term *coopertition* was coined by Watson and Morris (2008) to describe the duality of government incentives in economic development. On one hand, governments vigorously compete for economic development "prizes" since to prevail over other competitors means that the bulk of the benefits of that development are realized by the "winning" unit of government (Rubin 1988). When South Carolina was chosen in 1992 as the site of a new BMW assembly plant, the economic (and political) benefits of that project went to South Carolina and not to any of the competing states. The increased business taxes, higher property values, and new jobs as well as the economic benefits of the other companies that followed BMW to Spartanburg County, enriched South Carolina (Schunk and Woodward 2003).

The historical competition among states for economic development has often created clear winners and losers (Watson 1995). Increasingly, though, governments are coming to realize that they are better able to compete when they pool their available resources in ways that make the area (or region) more attractive to new businesses. While this (cooperative) practice has been in place among local governments for many years, state governments are just beginning to realize that the same benefits may apply on a larger scale.[1] The logic of coopertition in economic development is that while a particular unit of government may not secure a specific economic development project, the odds of securing any project are increased if that government becomes more competitive by cooperating with other governments.

Thus, economic development includes, at its core, a competitive element. Coopertition recognizes that competition is an integral part of economic development and yet also seeks to leverage the advantages of economies of scale by cooperating with neighboring governments. The net result of coopertition is the creation of a new economic unit that not only is larger in scope but also can offer resources unmatched by smaller units individually competing for the same development project. Size confers a certain advantage in the eyes of potential investors, so the probability of successful development outcomes for each individual participant increases. The balance of this article further develops the idea of coopertition and provides examples of how coopertition works in practice.

FEDERALISM AND ECONOMIC DEVELOPMENT

The American model of federalism creates distinct political entities with clear geographic boundaries. These boundaries are much more than lines drawn on a map; they represent very real political, and often cultural, boundaries as well. When the Founders drafted the Constitution, they envisioned a model of federalism that has both vertical and horizontal dimensions. While the literature is rich with variations on this basic model (see, e.g., O'Toole 2006; Wright 1988), it provides us with a useful heuristic through which to examine coopertition.

The vertical dimension of federalism posits a system in which the national government occupies the space at the top of the pyramid, with the states occupying the middle level and local governments at the bottom of the chain. This hierarchical structure also includes a vertical (downward) flow of authority, so that each level is subservient to the level or levels above. The focus in this model thus becomes the nature of the authoritative relationships between governmental entities at different levels within the structure. A diagram of such a model would also have a certain "silo-like" quality to it, in that each of the fifty states operates as a distinct entity, with its own local governments lined up underneath it. Most economic development activity in this dimension takes place between states and local government; states act to assist local governments in their quest to bring new businesses into their communities (and thus into the state).

The horizontal dimension focuses our attention on relationships among equals: state government to state government or local government to local government. In this conception authoritative, hierarchical relationships are replaced by cooperative, collaborative, or competitive relationships among coequals. It is in this dimension that much of the work in economic development is, at least implicitly, grounded; moreover, most of the early work in the economic development literature conceives of these relationships as being inherently competitive in nature (Bowman 1998). States compete against other states to be selected as the recipient of a new automobile assembly plant; cities compete against other cities to lure new businesses into their industrial parks.

When these dimensions are combined into a single model of federalism and applied to economic development relationships, we begin to develop a more complete understanding of not only the conduct of economic development policies and strategies but also the nature of the complex intergovernmental relationships that exist within the framework (see Figure 1). Vertical conceptions of federalism acknowledge the supremacy of state governments over local governments and make local governments accountable and responsible to state governments. Disputes between states are adjudicated at the national level. Likewise, horizontal conceptions of federalism acknowledge the real-world experiences of states and local governments, who regularly interact with one another across political boundaries. These interactions, however, are in turn governed by the vertical relationships in the model.

Cross-border relationships between states, or between local governments, are commonplace in America and have been since the founding of the Republic. The Port Authority of New York and New Jersey is a long-standing and successful interstate enterprise. The Hampton Roads Transit Authority is a successful regional enterprise that involves seven municipalities in southeastern Virginia, and many other examples of both interstate and interlocal agreements abound around the nation. These also tend to be cooperative (or collaborative) in nature, and all of the participants are perpetual "winners" in that they are continually better off as a part of the arrangement than they can be without participating. Economic development, however, necessarily creates

from territorial disputes to educational records for the children of military members (Council of State Governments 2009), the interstate compact has not proven a popular mechanism to address cooperation (or coopertition) in economic development. The reasons for this are unclear, although we posit that the formality of the interstate compact may, in part, be responsible for its relative unpopularity. Compacts carry the force of law and must often be sanctioned by Congress (Council of State Governments 2009), while states are free to enter into less formalized cooperative or collaborative agreements without potential interference from the national government.

Two examples of cross-state coopertition may be found in the northeastern United States. In the first, the greater metropolitan areas of Hartford, Connecticut, and Springfield, Massachusetts, entered into an agreement to market the regional airport and to develop and market the 1–91 corridor (dubbed New England's Knowledge Corridor) between the two areas. The Hartford-Springfield Economic Partnership encompasses six counties and is governed by a twenty-one-member steering committee. By working together to attract new businesses to the area, they are able to pool their resources to market to a broader audience than either could reach on their own. Any one business attracted to the area may choose to locate on one side of the state line or the other, but coopertition works because both are able to attract businesses they would not otherwise reach—in short, both are better off by working together, even though they may win or lose individual businesses. Since its inception the partnership has secured many projects across both borders and has resulted in joint funding from federal agencies on workforce development and transportation. The competing areas also joined forces to promote a workforce retention strategy to stem the outflow of emerging workers. The cooperative agreements are relatively informal and largely involve local resources (as opposed to state resources), which obviate the need for a significant role for state government.

In the second instance, Connecticut, Maine, Massachusetts, New Hampshire, Rhode Island, and Vermont have created a coalition to foster economic development. Known as Team New England, the arrangement seeks to leverage joint resources to attract new industry and new businesses to the region. As with the Hartford-Springfield relationship, the participating governments have concluded they can be more competitive by combining their resources at a regional level than they can be working against their neighbors. Such an arrangement means that in most instances all but one state will lose any one new business to its partners, but the expectation is that each individual state's overall competitiveness is heightened through cooperation. The end result is that each state will ultimately attract businesses that would otherwise not have been attracted. This informal coopertition is truly remarkable. Business attraction is at the core of most state economic development functions and provides substantial political capital to the winners. An interesting feature of both of these cross-border collaborations is the presence of a convener in the arrangement. In this case, the convener is a private utility company. NU's economic development department proposed the initial idea and worked to convince the participating state and local governments that such cooperation made sense. The utility's interests are clear in the Hartford-Springfield partnership: new businesses and industry require electricity, natural gas, and water, so an influx of new customers into the utility's service area means new customers and greater demand for its utility services. However, NU operates in only three of the states that make up Team New England. The NU economic development staff clearly recognized the historical and cultural ties of the greater New England region and convinced state economic development agencies of the importance of coopertition, even though the potential benefit of some projects may fall outside the utility's service area.

CONCLUSION

The multifaceted nature of economic development has generated much interest from academics and practitioners across a broad spectrum of disciplines and industries. Policy makers and administrators play a critical role in shaping the nature and scope as well as direction of practice. The extant literature is replete with references to the competitive nature of this activity and has criticized policy makers and practitioners for upping the ante associated with securing industrial investment. The "beggar-thy-neighbor" policy often associated with economic development practice to a large extent underpins the culture of economic development. The contentious nature of cross-border economic development casts competition and cooperation in "either-or" propositions. We suggest that economic development scholars and academics explore the idea of coopertition as a way to better frame our understanding of cross-border economic development success, however that success may be defined. Furthermore, practitioners may use coopertition to justify administrative actions that transcend state boundaries. Much like the literature on industrial clusters suggests, success is predicated on coopertition (cooperative competition) among private-sector firms (Malizia and Feser 1997). So too can governments at the local and state levels enhance their economic development success through coopertition. In the illustrative cases of cross-state-border economic development initiatives, coopertition had at its core a convener. We suggest that future research explore the need for and role of the convener in facilitating cross-border coopertition. Is a convener a necessary component of successful coopertition? What makes for a successful convener, and who defines the role of the convener? What are the pragmatic issues surrounding cross-border ventures? Clearly, systematic investigation of the effectiveness of cross-border coopertition cannot be achieved without further research and case studies.

between service types. These findings therefore tend to support our assertion that economic development is seen primarily by local officials as competitive in nature. The key to coopertition, then, is to convince local officials, particularly elected officials, that the increased benefits (greater competitiveness) of cooperation with neighboring governments for economic development outweigh the perceived political losses that might be incurred by cooperation. We are also hesitant to equate economic development functions with parks and recreation or policing (Andrew 2009; Williams 1971). Successful economic development is as likely to rest on the availability of suitable maintenance services—utilities, transportation networks, and so on—as it is on the amenities offered by a community. In other words, economic development may be more accurately thought of as the "engine" that drives both system maintenance and lifestyle services. While we agree that a perceived higher quality of life can help attract new businesses to an area (Florida 2005; Friedman 2005), economic development more likely transcends the distinctions between system maintenance and lifestyle services proffered by Williams (1971). These assertions are the subject of future research.

NOTES

1. The literature in interlocal cooperation (LeRoux and Carr 2007, forthcoming) or interjurisdictional agreements (Andrew 2009) distinguishes between "system maintenance" services and "lifestyle" services (see Williams 1971). System maintenance services—infrastructure, utilities, and transit systems—are generally perceived by both professional administrators and elected officials to be less contentious (or competitive); they are thus more willing to cede a certain amount of control over these services to other jurisdictions. On the other hand, lifestyle services (economic development, parks and recreation, etc.) are more likely to be perceived by elected officials as more competitive in nature and thus more worthy of local political and administrative control. Recent work (see LeRoux and Carr, forthcoming) appears to support these distinctions

REFERENCES

Andrew, Simon A. 2009. Recent developments in the study of interjurisdictional agreements: An overview and assessment. *State and Local Government Review* 41 (2): 133–42.

Bowman, Ann O'M. 1998. Competition for economic development among southeastern cities. *Urban Affairs Quarterly* 23: 511–27.

Bowman, Ann O'M. 2004. Horizontal federalism: Exploring interstate interactions. *Journal of Public Administration Research and Theory* 14: 535–46.

Caver, Floun'say R., and Grace Galluci. 2008. Transit-oriented development: The Euclid Corridor Transportation Project and the Greater Cleveland Regional Transit Authority. In *Building the local economy: Cases in economic development,* ed. Douglas J. Watson and John C. Morris, 143–56. Athens, GA: Carl Vinson Institute of Government.

Council of State Governments. 2009. 10 frequently asked questions, http://www.csg.org/knowledge center/docs/ncic/CompactFAQ.pdf (accessed December 30, 2009).

Feiock, Richard C, M. Jae Moon, and Hyung-Jun Park. 2008. Is the world "flat" or "spiky"? Rethinking the governance implications of globalization for economic development. *Public Administration Review* 68: 24–35.

Feiock, Richard C, Annette Steinacker, and Hyung Jun Park. 2009. Institutional collective action and economic development joint ventures. *Public Administration Review* 69: 256–70.

Florida, Richard. 2005. *The flight of the creative class: The new global competition for talent.* New York: Harper.

Friedman, Thomas L. 2005. *The world is flat: A brief history of the twenty-first century.* New York: Farrar, Straus, and Giroux.

Gordon, Victoria. 2007. Partners or competitors? Perceptions of regional economic development cooperation in Illinois. *Economic Development Quarterly* 21: 60–78.

Gordon, Victoria. 2009. Perceptions of regional economic development: Can win-lose become win-win. *Economic Development Quarterly* 23: 317–28.

Grady, Dennis O. 1987. State economic development incentives: Why do states compete? *State and Local Government Review* 19 (3): 86–94.

Hoyman, Michelle, Jennifer Weaver, and Micah Weinberg. 2008. Rural prison sitings in North Carolina: Competition and community leaders' attitudes. In *Building the local economy: Cases in economic development,* ed. Douglas J. Watson and John C. Morris, 233–48. Athens, GA: Carl Vinson Institute of Government.

Kapucu, Nairn. 2006. Interagency communication networks during emergencies. *American Review of Public Administration* 36: 207–25.

Kingdon, John W. 1984. *Agendas, alternatives, and public policies.* Boston: Little, Brown.

Lackey, Steven Brent, David, Freshwater and Anil Rupasingha. 2002. Factors influencing local government cooperation in rural areas: Evidence from the Tennessee valley. *Economic Development Quarterly* 16: 138–54.

Lambright, Kristina T., Pamela A. Mischen, and Craig B. Laramee. 2010. Building trust in public and nonprofit networks. *American Review of Public Administration* 40: 64–82.

LeRoux, Kelly. 2006. The role of structure, function, and networks in explaining interlocal service delivery: A study of institutional cooperation in Michigan. PhD diss., Wayne State University.

LeRoux, Kelly, and Jered B. Carr. 2007. Explaining local government cooperation in public works. *Public Works Management and Policy* 12 (1): 344–58.

LeRoux, Kelly, and Jered B. Carr. Forthcoming. Prospects for centralizing services in an urban county: Evidence from self-organized networks of eight local public services. *Journal of Urban Affairs.*

Lombard, John R. 2008. Crossing state borders: Utility-led interstate economic development cooperation in New England. In *Building the local economy: Cases in economic development,* ed. Douglas J. Watson and John C. Morris, 78–94. Athens, GA: Carl Vinson Institute of Government.

Malizia, Emil, and Edward Feser. 1999. *Understanding local economic development.* New Brunswick, NJ: Center for Urban Policy Research.

McCarthy, Linda. 2003. The good of the many outweighs the good of the one. *Journal of Planning Education and Research* 23: 140–52.

McNamara, Madeleine W., William M. Leavitt, and John C. Morris. Forthcoming. Multiple sector partnerships and the engagement of citizens in social marketing campaigns: The case of Lynnhaven River Now. *Virginia Social Science Journal.* volume? pages?

Morris, John C. 2007. The artist as environmentalist: Ansel Adams, policy entrepreneurship, and the growth of environmentalism. *Public Voices* 9 (3): 9–24.

O'Toole, Laurence J., Jr. 2006. *American intergovernmental relations: Foundations, perspectives, and issues.* 4th ed. Washington, DC: CQ Press.

Rubin, Herbert J. 1988. Shoot anything that flies; claim anything that falls: Conversations with economic development practitioners. *Economic Development Quarterly* 2: 236–51.

Schunk, Donald L., and Douglas P. Woodward. 2003. Incentives and economic development: The case of BMW in South Carolina. In *Financing economic development in the 21st century,* ed. Sammis B. White, Richard D. Bingham, and Edward W. Hill, 145–69. Armonk, NY: M.E. Sharpe.

Spindler, Charles J. 1994. Winners and losers in industrial development: Mercedes-Benz and Alabama. *State and Local Government Review* 26 (3): 192–204.

Watson, Douglas J. 1995. *The new civil war: Government competition for economic development.* Westport, CT: Praeger.

Watson, Douglas J., and John C. Morris. 2008. Introduction: Competition, coordination, or "coopertition?" In *Building the local economy: Cases in economic development,* ed. Douglas J. Watson and John C. Morris, 1–14. Athens, GA: Carl Vinson Institute of Government.

Williams, Oliver. 1971. *Metropolitan political analysis.* New York: Free Press.

Wright, Deil S. 1988. *Understanding intergovernmental relations.* 3rd ed. Pacific Grove, CA: Brooks/Cole.

Zimmerman, J. F. 2002. *Interstate cooperation: Compacts and interstate agreements.* Westport, CT: Praeger.

3

What Really Matters in Health-Care Reform

Donald F. Kettl

The federal government has undertaken the biggest reform of health care in generations. Actually implementing those reforms, however, depends on the states. Some states seem less than eager to make reform a reality.

Health-care reform has made for some strange battles, but none is stranger than the one Michigan Attorney General Mike Cox is having with himself.

Conservative opponents to the new health-care law were loaded and ready to fire before President Barack Obama had even signed the bill. They found an argument they think will work: They say the law forces consumers to buy a product—health insurance—which is an unconstitutional use of the Constitution's interstate commerce clause.

Cox headed a group that included 13 other attorneys general who filed suit against the new health-care reform bill. But Michigan Gov. Jennifer Granholm ordered him to file on the other side of the case. To paraphrase Abraham Lincoln, a Cox divided against himself cannot stand.

"On behalf of the interests of the people of Michigan," as the attorney general put it, he's trying to torpedo health-care reform. On Michigan's behalf, as the governor's lawyer, Granholm says Cox is obliged to advance her pro-reform position. Without an act of the legislature, he counters, how can the governor know she's speaking for the state?

And to steal from the movie classic *Casablanca*, we might be shocked—shocked!—to discover there's politics going on here. In Michigan and three other states, Democratic governors are battling Republican attorneys general. In Georgia and Mississippi, Democratic attorneys general are refusing to contest the law on behalf of Republican governors. Three of the attorneys general are running for governor and a fourth is considering a contest next time around.

From *Governing*, June 2010.

We've been down this state-nullification road before: In the '60s—the 1860s, that is—nullification didn't work out well for states below the Mason-Dixon Line that brought disputes, which had been simmering for decades, to a bloody battle over supremacy. In the 1960s, some states were painfully dragged to new federal civil rights and voting rights standards.

The health-care reform battle is a bit different, since it's grounded in an argument about whether individuals can be forced to *do* something (buy insurance) instead of be forced *not* to do something (discriminate). But it's unlikely to have a different outcome. Bit by bit, the federal government has chipped away at Thomas Jefferson's argument that the states were the Constitution's supreme arbiters. The upcoming row over Cox's competing loyalties will be great political theater, but it's unlikely to produce legal doctrine.

However, it would be a huge mistake to write this off completely as partisanship. Health insurance reform might be the federal law, but its implementation depends critically on the states. Beneath it all is the always-simmering question of federal pre-emption of state power.

On the implementation side, the cornerstone of the new program is a collection of state-run insurance exchanges. After the health-care fighting was over, the "public option" became a state option, which became a plan in which state governments will create online marketplaces—a kind of Hotels.com for health insurance. These exchanges don't have much of a track record. The plan is based on the Massachusetts Health Connector, created in 2006 under former Gov. Mitt Romney, who's now doing a quick tap dance trying to explain how his plan differs from the "Obamacare" program that followed in its steps. This plan creates strong government control over basic packages of care.

Utah created the nation's second exchange. This one relies far more on telling citizens which private plans are available, and it's already gone back to the drawing board for more tinkering. Utah House Speaker Dave Clark claims it's a better way, because, "not only can we run these programs adequately without federal oversight and interference, but we can operate them more effectively, more efficiently and serve citizens better."

Beyond the exchanges, the new health-care bill significantly expands eligibility for Medicaid, the nation's health program for the poor. Pre-health reform, Medicaid mostly covered health care for children and nursing home care for seniors. The law opens up the program to others under 133 percent of the federal poverty level, which will put states on the front lines of expanding coverage for many more Americans.

Of course, the states don't actually provide health care, either through Medicaid or the exchanges. They are brokers, leveraging and overseeing the behavior of private insurance markets, hospitals and health-care providers without actually hiring the doctors and hospitals that provide the care. This is where the real action in health-care reform will be—and it's why public battles over who is suing whom miss the big point.

We're in the process of rejiggering $1 of every $6 moving through the American economy and rethinking one of the few things—health—in which all of us have a strong and equal interest. The feds are changing the rules of the game. The big questions will be who gets what care from whom and how much it will cost—and they will depend on how the states set up and play the game.

The federal government will decide which state models meet the new program's national standards. So enjoy the on-stage Cox drama. The second act, where states and the feds fight out how to run something that's only barely been tried, will be where the real action is.

4

An End Run on the Electoral College

Emily Badger

The Electoral College strikes many as an unnecessarily complicated way to choose a president. A handful of states are trying to change that.

The Massachusetts state Legislature last week passed a law designed to circumvent what many consider the dysfunction of the Electoral College. Under the bill, all of the state's electoral votes would go to the presidential candidate who wins the national popular vote, whether that candidate also wins the local vote in Massachusetts or not.

The bill has a clever trigger mechanism — it would only go into effect if a majority of states (representing 270 electoral votes) adopt identical laws. No sane state would want to go this alone, in essence sacrificing its residents' votes to make a point about true democracy.

The bill's backers — who seem pleased they've come up with a legal alternative to dismantling the Electoral College by constitutional amendment — are slowly on their way. If Massachusetts Gov. Deval Patrick signs the law, his state will become the sixth (spanning 73 electoral votes) to line up for the experiment.

Some Republican leaders in the Bay State have cried foul. And the idea does suffer from a mild ideological tinge, if only because it recalls Democrats' bitter disappointment in the 2000 election. (So far all of the backers have been blue states.)

But according to the bill's grandfather, a doctorate in computer science with an expertise in genetic programming, this idea is less about who wins on Election Day than what occurs before then. Sure, John Koza says, it's problematic that the American system periodically puts second-place candidates in the White House (and he's not just talking about George W. Bush — this has happened in four of 56 presidential elections).

The bigger problem, he says, is that our existing system encourages candidates to ignore entire swaths of the country. And

From *Miller-McCune*, August 2010.

polling suggests both Democrats and Republicans agree with this.

"What struck us in the 2004 election was how extreme the concentration on the battleground states had become," Koza said. In the last six elections, and particularly the last three, he's watched candidates hold two-thirds of their campaign stops and spend two-thirds of their money in as few as six states.

In any given election, he adds, 98 percent of campaign money is spent in 15 or 16 states, leaving the vast majority of the country — and its concerns — out of the game.

"Of course, candidates concentrate on those states during the election," he said. "Then they get elected and they're thinking of re-election, and they concentrate on those same states while they're governing."

Koza wants to change this via interstate compact. States have the exclusive power to decide how to award their delegates to the Electoral College. Nothing in the Constitution requires them to use the winner-take-all formula that has become the norm. And so changing that formula would not require a constitutional amendment, as many people assume.

"I thought that, too, and I lost a bet when I was in college, a very embarrassing bet to a pre-law student," Koza said. "The winner-take-all system, not only is it not in the Constitution, but it was only used by three states in the first election. So it was not the choice of the founders."

Koza, then, dismisses the most common objection to his plan — that somehow, this seems like a sneaky subversion of the Constitution. (The idea could, however, be subject to litigation on the finer points of congressional approval of interstate compacts.) He also frequently hears fears that his system would undermine federalism, the balance of power between the states and the federal government.

"A state is no weaker or stronger if they count votes one way versus another," he said. Besides, the states would retain the right to change their systems at any time—as Massachusetts, for one, has done throughout its history.

Most unnerving, though, is the prospect that voters in Massachusetts, for example, could wind up overwhelmingly supporting one candidate, only to have their state's entire electoral trove awarded to the other guy. Such scenarios, even if rare, may only bolster the popular gripe that "my vote doesn't count."

"The opposition tries to make an issue of that," Koza said. "The truth is that's the entire point of the bill — to get away from the state-by-state outcome controlling the White House. If you want candidates to treat every vote equally around the country, if you want them to campaign around the country, then you need a national popular vote."

Think of it this way, he adds: Do you care how your county voted for governor, or do you just care if your candidate won the office?

II

Elections and Political Environment

Partisan electoral fortunes can certainly change in two years, but rarely as much as they did between 2008 and 2010. Back in 2008, the electoral future looked rosy for Democrats. Their popular presidential candidate laid claim to the White House; the party controlled both houses of Congress; and down at the state level, Democrats came out of the 2008 electoral cycle controlling more than half of state legislatures and 60 percent of state gubernatorial offices. The GOP seemed to be in retreat pretty much everywhere. Fast-forward two years, however, and it was Republicans piling up a historical haul of electoral victories. And it is the GOP's 2010 victories that are much more likely to shape the electoral and political environment for the next decade than the Democrats' short-lived victory of 2008.

The causes of the Democrats' fall from electoral grace over the past couple of years are not hard to fathom. In the simplest terms, a host of economic problems and the perceived ineffectiveness of government at any level to deal with the fallout—let alone correct the slide—resulted in deep voter frustration. That frustration was taken out on the people in office. Because of their big victories in 2008, that primarily meant Democrats. As President Barack Obama put it, his party took a "shellacking" in the fall 2010 elections, losing its House majority to the GOP and seeing its majority in the Senate chopped far below the filibuster-proof 60 the Obama administration enjoyed in its first two years. While 2010 electoral results were gloomy for Democrats at the federal level, at the state level, they were potentially disastrous.

The depth of the problem for Democrats goes much further than the erosion in elected members, although those certainly sting. By 2011, the Democrats' hold on state government had evaporated; Democrats had majority control of just 16 state legislatures, while 25 were wholly under Republican control (partisan control was split in 10, and Nebraska's unicameral is nonpartisan). Republicans held the keys to 28 governors' mansions. This GOP resurgence at the state level represents much, much more than a big electoral comeback for Republicans.

Their electoral resurgence was perfectly timed for Republicans to shape the political environment at the state and local level for the next decade. This is because of the 2010 census, the decennial head count used to apportion political districts for state legislatures and the U.S. House of Representatives. How those lines are drawn on the map, what mix of voters is or is not clumped together for purposes of representation, has massive implications for who can reasonably hope to get elected from a given district, and thus how power is distributed among various partisan, ideological, and policy interests. In 44 states, those lines are drawn by state legislatures. Thanks to their 2010 victories, Republicans are going to do most of the drawing.

READY, SET, DRAW

The essays in this section are designed to provide a quick overview of the 2010 elections and a more sustained examination of their potential implications for the political and electoral environment at the state level over the next decade. The first essay by Karen Hansen provides the details on the "red tide," the historical shift toward Republican control of state governments following 2010.

As already mentioned, one of the big jobs of those newly elected legislatures is going to be redrawing political districts. Emily Badger's essay covers an interesting and little-examined implication of demographic classifications and redistricting purposes; legislative districts that are drawn to include prisons carry disproportionate political power. This is because prisoners are counted as residents of those districts, not as residents of the communities they come from. The net impact of this demographic counting quirk is that urban black communities appear smaller while more rural (and more white) districts with prisons appear larger. For example, the vast majority of people incarcerated in New York state hail from New York City, but count for representation purposes as residents of the mostly upstate districts where they are incarcerated. Convicted felons cannot vote in New York state, so the incarcerated populations do not effect election outcomes. They do count for representation purposes. What this means is that prisoners artificially inflate the populations of districts that have prisons, giving those districts more political power.

While prison-based gerrymanders might help some less urban districts (albeit at the expense of diluting the voting power of African Americans), redistricting overall is not likely to be kind to rural areas. In many states, there have been significant population shifts from the country to the city. As goes the population, so goes the political clout. As a result of the 2010 elections, more state legislators are going to be from urban areas, and fewer are from rural areas. This creates a number of interesting political dilemmas, not the least interesting of which is the fact that those rural areas trend more Republican. Josh Goodman explores redistricting and the impact on the erosion of rural political clout and what that means for state policy priorities.

Finally, Micah Altman and Michael McDonald examine the ability of technology to increase public input into redistricting. Powerful computer programs now make it comparatively easy for a relative novice to take a crack at redrawing political boundaries in a realistic simulation. By facilitating more public input and less backroom wheeling and dealing, perhaps redistricting could become a fairer and less partisan process.

5

Red Tide

Karen Hansen

The 2010 elections give the GOP key gains in state offices. As newly elected state officials will be redrawing political boundaries, the "red tide" may be coming in for at least a decade.

From *State Legislatures*, December 2010.

The winds of change blew with hurricane force through America's state legislatures Election Day, changing the political landscape from blue to red in historic terms.

Just two years ago the barometric pressure reading couldn't have been more different. Democrats netted more than 100 state legislative seats across the nation, wresting control of 60 of the 99 chambers—the highest number in 15 years—in the Democratic sweep that won them the White House and solidified their control in Congress. But this Nov. 2—true to the predictions of prognosticators and pollsters—was demolition day for Democrats. Voters took their anger and disillusionment with the economy into the voting booth and shook up the political order from top to bottom.

Voters who decided to clean house in Congress handed Republicans a victory in the states, too. Midterm elections predictably swing against the party of the president, but the public's stunning repudiation of Democrats in 2010 put the GOP in control of the most state legislative seats since 1928. At the start of Election Day, Democrats controlled both chambers in 27 states, to the GOP's 14; eight were divided and Nebraska is nonpartisan. By the next morning, Republicans had taken control of at least 19 chambers, giving them the majority in 25 state legislatures. Three chambers—the Oregon, New York and Washington Senates remain—undecided at press time.

Election Night belonged to the GOP. Democrats did not win a single additional chamber, and saw their control slip to 16 legislatures. And the number of new seats for Republicans—some 675—was truly historic. It is the largest Republican win since 1966, even bigger than the post-Watergate surge by Democrats in 1974. There are now more Republican state legislators than any time since the Great Depression.

The widely reported enthusiasm gap among Democrats was reflected in the number of candidates each party fielded. In the states, 6,115 legislative seats were up this year. (Four states—Louisiana, Mississippi, New Jersey and Virginia—and three Senates— Kansas, New Mexico and South Carolina— did not have legislative elections.) Some 11,000 candidates ran for legislatures. This year Republicans put up 822 more than they did in 2008, while Democrats had 50 fewer candidates than two years ago.

Republicans successfully nationalized the election, expanding their congressional victories to the states. Polls before the election indicated that 75 percent of Americans believe things are going badly in the country. The old adage, "it's the economy, stupid," proved especially true Nov. 2. Voters by a 62 percent margin cited the economy as the most important issue, far overshadowing health care reform (19 percent) and immigration (8 percent). With one in nearly 10 Americans out of work and a drum beat against a growing federal deficit and expanded government, those lawmakers closest to the people were caught in the maelstrom of anxiety and

> ## "The economy was 75 percent of the explanation for everything that happened on Election Day."
> —Larry Sabato

demand for change that spelled doomsday for Democrats.

"The economy was 75 percent of the explanation for everything that happened on Election Day," says Larry Sabato, director of the Center for Politics at the University of Virginia. "The new GOP state legislators appear to have the same priorities as their federal counterparts—less spending, lower taxes and a strong opposition to debt. This is a group of fiscal conservatives who favor smaller government. This is the common ground between the longtime Republican party base and the Tea Party activists."

WASHINGTON AND THE STATES

The new congressional alignment will have significant impact on the relationship of the states and the federal government.

Norman Ornstein, resident scholar at the American Enterprise Institute and longtime observer of Congress and elections, believes the economy and "the brutal facts of life in the political world" promise "it's not going to be a pretty picture for states."

"All the pressure in Washington is going to be on decreasing discretionary domestic spending," he says.

Election 2010: State Legislatures By the Numbers

675
Seats Republicans added

1928
The last year GOP held this many seats

55
Chambers controlled by Republicans

120
Seats gained by Republicans in the 400-seat New Hampshire House

11
Democratic leaders who lost their re-election bids

32
Republican-controlled houses, compared with 17 before the election

15
Democratic-controlled houses, compared with 32 before the election

30*
GOP-controlled senates, compared with 24 before the election

19
Democratic-controlled senates, compared with 26 before the election

Source: NCSL, 2010
*The New York Senate remained undecided at press time.

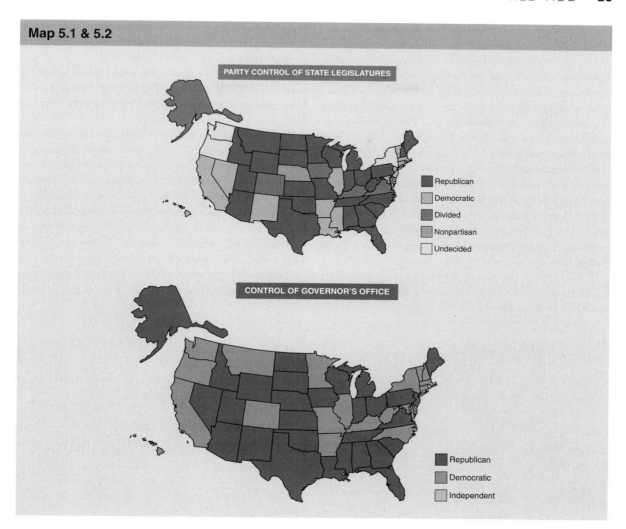

Map 5.1 & 5.2

PARTY CONTROL OF STATE LEGISLATURES

- Republican
- Democratic
- Divided
- Nonpartisan
- Undecided

CONTROL OF GOVERNOR'S OFFICE

- Republican
- Democratic
- Independent

"That means any state expecting help on Medicaid can forget about it. And the ability of Obama and the Democrats to keep extending unemployment benefits will be much more limited."

Even though the economy and the jobs picture are improving incrementally, unemployment remains stubbornly high. "If people don't have jobs and don't have unemployment insurance," Ornstein says, "much of the burden is going to fall on the states and cities. If you have no more Medicaid money when people are unemployed and going on Medicaid, and face other fiscal burdens, it's going to be tough to balance budgets."

RED IN THE MIDDLE

Republicans changed the political order in what was the largest midterm election turnout ever, with some 90 million people casting ballots, but still far less than the general election vote in 2008. And although people may have voted for divided government at the federal level, in the Midwest and the South they clearly wanted the GOP in charge. Republicans also made substantial gains in the East, where they won 233 new seats and the West, where they added 108 seats. Not since the Eisenhower era in 1952 have the Republicans controlled so many legislative chambers.

The electoral battleground in the Midwest, once the industrial bastion of Democrats, is now a swath of red.

In Michigan, Republicans have controlled the Senate since 1983, but the House has swung back and forth between the two parties. On election eve, Democrats held the majority in the 110-member House 64-42 with four vacancies. The next day, the GOP was in control 63-47. Term limits, retirements and defeats have changed the landscape of one of the nation's largest full-time legislatures. In the 38-member Senate, 29 lawmakers will be new, although many have come from the House. But the House is a completely different story. Of the 110 members, 95 have two or fewer years of experience. They will have to gain it quickly. First on the agenda is closing a $1.5 billion budget gap.

"We're ready to get to work," says Republican Representative Jase Bolger, who is poised to take the speaker's podium for the GOP. "I think the voters are very clear they want to see spending control, they want to see jobs. It's a huge task in front of us. But big challenges bring big opportunities."

For the first time since 1998, when John Engler was governor, the Michigan GOP controls everything—the Legislature, the governorship and even the state Supreme Court.

Wisconsin became the only state where Democrats lost the governor's mansion, a U.S. Senate seat and the entire Legislature. "It's just like '08 and '06 in reverse," says Reince Priebus, state GOP chair. Republicans' statewide sweep was the sweetest for the GOP there in 72 years.

The Minnesota Legislature fell to the Republicans for the first time in nearly 40 years. "This is an important, critical time in our state's landscape," House Republican Leader Kurt Zellers says. "We're going to get to work. This is about getting the state's economy back on track, people back to work and Minnesota back to being pro-business again."

CAPITOL TO CAPITOL

There are 43 former state lawmakers who were elected to Congress on Nov. 2. Additionally, former Kansas legislator Jerry Moran is moving from the U.S. House of Representatives to the U.S. Senate.

U. S. SENATE
Connecticut
Richard Blumenthal
Florida
Marco Rubio
Kansas
Jerry Moran *
West Virginia
Joe Manchin
*Moved from the House to the Senate
U.S. House of Representatives
Arizona
David Schweikert
California
Karen Bass
Jeff Denham

Louisiana
Cedric Richmond
Maryland
Andy Harris
Massachusetts
Bill Keating
Michigan
Justin Amash
Hansen Clarke
Bill Huizenga
Tim Walberg
Mississippi
Alan Nunnelee
Missouri
Vicky Hartzler
Nevada
Joe Heck

Colorado
Cory Gardner
Scott Tipton
Florida
Sandy Adams
David Rivera
Dennis Ross
Daniel Webster
Frederica Wilson
Georgia
Austin Scott
Hawaii
Colleen Hanabusa
Idaho
Raul Labrador
Illinois
Randy Hultgren
Indiana
Marlin Stutzman
Kansas
Tim Huelskamp
Kevin Yoder

New Mexico
Steve Pearce
North Dakota
Rick Berg
Ohio
Bob Gibbs
Steve Stivers
South Carolina
Jeff Duncan
Mick Mulvaney
Tim Scott
South Dakota
Kristi Noem
Tennessee
Diane Black
Virginia
H. Morgan Griffith
Robert Hurt
Washington
Jamie Herrera
West Virginia
David McKinley

Source: NCSL

Republicans also won the Indiana House, a chamber where control has switched 20 times over the past 110 years. They notched wins in the Ohio House and the Pennsylvania House, giving them control of both legislatures, and captured both governorships as well. Election night allows the GOP to shape the political terrain in the Midwest for the next 10 years when they begin drawing congressional and legislative maps next year.

> *Voters are "looking for something that works and when it doesn't work quickly, it's throw the 'ins' out and bring the 'outs' in."*
> —Norman Ornstein, American Enterprise Institute

GOP GAINS IN THE SOUTH

In the South, Republicans continued their march to majority. In 1990 Republicans did not control a single chamber in a Southern legislature. Now the geography is decidedly red. Republicans made history in Alabama and North Carolina, winning control of both states for the first time since Reconstruction.

In Alabama, Democrats had been in control for well over a century. They won the House in 1870 and the Senate in 1872 and never let go. Until election night when the GOP wrested both chambers.

"It's a big deal," said Auburn University at Montgomery political scientist Brad Moody. "The Alabama Legislature has been one of the last to switch from being Democratic controlled to Republican controlled."

North Carolina Republicans last held a majority in the Senate in 1870. "In serving the people, you understand a day like this may come," said Marc Basnight, the Democratic Senate president for 18 years. "You are hopeful that the change is beneficial, new ideas, different thoughts. This is only what the people want, so that means it's good."

The GOP also won the House. "It was just a wave," said Democratic Speaker Joe Hackney. "I was here for the national Republican wave in 1994, and this is like that." The new North Carolina Legislature will face a $3.5 billion budget gap.

Oklahoma Republicans maintain control of the Legislature, and their victory in the governor's race puts the GOP in control of state government for the first time. A Republican also won the governorship in Tennessee, a state already under GOP legislative control, giving the party total control there for the first time since Reconstruction.

MIXING COLORS

In New Hampshire, Republicans won a stunning net gain of more than 125 seats, giving them control of the House and Senate. The GOP also won the Maine Senate. In New York, Democrats achieved a slim 32-30 Senate majority just two years ago after some 50 years of Republican power. The final count was still in play at press time, with Republicans claiming 32 or 33 seats and the possibility of a tie looming.

In the West, the Republican rout was somewhat stymied. Colorado voters gave control of the House to the GOP, but not the Senate, and they put another Democrat into the governor's mansion. The GOP won the Montana House, which had been tied, and it already controlled the Senate. In Oregon, the only state to conduct all elections by mail, the House is split 30-30, and Democrats appear to have held on to a narrow majority in the Senate. Voters returned former Democratic Governor John Kitzhaber to his old office for an unprecedented third term. He was governor from 1995-2003 with a GOP majority in the legislature.

Democrats retained control of the Washington House, but the Senate was still undecided at press time. Nothing changed in Alaska or Hawaii. The Alaska Senate remained tied and Republicans kept the House. Hawaii continues to be one of the most Democratic states in the country.

POISED TO REDRAW

Sabato says when voters went to the polls to hand Republicans historic wins, most "clearly pulled the 'R' lever for state legislators, too," leading to one of the best Republican years at the state level on record. "And if you're going to have a great year at the state level, you want to pick the Census year in order to reap the redistricting bonanza," he says.

Republicans are in the redistricting cat bird's seat, and the prize is huge. The GOP will be in complete charge of remapping some 190 U.S. House districts when the Census data are released in February, solidifying congressional gains and their legislative victories. The GOP finds itself in the best position for redistricting since the landmark "one-person, one-vote" *Baker v. Carr* decision in 1962. Republican legislative wins in 2010 give them the upper hand in redistricting, so their victory could echo across the political landscape for at least the next 10 years.

The 2010 election was one for the record books, a realized dream for Republicans and a nightmare for Democrats. The pendulum will undoubtedly swing back some day, but for now, Republicans can enjoy making history before the reality sets in that state budgets are still on shaky ground, the hard work is only beginning, and the clock to the next election is ticking.

"When you get three wave elections in a row," Ornstein says, "it suggests that voters are simply more impatient. What they're looking for is something that works and when it doesn't work quickly, it's throw the 'ins' out and bring the 'outs' in."

The fingerprints of history are on the GOP.

6

Prison-Based Gerrymandering Dilutes Blacks' Voting Power

Emily Badger

Because prisoners can count for redistricting purposes, some state legislative districts include thousands of voters who cannot vote. One of the bizarre implications of that situation is the rural, mostly white districts with large prison populations draw political power from the incarceration of mostly urban blacks.

Sixty-six percent of the inmates in the state of New York come from New York City. But 91 percent of them are incarcerated upstate, in communities where they have long been counted by the U.S. census.

On paper, this means prisoners belong not to the communities from which they've come (and to which they eventually will return), but to places where they can neither vote, check out a library book or attend a local school.

The counting quirk sounds like a quandary for demographers. But it also means, come gerrymandering time, that many urban black communities look smaller than they actually are, a disproportionate number of their residents having been counted in the rural areas that are home to penitentiaries.

Most states redraw political districts every 10 years using census data, and so this counting practice has the effect of increasing the political power of anyone who lives near a prison, while decreasing the power of the communities where prisoners legally reside.

Critics disdainfully call the practice "prison-based gerrymandering."

During the 2000 census, 43,000 New York City residents were counted upstate in this way. Remove them, and seven state senate districts would not have met minimum population requirements and would have had to be redrawn, setting off a chain reaction throughout the state, according to a report released this week by the NAACP Legal Defense Fund.

This counting method "artificially inflates the population count — and thus, the political influence — of the districts where prisons and jails are located," wrote the authors of the report, "Captive Constituents: Prison-Based Gerrymandering & The Distortion of

From *Miller-McCune,* June 2010.

Our Democracy." "At the same time," they add, "this practice reduces the political power of everyone else. The viability of our communities, integrity of our democracy and basic principles of equality suffer as a result."

African-Americans comprise 12.7 percent of the U.S. population. But because they make up 41.3 percent of the federal and state prison population, this type of gerrymandering disproportionately affects black communities. Prisons are also often located in rural areas — non-metropolitan America houses 20 percent of the national population, but 60 percent of new prison construction, according to the report — further distorting political muscle.

"It is all too reminiscent," the report says, "of the infamous 'three-fifths compromise,' whereby enslaved and disfranchised African Americans were counted to inflate the number of constituents — and thus, the political influence — of Southern states before the Civil War."

The report also cites the Iowa town of Anamosa, which was divided in 2002 into four city council wards of about 1,370 people each. One ward, however, was home to a state penitentiary with 1,320 inmates. In effect, the district held only about 50 true constituents who had the same political representation as wards 45 times as large — a violation of the spirit of the Supreme Court's "one person, one vote" apportionment principle.

The census counts some other groups similarly: College students are recorded in their dorm rooms, not their parents' homes, and military personnel are counted on base, not at their permanent residence. But both are integrated into the community — and can use its public services — in a way prisoners are not.

In total, about 2 million prisoners in the country are counted this way — enough people, according to the NAACP, to qualify by themselves for five votes in the Electoral College. And in 173 counties nationwide, the report adds, "half of the purported African-American population are not true residents, but are actually prisoners imported from elsewhere."

The problem has grown with the rate of incarceration (the NAACP partly blames the "war on drugs"), and the Census Bureau for the first time this year is becoming attuned to it. The bureau will provide prisoner data to states following this spring's decennial census in time for officials to use it in their 2010 redistricting. And this April, Maryland became the first state to pass legislation requiring redistricting officials to count inmates at their actual homes, using the new census data to identify them. Delaware is poised to follow next.

Some argue it doesn't matter where we count inmates, because most states don't let them vote. But the census counts everyone — including non-voting illegal immigrants and children — and we apportion political districts by total population, not just voting residents.

The NAACP points to the two states that do permit inmates to vote: Maine and Vermont. Both send prisoners absentee ballots from their home communities, a common-sense sign of where their political muscle would most logically be exercised.

7

The Future of Redistricting and Rural America

Josh Goodman

The once-a-decade redistricting triggered by the decennial census is about to change the makeup of state legislatures. For one thing, there are going to be a lot more legislators from urban areas, and a lot fewer from rural areas. This is cause for concern for those who do not live near major urban centers.

P atsy Ticer is a pretty powerful Virginia state senator, representing an economically vital part of her state: the Senate's 30th district. That district includes Alexandria and parts of Arlington and Fairfax counties—inner-ring suburbs directly across the Potomac River from Washington, D.C. Her district is home to federal workers, defense contractors, immigrants and young middle-class couples. It has subway stations, dog parks, farmers markets and Ronald Reagan Washington National Airport.

But after the 2007 elections, when Ticer was named chair of the Virginia Senate committee in charge of agricultural issues, she found herself teased by a lobbyist.

The lobbyist asked, Ticer remembers, "Now Sen. Ticer, have you found out how many cows there are in Virginia yet?"

A senator from District 30 finding herself in charge of agricultural issues partially reflects the vagaries of the legislative committee system. Ticer's committee is Agriculture, Conservation and Natural Resources. Ticer has a long-standing interest in conservation issues, and agriculture comes with the territory.

But her chairmanship also reflects the way Virginia is changing. In a state once defined by its tobacco fields, Virginia's population and political power has moved to Northern Virginia and Hampton Roads. Those regions increasingly have become urbanized and suburbanized. Rural interests aren't as important in Virginia's Capitol as they once were. The story is the same in many other states such as Georgia, Illinois and Texas, where suburban and exurban areas have boomed while rural ones haven't.

Next year, that population shift will have lasting consequences. With the once-a-decade redistricting process, state legislatures will

From *Governing*, November 2010.

be charged with redrawing the nation's political lines to reflect where people live. A proportionally smaller rural population will mean that fewer state legislators and congressmen represent rural areas in the next decade — and likely for many decades to come. The shift will leave rural areas grappling with a future in which the fate of issues they care about are at the mercy of people who rarely catch a glimpse of a cow.

MAKING THE MOVE FROM RURAL TO SUBURBAN

The U.S. Census Bureau is still weeks away from reporting its numbers, but pundits already have declared the winner in this round of reapportionment: Texas. Preliminary estimates show that since 2000, the state grew more than twice as fast as the national average. That growth will put Texas in line for perhaps four additional seats in the U.S. House of Representatives and four extra votes in the Electoral College. But not all of Texas will win.

Texas' growth is powered by the outward expansion of its major metropolitan areas. The nation's 25 fastest growing counties over the last decade include Rockwall and Collin counties near Dallas, Williamson and Hays counties near Austin, and Fort Bend and Montgomery counties near Houston. Large parts of Texas are becoming one giant exurb, especially along the highway that connects Dallas to Austin to San Antonio. "If you look back 10 or 20 years ago and you were to drive the Interstate 35 corridor, there were vast areas where there really was very little," says Lloyd Potter, Texas state demographer. "Now you see developments of big box stores and subdivisions."

Texas' big cities aren't growing quite as fast as these surrounding counties, but they're still growing impressively. In Texas' five biggest cities, population growth this decade ranges from 9 percent in Dallas to 34 percent in Fort Worth. In this regard, Texas is a microcosm of the nation. Despite the exoduses from a few Detroits and Clevelands, the last decade has generally been kind to the nation's big cities. Overall, the nation's 50 largest cities have seen their populations grow by 7.5 percent, only slightly less than the national average of 9 percent.

Amid all the growth in Texas, it would be easy to miss that more than 100 counties in the state lost population over the last decade. Of these shrinking counties, only

two have populations of more than 100,000. Most of the shrinking counties are in the vast area west of I-35. Young people are fleeing these areas to look for jobs.

Kel Seliger knows better than most what these trends mean for political representation. Seliger is a state senator from Amarillo. His current district comprises 26 counties stretching from the Oklahoma border nearly all the way to the Mexican border — "slightly smaller than the state of Indiana" is how he describes it. Next year, when it comes time for redistricting, Seliger's old lines won't contain enough people to support a district, which means it will have to grow larger still. It may add another 10 to 15 counties. This massive area of West Texas will have only one state senator in Austin.

That's only half the trend. Rural areas aren't just losing some of their population — they're ceasing to be rural at all. Located about 35 miles from Washington, D.C., Loudoun County, Va., used to be known for its horse farms. Today, as the nation's fifth fastest growing county since 2000, it has become famous for its new subdivisions, town centers and traffic jams. Ticer's inner-ring suburbs are experiencing moderate growth, but Virginia's fastest population growth is in suburbs that weren't suburbs 20 years ago. The trend is similar in many other states, from Illinois and Minnesota to California, Georgia and Florida. Just six of Illinois' 102 counties, all of them suburbs and exurbs of Chicago, account for the entirety of the state's 500,000 net growth in population over the last decade.

THE EFFECTS OF THE POPULATION SHIFT

All of this is a source of economic and political anxiety for people who live far from the nation's population hubs. So it was considered a small coup for Texas' rural communities that the person picked to lead the Senate committee in charge of redistricting is a West Texan himself: Seliger.

The senator, though, doesn't want anyone to view him as the savior of rural Texas. "Numbers dictate redistricting," Seliger says. "That's something nobody can do anything about." Most rural legislators echo Seliger. The principle of "one person, one vote," prevents lawmakers from doing any more than manipulating lines along the margins to preserve rural power.

The shift has major implications for a variety of policy issues, most of which have little to do with counting cows. Will education funding formulas favor urban districts or rural ones? Will states spend on mass transit or rural roads? Will rural broadband and telemedicine be priorities? Those are the sorts of topics Seliger cites as his concerns. "I don't represent a district from the 1940s," he says. "I represent people that live and work and go to school today."

Georgia is a good case study for why the balance of power between rural areas and urban and suburban areas matters. Rural Georgians — or at least some of them — have long asked why Atlanta gets the lion's share of the state's roads, jobs and water. They view the city as a hotbed of corruption. For their part, many Atlantans have long viewed the rest of the state as backward, unappreciative of their economic contributions and probably at least a little bit racist. Some of the tension has centered on Atlanta itself — a bastion of liberalism in a conservative state — but tension also exists between the broader Atlanta metro area and the rest of the state. "There has been a long-standing saying in Georgia that there are two Georgias," says state Rep. Jay Roberts. "You have Atlanta, and you have outside the doughnut."

As chairman of the Georgia House of Representatives Transportation Committee, it was Roberts' job early this year to make the two Georgias one on the nettlesome transportation funding issue. For the last few years, the top priority of Atlanta's business leaders has been to find new money for roads. They worried that congestion was slowly killing the economic vibrancy of the South's capital. But rural Georgians didn't want their tax dollars to fund roads in a part of the state that, in their view, already received more than it deserved. Efforts to raise the sales tax statewide stalled.

Finally, this year lawmakers reached a compromise. There won't be two Georgias, but 12. Each region will vote on whether to raise its sales tax to fund a list of transportation projects in its own region. Atlanta's leaders celebrated the breakthrough as a historic victory. Still, they had to battle for years merely to gain permission to tax themselves. Rural lawmakers held enough sway to veto any plan that put their communities at a disadvantage.

After Georgia elects a Legislature with the redrawn lines in 2012, that power will be diminished. State Rep.

Roger Lane, chairman of the Georgia House's Legislative and Congressional Reapportionment Committee, says the 29-county Atlanta region could control as many as 100 of the House's 180 seats, giving the region a clear majority for the first time. That won't mean that Atlanta will simply be able to run roughshod over the rest of the state. Those 100 representatives will come from different parties and different jurisdictions with different interests. Still, on topics like water and transportation policies, rural Georgia may be playing defense. "It can't be us against metro Atlanta," says Lane, whose district is nearly 200 miles southeast of Atlanta, "because they have the votes."

PROTECTING RURAL INTERESTS

The question for rural legislators is how to protect their interests with the members who are left. One option is solidarity.

That's the message preached by Maryland Delegate Sally Jameson, who recently chaired the National Conference of State Legislatures' (NCSL) Agriculture and Energy Standing Committee. Jameson says the creation of the Maryland Legislature's Rural Caucus about a decade ago helped check the power of lawmakers from Baltimore and the big Washington, D.C., suburbs. Legislators from the state's far-flung places — southern Maryland, the Eastern Shore and western Maryland — realized that they shared common interests on subjects like rural broadband. They also realized that together they controlled about half the seats in the House of Delegates. "It doesn't matter that we're Republicans or Democrats," says Jameson. "If we pull together as rural legislators, with just a couple of people from other parts of the state, we can win a vote." This summer, Jameson preached the value of active rural caucuses at NCSL's annual meeting.

If you know Maryland's geography though, Jameson is a somewhat unlikely rural champion. She represents part of Charles County, a jurisdiction in southern Maryland that's directly across the Potomac River from Fairfax County, Va. Charles County isn't shrinking — its population has jumped from around 120,000 in 2000 to more than 140,000 today. That's because it's quickly suburbanizing. "Sixty percent of my community commutes out of my county every day," Jameson says. "They drive into Washington, Baltimore, Northern Virginia to jobs."

That a lawmaker for Charles County still thinks of herself as rural is a hopeful sign for the future of rural interests. Lots of lawmakers in booming suburbs and exurbs still will have rural pieces to their districts after redistricting. Many of them may still have an affinity for rural life, even if it's disappearing around them. Whether these legislators are oriented toward the cities or the country will likely determine the fate of rural causes in legislatures over the next decade. "We don't have but five or six truly rural members left," says Texas state Rep. Sid Miller, a former chair of the state's House Agriculture and Livestock Committee, "but we don't tell them they're not rural."

Even if some suburban lawmakers continue to think of themselves as rural — and at times, vote like their rural colleagues — some rebalancing of political power will come with redistricting. Many legislatures have been dominated by rural members for decades. In most states, those days are over. To get anything done going forward, rural lawmakers will have to find common interests with suburban colleagues or even urban ones.

Ticer, for one, says she's eager for compromise. She notes that in Virginia, environmentalists and farmers have joined together to prod the state to provide more funding for efforts to limit runoff into the Chesapeake Bay. She'd like to see more efforts like that. "I really do subscribe to the idea that we are a commonwealth, and it's very important what happens in all parts of the state," Ticer says. "And certainly agriculture is a very important part of our economy."

But did Ticer ever find out how many cows there are in Virginia? "No, I didn't," she says. "Quite frankly, I didn't make too big of an effort."

The Dawn of Do-It-Yourself Redistricting? Online Software Puts Redistricting Tools in the Hands of the Public

8

Micah Altman and Michael P. McDonald

New software now allows pretty much any computer literate citizen to try their hand at drawing political districts. Should states be paying attention to boundary lines drawn by citizens?

From *Campaigns & Elections,* January 2011.

Arizona's 2nd congressional district is one of the most bizarrely shaped in the country. It consists of a head-shaped chunk in the state's eastern half attached by a long, thin neck the width of the Colorado River as it snakes for a hundred miles through the Grand Canyon to a body-shaped portion that hugs the state's border with California. Indeed, for sheer formal chutzpah, it may just outdo the salamander-shaped 19th century Massachusetts district drawn to benefit Governor Elbridge Gerry and dubbed a "gerrymander" by critics. Unlike most gerrymandered districts, though, the rationale for the odd shape of Arizona's 2nd is not to protect an incumbent or to favor a particular party, but to separate members of the small Hopi Tribe from their longstanding, more numerous rivals in the surrounding Navajo Tribe.

The desire to protect the voice of communities is just one among a number of competing concerns that factor into drawing congressional districts. Federal rules require that districts have equal population and that they promote minority representation under certain circumstances as established by the Voting Rights Act. State requirements vary, but may include respecting community interests, as Arizona does; following existing political boundaries or geographic features; making districts as compact as possible; promoting fairness, by not favoring one political group or candidate over another; and fostering competition, which is usually achieved by creating districts that have a relatively equal number of partisans.

The authorities tasked with drawing congressional districts while balancing these concerns vary. In most states, state legislators draw districts, which are subject (in many cases) to gubernatorial approval. In a few instances, an advisory commission proposes maps for legislative consideration. A small number of states give all the authority to a commission, which may be composed of elected officials or their designees, or of citizens who have minimal connections with political leadership. Overshadowing all are the courts, which may review redistricting plans to ensure that they meet legal requirements.

Arizona is one of two states with a citizens' redistricting commission that requires commissioners to solicit public input. During the redistricting a decade ago, Chairman Wayne Taylor of the Hopi Tribe testified that "our ability to create a bright future for Hopi hinges in part on our own strong representation in the political process unfettered by another countervailing interest that drowns [ours] out." The commission considered this and other testimony in carving Arizona up into congressional and state legislative districts with the aim of respecting the interests of all communities, as required by its constitutional mandate. One result was the oddly-shaped 2nd congressional district.

In other states, unlike Arizona, the public has little input into the redistricting process, and as a result district lines tend to favor political interests over the public interest. Perhaps the most infamous example in the past decade was the Texas re-redistricting saga. In 2003, Democratic state legislators dramatically fled the state in an unsuccessful attempt to thwart a Republican congressional gerrymander engineered by U.S. House Majority Leader Tom DeLay. DeLay was later convicted of Texas campaign finance violations committed with the aim of gaining control of the

> *"There is only one way to do reapportionment—feed into the computer all the factors except political registration."*
> — Ronald Reagan

state legislature in order to implement the re-redistricting, which helped Republicans win an additional five congressional seats in the next election.

In California's last redistricting, the two parties colluded to draw districts that protected all incumbents. As a result, over the past turbulent decade of American elections, only one of the state's fifty-three congressional seats has changed hands between parties. The public's inability to produce change despite dramatic shifts in its voting patterns was a key argument for congressional redistricting reform, which has since been approved via state ballot initiative.

California now joins Arizona in establishing a citizens' commission tasked with soliciting public input. The idea is that public engagement in the redistricting process can help produce districts that better fulfill the representational needs of communities—and the round of redistricting beginning this year holds the potential for an unprecedented public role in this arcane process. Readily accessible computer software has advanced such that anyone with an interest can draw legal redistricting plans for their states and localities that they can then submit for consideration by redistricting authorities.

> *"With sophisticated computer programs, politicians can draw lines to maximize precisely their party's representation and minimize the other's. The result is sham legislative elections in which fewer and fewer seats are competitive and moderates of both parties get squeezed out of office."*
> —The Washington Post

COMPUTERS: REDISTRICTING HERO OR VILLAIN?

As the quotes at the beginning of this article suggest, computers have been cast as both potential heroes and villains of redistricting. One view sees them as capable of automatically drawing the fairest districts, while the other sees them as enhancing politicians' ability to draw districts rigged in their favor. Having been involved in redistricting for the last two decades as consultants, observers and scholarly analysts, we know firsthand that both the promise and peril of computers have been greatly exaggerated.

Our research—much of it conducted with colleague Karin MacDonald—has shown that computers have enabled authorities to create redistricting plans more quickly and cheaply, but have not substantially affected plans' content. Contrary to the doomsayers, we have observed that computers produce modestly more compact and more politically competitive districts—perhaps because they enable politicians to gerrymander by creating districts with a more pleasing shape in a manner that wastes fewer votes. In short, computers don't gerrymander, people do. Politicians and consultants know perfectly well how to draw districts to their advantage without the help of a machine.

Those who have tried to use computers to produce fairer districts have likewise met with little success. Indeed, the first automated redistricting attempts in the 1960s produced spaghetti-like districts that failed the giggle test. Part of the problem is that there is no consensus on what constitutes "fair" representation, or how to define "fair plans" sufficiently for evaluation by a computer program. Further complicating matters, it is often mathematically intractable to determine whether a computer has yielded an "optimal" plan, even when a criterion is easily measurable. For these reasons, practical automated redistricting software always builds in "heuristics," which are essentially educated guesses about how to draw plans—and these heuristics may implicitly favor some criteria over others.

Ultimately, computers can't do the hardest work of redistricting for us: balancing the competing concerns described above. An additional concern is that certain criteria that might appear to be neutral turn out to have significant political consequences. It is generally true, for example, that Democrats are inefficiently concentrated in urban areas from a partisan gerrymandering standpoint. With this fact in mind, the Supreme Court has recognized that emphasizing compactness or respect for political boundaries may favor Republicans by wasting Democratic votes in uncompetitive urban districts.

MAXIMIZING PUBLIC PARTICIPATION

We believe that the best approach to redistricting is to maximize transparency by encouraging public participation and debate over what we as a society value in drawing districts. We also believe that the true promise of computers is to serve as a means to these ends, and that this promise has the potential to be fulfilled in the upcoming round of redistricting when, for the first time, redistricting software will be freely available to and easily usable by the public. In the 1980s and 1990s, only state governments or political parties could afford the million-dollar-plus price tag of a redistricting system's components: high-end computers, a geographic information system and a combined database of census and political data. Some states made these systems available to the public, but they were typically located in a government building at the state capital, which deterred widespread public participation.

Twenty years ago, a computerized redistricting system cost more than a home and could only be operated by experts. Ten years ago, the software was about as cheap as a used car and could be navigated by determined laypeople. Today these bars to public access are practically nonexistent. During the round of redistricting starting this year, the software will be freely available through Web browsers, and will be usable by non-experts with minimal training.

Technology may no longer pose a barrier to public participation in redistricting, but the legal questions surrounding it can be so complex that they pose a barrier in their own right. Anyone can draw a district; the trick is drawing one that satisfies all federal and state legal constraints. On that front, too, the bar has lowered, with a number of online resources offering guidance. For instance, A Citizen's Guide to Redistricting, available from New York University Law School's Brennan Center, provides a comprehensive overview of each state's redistricting process and the applicable federal and state rules. Even more accessible is the documentary Gerrymandering, which introduces many of the issues around redistricting. Over half a million copies of the film were distributed to educate California voters about the state's recently passed redistricting reform, and a DVD will be widely available this spring.

WILL THE PUBLIC PARTICIPATE?

So, anyone can engage in redistricting if they want to, but will they? Public opinion surveys routinely find that the public knows little about the redistricting process. (They often confuse legislative redistricting with school districting, which hits closer to home for many parents.) While we do not expect every American to spend their free time drawing districts—heck, many abstain from the far simpler and more basic act of voting—we do suspect that there exists a cadre of activists and students who will take the time to draw their own redistricting plans.

Our belief stems from a 2009 public competition in Ohio held by the secretary of state's office and reform advocates in which participants submitted congressional redistricting plans for the state. Even though the competing plans had no chance of being adopted, fourteen were submitted, of which eleven deemed to satisfy legal requirements. From these, three winners were selected that included districts that met a laundry list of legal requirements: they had roughly equal population, met Voting Rights Act requirements, were sufficiently compact, respected political boundaries, were politically fair and would foster political competition. Significantly, all three winning plans equaled or surpassed the current Ohio congressional districts on all these criteria.

In the upcoming round of redistricting, we are aware of similar plans among reform advocates in a number of states. In Ohio and Virginia, advocates are planning to conduct redistricting competitions. In New York, advocates hope to convene a shadow commission to draw districts in parallel with the legislature's efforts. And, in many other states, advocates aim to open the process to anyone who wants to draw a map.

Collaborative mapping has the potential to fundamentally change redistricting. A state's redistricting authority—be it the legislature or a commission—can solicit public input to draw lines that are in communities' stated interests. And, if a member of the public creates a redistricting plan that exceeds a state redistricting authority's plan in meeting the legal requirements, the media and the courts may take a jaundiced view of the state's original plan.

PLANS FOR PARTICIPATION

As discussed above, some states already have mechanisms in place to formally consider public plans during redistricting. We expect that Arizona and California's citizens' commissions will accept redistricting plans through public hearings. Even more innovative is Florida, where the state House is creating a Web-based mapping tool that will enable anyone to draw a plan and submit it to the state legislature with a few mouse clicks.

Although Florida's tool covers only one state, there are a number of other systems under development across the nation designed to foster participation in redistricting. In collaboration with the firm Azavea, we have developed the open-source DistrictBuilder software (available at www.publicmapping.org), which aims to enable anyone with a Web browser to easily produce a valid districting plan for the state of their choice.

As redistricting software becomes more widely available, one pitfall to look out for is "black box" gerrymandering, whereby computers are programmed to produce districts that are skewed in one way or another, either by design or error. To guard against this problem, our DistrictBuilder software follows principles for transparency in redistricting generated through discussion with redistricting experts and good government groups. We recommend that other software projects follow these principles as well, which include making public the code or algorithms used to "score" districts; offering users the ability to obtain data and redistricting plans in nonproprietary, machine-analyzable formats; and clearly disclosing any organizations providing financial backing.

We hope that the experience of drawing their own redistricting plans offered to members of the public by software such as ours will provide a jumping-off point for a broader discussion of how to draw better districts. An important part of that discussion should be the tradeoffs between the competing concerns described above, such as the tensions between ideals of compactness and fairness and between meeting Voting Rights Act requirements and fostering competition. As more people grapple with these tradeoffs firsthand, public dialogue on how to approach redistricting will inevitably grow richer.

III

Political Parties and Interest Groups

Political parties have never been hugely popular with the public, but over the past couple of years, the two major partisan flavors managed to leave a historically bad taste in the mouths of many. In reaction, a lot of voters seemed to be using tea as a sort of partisan mouthwash, swishing out traditional centralized Republican or Democratic approaches in favor of a do-it-yourself, bottom-up approach that prided itself on not being anything like a traditional party.

While the rise of the Tea Party and its shake-up of the political landscape in 2010 and 2011 has energized a lot of voters, it has left a lot of scholars and observers of politics scratching their heads. The Tea Party clearly added a jolt to the most recent electoral cycle as its activists targeted some conservative Republicans (mostly in primary elections) and some liberal Democrats (mostly in general elections). It wasn't just seeking to win elections; its members wanted government to respond to its demands, and separate Tea Party caucuses have started to spring up in Congress and state legislatures.

Yet for all this, the Tea Party is not a party, at least not by traditional definitions of a political party. The most widely accepted definition of a political party in the United States is an organization that runs candidates for office under its own label. The Tea Party does not, for the most part, do that. Mostly what it does is support candidates who run as Republicans. Some traditional Republicans are not too comfortable with that and are leery of some of the more extreme demands made under the Tea Party banner (calls to ban the Federal Reserve, for example, make a lot of people nervous).

So if it's not a political party, what is it? A loosely organized wing of the Republican Party? If so, it's an odd sort of political party faction. It has no clear leader and has been accused of having an incoherent agenda. People are clear on what Tea Partiers don't like—government spending, government regulation, and, well, government in general—but there is no universal platform of policy specifics. The Tea Party might be described as a special interest group; it is, after all, undeniably lobbying government hard for its interests even if it's not always clear what those interests are. Perhaps it's a mash-up of both. If that's the case, the Tea Party is a truly remarkable phenomenon; it's managed to take elements of the two most mistrusted and disliked elements of the political system—political parties and special interest groups—and turn them into a popular grassroots movement.

As the readings in this chapter will show, the Tea Party is not simply a movement aimed at the federal government. It has been active in a wide array of state races, and the movement itself is much more state and local than nationally based.

POLITICAL PARTIES AND INTEREST GROUPS: DIFFERENCES AND SIMILARITIES

Political parties and special interest groups are alike in many ways. For example, both raise money, endorse candidates, and mobilize support for or opposition to particular issues and causes (and the Tea Party has done all of this in spades). Yet, there are also fundamental differences.

The most important difference is that political parties run candidates for office under their own label and help organize the government. The Tea Party has not yet done this. It mostly has backed Republicans rather than nominating its own candidates. Special interest groups might try to help get candidates elected, and they certainly try to influence government. They do not, however, nominate candidates; nor do people organize the government under their name. For example, the National Rifle Association (NRA) may contribute to a candidate's election campaign and try to persuade that candidate to support its position on legislative proposals if elected to office. That candidate, however, is likely to be elected as a Democrat or a Republican and will not be identified

formally as an NRA representative. If elected, that candidate's role in the legislature—committee assignment, relative power—will be determined by his or her party affiliation, not by the NRA. In this sense, then, the Tea Party seems more like a special interest group.

Regardless of the hybrid nature of the Tea Party (i.e., it seems to be part political party, part special interest group), political parties and special interest groups are generally seen as natural byproducts of a representative democratic system. If people have a representative form of government along with freedom of expression, freedom of assembly, and the right to petition government for redress of grievances, they have a gold-plated invitation to form parties and special interest groups.

While they are a natural outgrowth of representative democracy, political parties and special interest groups have never been particularly popular with citizens. Too often ignored in such judgments are the positive services these organizations provide to democracy. Both organizations play a critical role in aggregating interests and connecting them to government. A single individual is unlikely to gain the attention of a legislature or a governor, but a well-organized interest group that can mobilize voters, gain prominent news coverage, and wage effective public opinion campaigns is much harder for a government to ignore. Whatever it is, the Tea Party serves as a good example of this sort of thing. Yet while they provide important services to democracy, political parties and special interest groups are viewed with suspicion, especially when it comes to their relations with each other. The scramble to win elections, control the key offices and institutions of government, and influence the decisions of policy makers create a negative image of political parties and special interest groups. And the fact is, political parties do try to tip the electoral scales in their favor, and lobbyists sometimes do cross the line from persuasion to less ethical—and less legal—means of trying to line up legislative support for their favored policies.

The readings in this section take a snapshot of the current state of political parties in states and localities. The first essay by Lara Brown, a political scientist at Villanova University, is basically trying to answer the question of what, or at least who, the Tea Party is or (more interestingly) is not. The rank-and-file members of this suddenly potent force do not necessarily reflect its popular image.

The second essay by Pamela Prah takes a look at the Tea Party's attempts to influence state political races. Though typically viewed as being more federally than state focused, the Tea Party clearly has its sights set on the state level as well. An essay by Louis Jacobson points out that the rise of the Tea Party and similar minor-party movements at the state level could have serious ramifications for traditional political parties at the state level, especially the Republican Party. The Colorado GOP came alarmingly close to losing its major party status in 2010 because its gubernatorial nominee, Dan Maes, ran so poorly in the general election. Colorado's gubernatorial race was essentially between Democrat John Hickenlooper and Tea Party favorite Tom Tancredo, formerly a Republican but running under the banner of the American Constitution Party. The final essay takes a look at how the major parties are getting along in state legislatures. The short answer is not very well. Tea, anyone?

9

Restlessness Unleashed: The Tea Partiers and the Lessons of History

Lara Brown

The Tea Party is stirring up politics. Who are these guys and what do they want?

Members of the Tea Party movement, according to liberal pundits, are angry right-wing extremists. The progressive news website Alternet describes the movement as being "built on fear, violence, and race resentment." New York Times columnist Frank Rich views the Tea Party as an invention of ultra-conservative billionaires and plugged-in operatives. Washington Post columnist E.J. Dionne thinks it is merely a "successful scam." A Rasmussen Reports survey reveals that "a plurality (46%) of the political class says most members of the Tea Party are racist, but 53% of mainstream voters disagree."

This fear and loathing of the Tea Party movement is clouding too many peoples' judgment. If you don't understand the Tea Party, you can't develop political strategies that capitalize on the voter sentiment underlying it.

It's helpful to gain some historical perspective in order to think about how campaigns may tap into what is better understood as a century-long brewing Jeffersonian reaction to the triumph and overreach of Hamiltonian nationalism. What? Exactly. Read on.

Although 73% of Tea Party supporters are conservative and 53% are angry, according to a recent New York Times/CBS News survey, 71% do not believe it is ever justified to engage in violent action against the government. Eight percent consider themselves Democrats, 43% Independents, and 49% Republicans, according to recent Gallup polls.

Even though a large plurality of members (48%) in past elections have "usually voted Republican," according to recent surveys, it should not be overlooked that only a few Tea Partiers have been consistently faithful to the GOP. In fact, more say they have voted

From *Campaigns & Elections,* October 2010.

equally for both Republicans and Democrats (25%) in past elections than say they have always voted Republican (18%).

Take away #1: Ideology is more important to these voters than party. They can be persuaded to support a candidate who agrees with them.

But this conservatism is not synonymous with social conservatism. Tea Partiers are most in agreement about the role of government and least in agreement on social issues. Ninety-two percent prefer a smaller government with fewer services over a larger government with more services, but only 32% believe that abortion should not be available. A total of 57% believe that gay couples should either be allowed to marry (16%) or form civil unions (41%). Although more conservative (traditional may be a better descriptive) than the public as a whole, the Tea Party is not the religious right. Only 39% of Tea Partiers identify themselves as evangelical or born-again Christians and only 38% say they attend religious services every week. Moreover, they admire Newt Gingrich (10%) more than Sarah Palin (9%) or Glenn Beck (1%).

Take away #2: An attractive candidate to Tea Partiers focuses his/her campaign on limiting the role of the federal government, reducing the federal debt, empowering the states, increasing individual liberty, ending political corruption, and ousting the elitists from the nation's capital. This – by the way – is Jefferson (see his presidential campaign in 1800).

Although veteran reporter Dan Balz of the Washington Post explains that Tea Partiers share some characteristics with Perot's voters (more male than female, mostly white, and about a third with college degrees), he sees little overlap. But his assessment only compares "snap shots" of the movements. He fails to consider how Perot's voters have changed over time – after enduring a "Republican Revolution," a presidential scandal and impeachment battle, a nearly tied presidential election, a terrorist attack on American soil, an incompetent governmental response to Hurricane Katrina, a near tripling of the federal debt (from about $4 trillion in 1992 to $11 trillion in 2009), and two long wars far outside our geographic region (Afghanistan and Iraq).

Balz asserts that "age" is a "revealing" difference between the two groups – 63% of Perot's voters were 18-44, while only 44% of Tea Party supporters were under 45 – but he forgets that Perot's voters who were between 27-44 in 1992 are now, eighteen years later, between 45-62. He then notes that Tea Partiers are wealthier than Perot's voters. Yet one would assume that as Perot's voters aged and neared retirement, as is typical of most Americans, they earned higher salaries and accumulated more wealth especially during the "boom years" of the late 1990s.

He also states that Perot's voters were not as conservative, nor as Republican as the Tea Partiers. But then again, according to Gallup, the percentage of Americans who identify as conservative has grown from 36% in 1992 to 40% in 2009. Also from 2000 to 2009, the percentage of Republicans who consider themselves conservative has grown from 61% to 69% and the percentage of Independents who consider themselves conservative has grown from 29% to 35%. In this past year, Gallup found that the percentage of independents who lean Republican has grown from 11% to 17%. Beyond these numbers, one should consider that in 1992 the incumbent president was a Republican and in 2009 the incumbent president was a Democrat, meaning that one would expect a greater number of the voters who are dissatisfied with government and the incumbent president's administration to identify more with the party out of power.

Take away #3: Many Tea Partiers are Perot voters who have grown older, wealthier, more conservative, and angrier about the governmental and partisan failures they've witnessed. If you want to know more about these voters, focus your attention on Ohio's presidential vote since 1972. While the number of voters has increased by approximately 1.5 million, the turnout and the swings in support reveal a penchant among Ohioans for small government, fiscal conservatives who are somewhat anti-establishment – including some Democrats and Independents. They're also not opposed to staying home when no candidate fits the bill (see 1988 and 1996).

Take away #4: The Tea Party voters you thought were part of the far-right "fringe" should really be thought of as part of the Republican-leaning Independent "swing."

None of this is new in American history. Today's restless political environment bears a striking resemblance to the historical period that spawned the progressive movement.

In 1906, President Theodore Roosevelt said: "At this moment we are passing through a period of great unrest

– social, political, and industrial unrest." Yet by the time he implored reformers to do more than "muck rake" and to pursue "a resolute and eager ambition to secure the betterment of the individual and the nation," the people's "fierce discontent" had been roiling the country for 30 years – since the highly controversial 1876 presidential election.

In 1884 Democrat Grover Cleveland won the presidency. Ousted in 1888 by Republican Benjamin Harrison, Cleveland retook the White House for the Democrats in 1892. These partisan oscillations were not confined to the executive branch. In 1882 Republicans lost majority control of the House. In 1888 the Democrats turned back control to the Republicans. But two short years later, in the 1890 midterm, the Republicans not only failed to secure the majority, but lost 93 of the 332 seats in the House. All this occurred before the Panic of 1893.

The historical record shows that these elections were brutally competitive and appallingly corrupt. Disgusted with state and local political bosses and their patronage-fueled machines, middle-class voters swung from party to party, hoping a true reformer would make good on his promises to transcend partisanship, control big business, and cleanse government.

Aside from these tumultuous elections, two presidents were brought down by assassins' bullets. In 1881, James Garfield was shot by a "Stalwart" who believed Garfield insufficiently grateful (he had not awarded enough of the presidential spoils) to his faction of the Republican Party. In 1901, William McKinley was shot by an anarchist who was convinced that McKinley's only concern was the wealthy industrialists.

Similarly turbulent, these last 30 years show popular support swinging bizarrely from Carter to Reagan to Perot to Clinton to Gingrich, and back to Clinton again. The partisan wrangling over the presidency in 2000 was also eerily reminiscent of 1876. Despite Bush's reelection in 2004, the Democrats prevailed in Congress in 2006 and captured the presidency in 2008.

Tellingly, over the last three years, an average of only one in five Americans have said they were satisfied. Somewhat ominously, since 1979 when Gallup began this measure, there have only been eight years when the average percentage of Americans who are satisfied has reached 50% or higher (1984, 1985, 1986, 1998, 1999, 2000, 2001, and 2002).

Though the Progressives argued for empowering the national government and employing more administrative professionals and the Tea Partiers argue for emboldening state governments and electing more ordinary citizens, both hope to root out the partisan corruption in politics (the NBC/WSJ poll found that 42 percent of Tea Party supporters viewed their involvement as a protest against "business as usual in Washington").

Take away #5: When popular support swings wildly, the people are trying to send a simple message ("listen to us"), not endorse a partisan platform.

After McKinley, Theodore Roosevelt ascended the presidency and won reelection in 1904. Although Roosevelt did not run as a Progressive until 1912, he had been a champion of their cause since President Harrison had appointed him to the Civil Service Commission in 1889. This is Hamilton (see Roosevelt's "New Nationalism" platform in his 1912 campaign).

By the time Democrat Woodrow Wilson became president, Progressives were a significant force challenging the two-party system. In 1912, nine Progressives won seats in the House and one Progressive earned a seat in the Senate. Wilson knew that he should adopt much of Roosevelt's "New Nationalism" and set aside his own "New Freedom" doctrine (a recasting of Jefferson's philosophy), if he hoped to win reelection in 1916. Wilson did and he won.

Since that time, both Democrats and Republicans, until about the mid-1960s, continued to support an ever-expanding Progressive vision of the federal government.

Remaking America, Progressives passed constitutional amendments that levied a federal income tax on individuals, enfranchised women and young voters, and outlawed alcohol and the poll tax. Franklin Roosevelt grew the size and jurisdiction of the federal government far beyond what Hamilton would have ever endorsed, establishing numerous programs and agencies. Progressive presidents led America into not one, but four wars (World Wars I and II, Korea, and Vietnam). Over a 20-year period, presidents Harry Truman, Dwight Eisenhower, John Kennedy, and Lyndon Johnson worked to secure the civil rights of African-Americans, while the Supreme Court applied the 14th Amendment to the civil liberties of all Americans.

The conservative backlash began in 1964, when Barry Goldwater sided against the Civil Rights Act, believing that the legislation stretched the federal government's power too far. Although Republicans currently carry the torch of small government conservatives, every Republican president since Nixon has presided over an increase in the national debt as a percentage of GDP. No wonder Tea Partiers are so dissatisfied with their political choices.

Taken Together: Tea Partiers are the flip side of the Progressives' coin. Their votes are not locked up, but they do favor Republicans and small government conservatives. They want principled candidates willing to take on government spending and reduce the federal debt. More generally, they're looking for hope because they're disgusted with the current political system which they view, according to Stanford political scientist Larry Diamond, as comprising "two bankrupt parties bankrupting the country."

10

Tempest in a Tea Party

Pamela M. Prah

The Tea Party is mostly seen as a movement trying to influence what thefederal government does. That's only half right. Tea is being served in the states, too.

Anyone who is following the 2010 midterm elections knows that tea party activists are angry, motivated and determined to create a low-spending, low-taxing Congress. It's anybody's guess just how successful they will be. But an equally compelling question is just what impact the movement will have on gubernatorial and other state elections this fall.

Dale Robertson, president of Teaparty.org, admits that his movement is thinking more about Washington right now than about the states. But he is trying to shift that emphasis a few degrees. "We are trying to focus on the state races," he says. "We are getting candidates set up every day."

Both parties are taking tea party activists seriously and are wary of offending them – if they are not already actively wooing them. Just look at the governor's race in Ohio. Republican gubernatorial candidate John Kasich openly touts his tea party credentials in his bid to defeat incumbent Democrat Ted Strickland. "I think I was in the tea party before there was a tea party," Kasich famously told a Columbus crowd earlier this year. "This is a real movement with a real message about people's frustrations by broken promises that leaders on both sides of the aisle would be foolish to ignore," he went on to write in a blog posting.

For his part, Strickland says he agrees with some of the very same things that upset the tea party folks, including high taxes and inefficient government. "I would ask them to evaluate my performance, and I think there is much they could find positive," he said while he was in Washington in February, noting that he has cut taxes and reduced state government by more than 5,000 employees.

From *Stateline.org,* March 2010.

The Iowa Tea Party doesn't have a candidate in the race between incumbent Governor Chet Culver, a Democrat, and former Governor Terry Branstad, a Republican who is leading in some polls. "We don't have the money," says Ryan Rhodes, a party activist in Des Moines. But the tea partiers have a candidate for secretary of state in Matt Schultz, a Republican city councilman from Council Bluffs, who hopes to unseat incumbent Democrat Mike Mauro.

Schultz will first have to beat two opponents in the June 8 Republican primary in a race that party insiders say will be competitive. Schultz, a life-long Republican, calls himself a tea party member because "the Republican Party has strayed away" from fiscal conservatism.

Mississippi Governor Haley Barbour, a GOP strategist who helped engineer the Republican takeover of both chambers of Congress in the 1990s, sees an important role for the tea party movement in what he hopes will be a GOP comeback in 2010. "Republicans have a huge obligation to reach out and include the tea party activists because they ought to be with us. And if they're not, it's our fault," he told a roundtable of reporters last month as head of the Republican Governors Association.

Barbour compares today's tea partiers to the supporters of Ross Perot who rallied behind the Texas businessman's crusades against deficits and free trade as an Independent candidate during the 1992 presidential election.

"The worst thing that could happen to the conservative movement and the best thing that could happen to Barack Obama and the Democratic Party would be is if any substantial number of tea party voters became a third party," Barbour said. "Why split up the conservative vote? We can all work together."

But some tea party activists aren't buying it. "If the Republican Party were actually providing constitutionally conservative candidates, then it wouldn't be an issue, but when you look at both parties they seem to be more of the same," says Robertson of Teaparty .org. "The only reason the tea party exists today is because the political parties have lost track of their platforms."

In West Virginia, Elliot Simon, who has been both a Democrat and Republican, is now a tea party candidate running for a seat in the state House of Representatives. He calls Barbour's comments "political strategizing." He says the tea party's basic tenets of lower taxes and less government fit better under the Republican banner but that anyone is welcome who stands behind the movement's principles. He insists "we're not a radical movement . . . We are very mainstream."

G. Terry Madonna, director of the Franklin and Marshall College Poll in Lancaster, Pennsylvania, says that liberals who call the tea party " 'kooky right-wing crazies' seriously mischaracterize the movement." Madonna's latest poll shows more voters in Pennsylvania were likely (45 percent) than unlikely (34 percent) to vote for a candidate who supports the tea party movement's goals. To Madonna's surprise, nearly a quarter of Democrats said they were somewhat likely or very likely to vote for a tea party candidate. "I think they are underestimated," he concludes.

Delaware Governor Jack Markell, who heads the Democratic Governors Association, says Democrats' message to tea party supporters will be the same as the party's message to everyone else. "We are going to fight for every single job and we are going to do our best to ensure every single dollar of taxpayer's money is spent wisely," he said last month. "I guess there will be some tea party activists that don't like that message and that's fine. We are never going to get everybody on board."

Tea party candidates failed to deliver many knockout punches in the two states that have already had their primaries. In Illinois, Republican and tea party activist Adam Andrzejewski got 14 percent of the vote for the Republican gubernatorial nomination, coming in fifth in the Feb. 2 GOP primary. In Texas, Republican gubernatorial hopeful and tea party activist Debra Medina was polling strongly until her appearance on the Glenn Beck radio show, where she refused to take a position on whether the U.S. government was behind the 9/11 attacks on the World Trade Center. Medina finished third with 18 percent of the vote in the March 2 primary.

But at the legislative level in Texas, David Simpson, a tea party candidate, beat Republican incumbent state Rep. Tommy Merritt in a bid to represent Longview in East Texas. And an April 13 runoff will decide if another Republican tea party candidate, Charles Perry, will unseat GOP Rep. Delwin Jones, who has been in the Texas Legislature for nearly three decades, in a contest to represent Lubbock.

It's too early to tell whether tea partiers will be spoilers or kingmakers in important state elections this year. But their mere presence in a campaign could force candidates of both parties to make more detailed statements on spending, state sovereignty, gun rights and illegal immigration, and may very well shake up key statewide races.

And then there is the issue of voter turnout. Tea party activists in Texas are taking credit for the record number of voters who showed up for the GOP gubernatorial primary in March. Dennis J. Goldford, professor of politics at Drake University, says there's a simple reason. "Angry people turn out to vote," he says.

11

The Great Divide

Garry Boulard

Compromise used to be the way things got done in state legislatures. These days? Not so much. State legislators seem more inclined to toe the party line than step across the aisle.

From *State Legislatures,* February 2011.

Former Nevada Senator Bill Raggio isn't sure exactly when things changed. But sometime in the last decade, he began to think almost everything in the Nevada Legislature was being decided on a partisan basis—and not just as it pertained to head-line-making issues such as gay rights, immigration and abortion, but with the very process of the Senate itself.

Even decisions on organization and procedure and the makeup of committees have taken on a partisan tone, says Raggio, who was first elected to the Nevada Senate in 1972.

"There is no doubt about it: Things are much more partisan here today than they used to be," he says. "And the divisiveness is not only between parties, but even within parties."

Across the country, Tennessee Representative Jimmy Naifeh has been frustrated by the same trend.

"When I was speaker and we were dealing with a major issue, I would bring in both Democratic and Republican leaders, and we would sit at my conference table and work our way through things," Naifeh says.

"We did that over and over again on any number of issues. And by and large that worked out well."

Now, "talking things out is regarded by some as a bad thing," he says. "You have to be a Democrat or Republican, no matter what.

"I don't like it one bit."

Are state legislatures—long regarded as more civil assemblies than the national Congress because of close working relationships between members of both parties—going the way of Washington? Is that D.C. phenomenon known as gridlock now a regular feature of life in many statehouses?

A number of legislators say yes. They point to the growing role of big money in state campaigns, greater integration of state and national party leaders, term limits, and an electoral system tilted toward ideological extremes.

"I've been in the Kansas Legislature for 12 years, and the partisanship has gotten steadily worse the whole time," says Kansas Senator John Vratil. "More and more legislators think that this is all some kind of game and that the objective is to acquire power and dominate the other party."

In fact, the shift to a more partisan tone under the statehouse dome has been under

> "I've been in the Kansas Legislature for 12 years, and the partisanship has gotten steadily worse the whole time. More and more legislators think that this is all some kind of game and that the objective is to acquire power and dominate the other party."
>
> —John Vratil

way since the turn of the century, says Michael Dubin, author of "Party Affiliations in the State Legislatures."

"It's really a matter of the statehouses finally catching up to Washington," he says. "For more than a decade now, the legislator who revels in bipartisanship and moderation has been on the outs. The person who is more confrontational has become a driving force and gets all the attention."

What's more, he says, the age of instant and constant information has empowered the people at the extremes of the political spectrum. "Politicians both in Washington and at our state

Partisanship: The Bad Old Days

Maybe the most memorable partisan moment in congressional history came on May 22, 1856, when Representative Preston Brooks of South Carolina entered the Senate chamber and proceeded to beat Massachusetts Senator Charles Sumner with a cane.

The attack followed Sumner's "Crime Against Kansas" speech in which he vilified two other senators in a debate over whether Kansas should enter the union as a free state or slave state. Brooks took umbrage at Sumner's characterization of his fellow South Carolinian, Senator Andrew Butler.

Although such physical attacks were rare, historians often point to two dramatic congressional debates over slavery when making the point that partisanship and angry divisions are nothing new to Washington.

The Missouri Compromise of 1820 and the Compromise of 1850, both dealing with slavery, were forged only after weeks of parliamentary maneuvering, angry speeches and back-room deal-making. Participants in both battles felt the partisan and sectional rancor had become so great that both Congress and the country itself were on the verge of coming apart.

Congressional resentments simmered for the rest of the decade and were most conspicuously on display when the young Republican John Sherman was denied the speakership for endorsing a book called "The Crisis of the South," which argued that slavery was no longer economically viable.

For two months, vote after vote saw Sherman falling just short of a majority. The prolonged battle meant paralysis; members could be not paid until Congress was officially organized, resulting in large hotel and bar tabs, prompting the sergeant-at-arms to ladle out cash—said to eventually total more than $50,000—to tide them over.

The members finally selected a new speaker in February 1860 after Sherman withdrew. The likelihood of continued congressional rancor was greatly reduced when all the Southern members of both the House and Senate resigned their seats one year later when the states they represented seceded.

But congressional paralysis was hardly over. For a period of nearly three decades beginning in the late 1870s, a series of elections left either the Senate or House, or both, narrowly divided, creating a sort of permanent gridlock, says political scientist Bruce Oppenheimer.

"What was different in that era was that a large number of seats were highly competitive, so there were swings back and forth with partisan shifts in the electorate," Oppenheimer says. "Today we have a smaller number of seats that are highly competitive, along with a large base of seats that are electorally safe."

Author Michael Dubin contends the modern era of excessive partisanship began to appear in both Washington and the statehouses with the emergence of issues such as civil rights and Vietnam in the 1960s and abortion and gay rights after that.

"These issues greatly sharpened the partisan divide," says Dubin. "But the difference now is that even on economic matters we are also seeing similarly angry confrontations and debates."

capitols are playing to the folks who are most interested in what they have to say, who also tend to be the most ideological."

GROWING CLOUT OF MONEY

The change to a more partisan tone has been a long time coming and the rising cost of running for office is part of the reason, according to Dan Glickman, a senior fellow at the Bipartisan Policy Center in Washington, D.C.

"It's getting very expensive," he says. "Many state legislative races today cost what congressional races used to cost about 25 years ago. When you have a lot of money coming into politics, particularly outside money, it discourages people in a legislative setting from working together."

The reason?

Big money—national party money—often comes to those who get the most attention and are the most confrontational, because they have the most potential as possible candidates for Congress, says Nicole Mellow, a professor of political science at Williams College.

"There are more linkages now at the state level with what is happening in Washington," says Mellow, who is the author of "The State of Disunion: Regional Sources of Modern American Partisanship."

"There is greater integration between national party leaders and state party leaders," she says. "Once that cycle is in motion, it only intensifies conflict.

> *"Term limits are one of the reasons so much of this is happening. Members who are not going to be here for very long soon decide they are not all that interested in working with people on the other side of the aisle."*
>
> —Bob Burns

"And that integration very much includes the way money flows and communication works."

TERM LIMITS, NATIONAL ISSUES

Former Arizona Senator Bob Burns thinks structural changes in state legislatures also have contributed to the problem.

"Term limits are one of the reasons so much of this is happening," he says. "Before, people were concerned about being re-elected, which meant it was important for them to get things done and, by so doing, develop relationships with other members, regardless of their party and philosophy," he says.

"The imposition of term limits changed all that," says Burns. "Members who are not going to be here for very long soon decide they are not all that interested in working with people on the other side of the aisle."

Burns also thinks the decline in nonpartisan social activities, often hosted by a lobbyist or interest group, has made things worse. Such events are less frequent because of media scrutiny and ethics rules.

"We don't get to know each other the way we used to," Burns says. "And I think that's to our loss."

Naifeh says the political aspirations of some members also have not helped. "Whenever one of the members starts to run for Congress or governor or some higher office, that's when the trouble really starts," he says. "Their whole attitude changes about their votes and what they are doing. They tend to become much more partisan than before."

Raggio also points to what he describes as a nationalization of state issues as a source of conflict.

"Practically everything we do here has some sort of national significance today," he says. "Very few issues are entirely local. Certainly the economy is not just local. And that's one of the main reasons members at the state level have begun to adopt the talking points of their national parties."

MIXED MESSAGES

It may be of scant comfort, but for those who think the current level of partisanship is something new, think again.

"We've been here repeatedly throughout our history," says Dubin. "When you think about issues like Vietnam and civil rights, I would argue that in some way we are less confrontational than we used to be. The only difference now is that the fighting seems to go on nonstop." Against this wave of partisanship are several studies released this year by Allegheny College that found voters dislike the excessive partisanship of their elected leaders. In one survey, 85 percent said they wanted their representatives to "Be friends with individuals of the other party."

"People are turned off by all the negative campaigning and attacks," says Daniel Shea, director of the Center for Political Participation at Allegheny College.

But Shea acknowledges that constituents send conflicting messages.

"Most people say they want their representatives to be more moderate, but it is the fired-up and angry supporters who are the ones sending e-mails and calling on the phone, encouraging their elected officials to be just as hard core as possible."

He points to the effectiveness of groups such as MoveOn.org and the Tea Party in primary campaigns. "In both parties, if you don't toe the line, you might well be thrown out of office. And that is true at the state legislative level as well."

Nonetheless, a certain amount of partisanship may be a good thing.

"Theoretically, our system functions best when competing ideas are forced to be hashed out and when people argue ideas forcefully and with conviction," says Mellow. "People get frustrated with how long it takes to get legislation through in Washington or in the statehouses, how difficult it may seem to make changes. But the good side to that is the opportunity for deliberation."

Raggio takes a long view.

"I remember the days when the John Birch Society controlled the Republican Party. But they finally wore out their welcome," he says. "The Democrats have also gone through periods of time when different factions were controlling them.

"These are just phases that our country has had to get through," he says. "The only problem is that we don't know how long this particular phase is going to last."

12

State Political Parties Stand the Risk of Losing Major Party Status in Future Elections

Louis Jacobson

The rise of third party movements like the Tea Party may lead to Republicans losing majority party status in some states.

O n Election Day 2010, the Colorado Republican Party came within 20,000 votes of losing its major-party status in the state. This week, state Republican Party chairman Dick Wadhams decided against seeking another term, citing "nuts who have no grasp of what the state party's role is." His departure highlights a growing schism in state GOP parties nationwide, one that other state Republican parties face if the Tea Party's growth continues. The risk? The loss of major party status.

The differences between major- and minor-party statuses vary by state. In Colorado, political experts say that minor parties face greater challenges in petitioning for ballot access and for holding primary elections. If parties do not hold a primary, then donors can only give to candidates for the general election, effectively halving potential candidate donations.

To be sure, the 2010 gubernatorial election in Colorado was somewhat unusual, due to a problematic GOP gubernatorial nominee and a strong third-party bid by a former congressman. The initial frontrunner for the GOP gubernatorial nomination, former Rep. Scott McInnis, saw his candidacy derailed after allegations that he had plagiarized reports on water policy. That enabled a little-known challenger, Dan Maes, to win the GOP nomination.

Eventually, Maes' own credibility plummeted when the media raised questions about his claim that he had worked "undercover" 25 years earlier with the Kansas Bureau of Investigation. This enabled former GOP Rep. Tom Tancredo to become Democratic Denver Mayor John Hickenlooper's main challenger. Tancredo ran under the banner of the American Constitution Party (ACP).

From *Governing*, February 2011.

53

On Election Day, Hickenlooper cruised to victory with 51 percent of the vote, followed by Tancredo at 36 percent and Maes at 11 percent. If Maes had failed to receive 10 percent, the GOP would have lost major-party status. This is striking because Republican candidates in the same election defeated two Democratic members of Congress, the secretary of state and the state treasurer; and flipped the previously Democratic state House.

Minor party status in Colorado applies to all candidates up and down the ticket, and it lasts until the next gubernatorial election. Had Maes' won just 20,000 fewer votes out of almost 1.8 million cast, all Republican candidates — for whatever county, legislative, or statewide office they sought in 2012 and 2014 — would have been deemed minor party candidates, with all the additional challenges that entails.

The last time a Democratic or Republican state party lost its legal status as a majority party was in Virginia in 1990, says Richard Winger, the publisher and editor of Ballot Access News. At the time, Virginia law said that a "party" was a group that had polled 10 percent in any statewide race during the last election. In 1990, the Democrats decided not to run against Republican Sen. John Warner, a popular moderate. But that was the only statewide race that year, and Democrats realized too late that doing so would force their party off the ballot in the next election. Virginia's Legislature saved the party by changing in a special session the definition to any group that had polled 10 percent for any statewide race in either of the last two elections, "Winger says".

That same year, Democrats in Connecticut were on thin ice. During the 1990 election, former Sen. Lowell Weicker, running under the banner of a third party, won the governorship, and the Democratic nominee, Bruce Morrison, barely cleared the 20 percent threshold needed for major-party status.

Today, state Republican organizations, dominated by conservatives whose taste runs to the right of what voters in the state prefer, puts the GOP at risk. Wadhams added that "the ability of Colorado Republicans to win and retain the votes of hundreds of thousands of unaffiliated swing voters in 2012 will be severely undermined."

Of course, there's no certainty that the same pattern will hold in 2012, a year in which there are fewer elections for statewide offices. But the 2010 election featured a confluence of both three-way races and Tea Party victories over establishment candidates in party primaries and conventions. Independent Lincoln Chafee won the governorship of Rhode Island, while third-party candidates for governor took significant (if losing) vote shares in such states as Maine, Massachusetts and Minnesota. In a rash of Senate contests, Tea Party-affiliated candidates prevailed in intra-party contests over establishment-backed candidates, including Colorado, Florida, Kentucky, Nevada and Utah.

According to an account in the *Atlantic*, of the 3,500 or so delegates to Colorado's state GOP convention, Wadhams estimated that in 2010 "about 40 percent of that state assembly were delegates for the first time," and that "the vast majority" were affiliated with the Tea Party or similar groups. Tancredo, for his part, returned to the GOP after the election, and it's not clear that the ACP, with its small infrastructure, can benefit from its new-found major-party status.

IV

Legislatures

State legislatures really only do three basic things: They pass laws, they represent the people, and they oversee public agencies in other branches of government. Those three things, though, represent an incredible workload and a phenomenally complicated juggling act. It's a tough enough job in normal times, and these are anything but that.

Consider that the average state legislature deals with at least a thousand proposed laws in any given year.[1] Those bills cover everything from education to regulation, from property taxes to the death penalty. All of that "regular" stuff still has to be done in 2011–2012, but also on the to-do list is dealing with the biggest set of economic challenges to face five generations. People clearly expect a lot from their legislators as the job means being an expert on, well, just about everything.

Representing constituents is, if anything, harder than attending to the (literally) thousand and one bills competing for legislators' attention. Constituents tend to be a tough crowd. For one thing, voters tend to have very low opinions of the work habits, ethics, and general character of those in elected office, and, for another, there are a lot of voters. Constituents outnumber state legislators by tens of thousands, even hundreds of thousands, to one. Ever try pleasing a hundred-thousand people? It doesn't matter what side you take on an issue; you upset someone (usually a lot of someones) who takes your vote, speech, media interview, or expression of support/opposition for a bill, an issue, or a proposal as just one more piece of evidence of what a lazy, unethical, and generally bad character you are.

And if that isn't enough, legislators are expected to keep an eye on pretty much all state agencies. One of these organizations makes a bad mistake or fritters away the taxpayers' dough, and it's not just the bureaucrats who get in trouble; voters want to know who in the legislature was sleeping at the switch while the Department of Dubious Behavior was up to no good.

Given all this, it's understandable that being a state legislator is a full-time job—except it's not a full-time job, at least not in the sense of getting a full-time paycheck. The National Conference of State Legislatures estimates that in roughly 40 states, most legislators cannot make a living on the salaries they get for being in elected office.[2]

The thanks for the hard work and generally low pay is mostly no thanks at all from your boss (i.e., the voting public). It used to be that you could at least count on some measure of job security, but that's not true anymore. Incumbency still has its advantages, but between term limits and an electoral, throw-the-bums out mood, it's not what it used to be. Long hours, low pay, big problems, and small praise kind of make you wonder who'd actually want to be a state legislator.

Yet despite being a pretty tough gig, being in a state legislature has one huge positive: If you want to make a difference (for good or ill), it's the place to be. Because their policy portfolios are so comprehensive and because their constitutional jurisdiction makes them the chief revenue raisers of state government, state legislatures probably affect the daily social, economic, and political life of U.S. citizens more than any other institution outside of family. That's reason enough to pay close attention to current trends in state legislatures.

RECENT TRENDS

The central theme of this section's readings is change: changing leadership, changing party control, changing agendas, and a general changing of the guard.

First up is an overview of change by Alan Greenblatt. A primary agent of that change is the 2010 elections. After all the votes were counted, many state legislatures had new leaders, new party control, and a new policy orientation. They also had a lot of new members; roughly a quarter of all state legislators in 2011 are freshmen.

Second is an examination of a second agent of change by Russell Nichols. Term limits were adopted with enthusiasm by the states over the past decade or two. By now, the implications of putting turnover on autopilot are beginning to become fully apparent. Two of the big downsides are getting rid of experienced policy makers just as states face the biggest economic challenge in five generations and getting the rookies up to speed fast enough to deal effectively with that challenge.

The third essay, by Karl Kurtz and Brian Weberg, takes an extended look at legislative reform. The big efforts to institutionally refashion legislatures to make them better at their jobs—notably term limits—either have not worked or are out of date. How do we deal with the issues of deepening partisan gridlock, ethical conduct, and increasing partisan cynicism?

Finally, Melissa Maynard examines how newly elected legislators are increasingly being given intensive training to get them ready for the complicated job of democratic representation. Winning a campaign and being an effective—or even merely a competent—legislator are two very different things. As legislative freshmen find out quickly, there is a lot to learn.

NOTES

1. Kevin B. Smith, Alan Greenblatt, and John Buntin, *Governing States and Localities* (Washington, DC: CQ Press, 2005), 178.

2. National Conference of State Legislatures, *Full and Part-Time Legislatures*, June 2009, http://www.ncsl .org/?tabid=16701. Accessed June 2, 2011.

13

Newly in Charge

Alan Greenblatt

The 2010 elections changed state legislatures: New members, new leaders, new party balance and a new agenda.

Employers still aren't much in the mood for hiring, and it's unusual to see a lot of new faces around most workplaces. But state legislatures aren't like most other places.

About a quarter of all state lawmakers are freshmen this year. Combined with the effects of term limits in 15 states and the flood of newcomers who first took office with the elections of 2008 and, especially, 2006, it quickly becomes clear that state capitols these days aren't populated by very many old hands.

For that reason—and because of the sizable number of chambers that switched party control last November, all from Democratic to Republican or to tied—an astonishing number of new leaders are now in charge.

There are 24 new house speakers around the country, or 25 if you count the two co-speakers in Oregon's tied House. The numbers are similarly high in state senates, with 17 new senate majority leaders, eight new senate presidents and 16 new presidents pro tem.

Any way you slice it, going down the ranks from presiding officers to assistant floor leaders, about half the nation's legislative leaders are new to their positions this year.

Politics aside, there's some risk in losing experience. Loss of institutional memory can often lead lawmakers to spend time rehashing old arguments. Less-experienced legislators also are likely to take a back seat to governors when it comes to setting choices about important matters such as crafting the budget.

From *State Legislatures,* April 2011.

But there are also positives borne out of having so many newcomers, perhaps particularly in the leadership ranks. People who are new to the game aren't as beholden to the status quo. They certainly won't expend as much energy defending policies of the past.

That might be helpful this year, as states face what is likely to be the most challenging budget season in living memory because of still-sluggish revenues and the drop-off in federal funds available through the American Recovery and Reinvestment Act. It's certain states are going to rethink their priorities and quite possibly reshape much of their mission over the coming years because of budget pressures.

"Normally, I would say that experience counts a lot," says Alan Rosenthal, an expert on state legislatures at the Eagleton Institute of Politics at Rutgers University. "But having people who are new at leadership might not be as much of a problem as during normal times. The budget in most states is just so overwhelmingly difficult that the old way of doing things isn't going to work.

BUDGETS AND JOBS

This year's crop of new leaders has at least one thing in common: They all recognize that they were elected on a platform of dealing with the budget and helping to create new jobs among those who don't happen to be state legislators.

"Having our focus on job creation and economic recovery has clarified our purpose in the legislature," says Frank McNulty, Colorado's new House speaker.

Scott Bundgaard, who returned to the Arizona Senate as its new majority leader this year after an eight-year hiatus from office, says his Legislature will spend less time this year on "divisive" social issues than it has in the recent past. "The focus has to be on those bread-and-butter issues," Bundgaard says. "We have a whole lot of work to reinvigorate the economy."

> *"The focus has to be on those bread-and-butter issues. We have a whole lot of work to reinvigorate the economy."*
> —Scott Bundgaard

In addition to trying to find ways to promote job growth—often through business-friendly tax cuts, despite the ongoing budget shortfalls—legislative leaders are on the hunt for ways to save money and streamline government. Kirk Adams, the rookie House speaker in Arizona, has unveiled a package designed to address the state's pension gap, shifting more of the cost from taxpayers onto state employees.

Similar ideas have been tried in other states. It's become fashionable for state officials to talk about zero-based budgets and value-added budgets and "priority of government" budgets. All these different catchphrases are meant to describe the idea that spending should not be based on last year's budget but on those programs identified as performing most efficiently and best meeting the needs of the state.

"Why can't we just ask whether we are getting the best return for the dollar?" says Kurt Zellers, Minnesota's new speaker. "If not, can we do away with the program and shift the money elsewhere?"

FRESHMAN CLASS

In Minnesota, a striking number of freshmen have been introducing high-profile legislation during this session, addressing everything from how agencies budget to teacher pay and abortion funding. Given the fact that 33 of the 72 House Republicans are new, they are making their mark early.

It's not unusual this year for Republican caucuses to be composed of 30 or 40 or even 50 percent newcomers. In Michigan, 61 of the 110 House members are new, which sounds like an awful lot until you realize that 29 of the 38 state senators are new.

"It's a clean slate," says Michigan's first-time speaker, Jase Bolger. "Everybody is new at the same time, which calls for us to do bold things and not be afraid to take on things because they're uncomfortable."

Like Bolger and many of his peers, Zellers likes to brag that the newcomers have brought valuable private-sector perspective with them to government. Many are small businessmen who have had to balance their own books and want to do the same thing for the state—without raising taxes.

"Quite honestly, if these guys were to lose their election or had to retire for some other reason, they'd be just as happy to leave as they were to get here," Zellers says. "They don't see this as a career; they see it as, they've come down here to fix the problem."

> *"Having people who are new at leadership might not be as much of a problem as during normal times. The budget in most states is just so overwhelmingly difficult that the old way of doing things isn't going to work."*
> —Alan Rosenthal, Rutgers University

NOT EVERYTHING CHANGES

Not everyone is convinced states are going to be able to fix their budget problems without raising taxes.

"There have been any number of times when people were elected on a platform of not raising taxes, and then in their first year they raised taxes," says Jon Shure, deputy director of the state fiscal project at the Center on Budget and Policy Priorities, a liberal-leaning group in Washington. "Once you're the stewards of the state's economic future, you do what you've got to do."

This may be the key question in state government this year: Can tax increases be avoided? They haven't gotten any more popular politically, and the enormous class of GOP freshmen elected this year certainly didn't come into office intending to expand government or raise taxes.

That may create a challenge for the new crop of leaders overseeing huge numbers of new, noncareer legislators who feel they were elected with a mandate.

"The people who were elected this time are not coming to the capitol to be told what to do," says Representative Joe Hackney, who lost his post as House speaker in North Carolina when the Democrats lost their majority in November.

People used to joke during Vern Riffe's 20-year reign as speaker that Ohio had a House of Representative, singular, because only his opinion counted. Some longstanding powerhouse chamber leaders remain around the country, but not nearly as many as there used to be.

That may shift some power from the legislature to the governor. Newer leaders are less inclined to stand up to the governor than older leaders who have seen a governor or two come and go and have a different sense of themselves and their position.

"I don't care who the governor is in Illinois. No one is going to roll over Mike Madigan because he's been there so long," says Robert Hertzberg, a former California Assembly speaker. Madigan has been speaker of the Illinois House for all but two of the past 28 years.

But if many of today's leaders face a challenge in having to grow into the job, perhaps they will be helped by the energy exuded by their comparatively young caucuses. The desire to do things differently may offer leaders leverage, along with occasional frustration. Most of the important decisions in legislatures these days are more apt to be made by the majority caucus, after all, than by committees.

The large cohort of new legislative leaders is likely to pursue what Hackney describes as the "collaborative model"—leading by listening and figuring out where the caucus stands and how much it's willing to compromise with the other chamber or the governor. Ideally, says Rosenthal, the Rutgers political scientist, you can't tell where the leader ends and the caucus begins.

"It's important that all 65 members have their input," says McNulty, the Colorado speaker, "that their views have a fair hearing and that their input is real and substantive and not just brushed off."

New Presiding Officers

In last November's election, party control changed in 20 chambers in 14 states.

Alabama
House Speaker Mike Hubbard (R)
Political career: First elected to the House in 1998.
Occupation: Small business owner

Lieutenant Governor/Senate President Kay Ivey
Political career: Elected state treasurer in 2002; re-elected in 2006. Elected lieutenant governor in 2010.
Occupation: Lieutenant governor

Colorado
House Speaker Frank McNulty
Political career: First elected to the House in 2006.
Occupation: Attorney

Indiana
Speaker Brian Bosma
Political career: First elected to the House in 1986; elected speaker 2005-06, 2011.
Occupation: Attorney

Iowa
Speaker Kraig Paulsen
Political career: First elected to the House in 2002.
Occupation: Attorney

Maine
House Speaker Robert "Bob" Nutting
Political career: First elected to the House in 1998; served through 2006 and then returned to the House in 2008.
Occupation: Pharmacist

Senate President Kevin Raye
Political career: First elected to the Senate in 2004.
Occupation: Small business owner. Previously served as a top aide to U.S. Senator Olympia Snowe.

Michigan
House Speaker James "Jase" Bolger
Political career: First elected to the House in 2008.
Occupation: Small business owner

Minesota
House Speaker Kurt Zellers
Political career: First elected to the House in a 2003 special election.
Occupation: Public relations

Senate Majority Leader Amy Koch
Political career: First elected to the Senate in a 2005 special election.
Occupation: Small business owner

Montana
House Speaker Mike Milburn
Political career: First elected to the House in 2004.
Occupation: Rancher and farmer
(The Montana House shifted from tied to GOP control.)

New Hampshire
House Speaker William "Bill" O'Brien
Political career: First elected to the House in 2006.
Occupation: Attorney

Senate President Peter Bragdon
Political career: Served in the House 2000-02; elected to the Senate in 2004.
Occupation: Operations manager

New York
Senate Majority Leader and President Pro Tem Dean Skelos
Political career:
Elected to the Assembly in 1980; elected to the Senate in 1984.
Occupation: Attorney

North Carolina
House Speaker Thom Tillis
Political career: First elected to the House in 2006.
Occupation: Full-time legislator

Senate President Pro Tem Phil Berger
Political career: First elected to the Senate in 2000.
Occupation: Attorney

Ohio
House Speaker William "Bill" Batchelder
Political career: First elected to the House in 1968 and served until 1998; ran again and was elected in 2006.
Occupation: Attorney

Pensylvania
House Speaker Samuel Smith
Political career: First elected to the House in 1986.
Occupation: Full-time legislator

Wisconsin
Assembly Speaker Jeff Fitzgerald
Political career: First elected to the Assembly in 2000.
Occupation: Small business owner

Senate President Mike Ellis
Political career: Served in the Assembly from 1970-80; first elected to the Senate in 1982.
Occupation: Full-time legislator

Note: The Oregon House shifted from Democratic control to tied and now has co-speakers from each party.

14

Dealing With Term-Limited Legislators

Russell Nichols

To some it seemed like a good idea at the time, but term limits turn out to have some big downsides. Triggering massive legislative turnover means there are less experienced and knowledgeable policymakers in the state house. They are being forced to leave, just as states struggle with the biggest economic challenge of a generation.

There's an expansive view from the 10th floor corner office of state Sen. Dennis Olshove. From his suite in Lansing, Mich., you can see the main entrance of the state's Capitol, the impressive courtyard that leads up to it and the off-white Capitol dome that reaches into a canvas of clouds.

On a recent early winter afternoon, the view inside that corner office, however, is bleak: Boxes and folders clutter the floor. Files, mementos and thank-you letters litter a wooden desk. In the adjacent room, a paper shredder groans.

"Come back in three weeks," Olshove says, "and this room will be completely empty. The walls will be painted, and the history will be gone."

For the past eight years, Olshove walked from this legislative office building to the Capitol, where he pushed pieces of legislation on various matters like fire safety and renewable energy, medical issues and emergency unemployment benefits. Some bills passed, others never saw the light of day. But Olshove's days in the Michigan Legislature now are finished forever.

It's not by choice, however.

Olshove was elected to the state House of Representatives in 1991, took a break and then migrated to the Senate in 2002. Now he's been kicked out due to the state's term limits, which put a cap of three two-year terms for the state House and two four-year terms for the state Senate. Never again can Olshove run for the Legislature, and he and his fellow Michigan legislators aren't the only ones prohibited from being state legislators again.

Across the country, term limits are throwing lawmakers out of office and forcing extreme makeovers in several state legislatures. In

From *Governing*, January 2011.

61

the United States, 378 legislators in 14 states were term-limited this past year, according to an analysis by the National Conference of State Legislatures. But the face-lift in the Michigan Legislature has been the most extreme: Due to term limits, 29 of the 38 senators will be replaced along with 34 of 110 House members. In addition, the state will have a new governor, attorney general and secretary of state.

All of this is taking place at a difficult time in state governance: Financial turbulence clouds the future and raises questions about the need for experienced legislators — ones who know the ins and outs of passing laws in a timely manner and finding solutions to problems through the legislative process. A steep learning curve may be a luxury in times such as these. That's why, whatever state leaders believe about the merits of term limits, they are in agreement on one point: If term limits are in place, action should be taken to counteract the negative effects of high turnover and an inexperienced legislative body. That is, new legislators must be equipped quickly and effectively with the tools and tactics to handle the tasks they face. Nobody wins if lawmakers are forced to sit idly through their terms because they never learned the ropes.

THE ORIGIN OF TERM LIMITS

Formal limits for state officials date back to Colonial days, but it wasn't until the early 1990s that legislative term limits became a target of government reformers. Spurred by voter mandates, 15 states put legal restrictions on the number of terms a member may serve in a particular office. The underlying idea was that term limits could bring new faces to the legislature — thus a constant flow of fresh ideas to state government. Moreover, term limits, its proponents suggested, would keep legislators from hogging valuable seats as "career politicians."

When Michigan voters enacted term limits in 1992, it wasn't just the fresh ideas and new faces that voters were concerned with. They hoped term restrictions would sever ties between legislators and lobbyists, and open the door to a new world of policymaking possibilities.

Some hopes have been realized. Term limits have reportedly pumped life into the Michigan Legislature by improving diversity and helping local residents connect to a government that has a more everyday-citizen look to it. "I hear stories of the old days and the legislators were

treated literally like royalty," says state Rep. Tom McMillin, a certified public accountant who just finished his first term. "Everybody bowed to these people. Term limits guarantee that we get away from the whole idea of kings and princes. We gain much more in having a citizen legislature."

The legislative ticking clock, supporters say, also keeps the governing body from falling into a stale political routine, and it forces legislators to focus on the task at hand. There isn't time for new legislators to buy into conventional wisdom and inside-the-box thinking, suggests Jack McHugh, senior legislative analyst for the Mackinac Center for Public Policy, a free-market think tank based in Midland, Mich. "That's a good thing," he says. "If you don't have term limits, you're guaranteed to get a whole bunch of guys and gals whose thinking never veers outside the box, and they remain there for decades."

But there has also been an outcry over the counter-productivity of term limits. Term-limit opponents say experience matters, and when veterans term out, rookie lawmakers lose the vets' institutional knowledge. That, in turn, promotes short-term thinking. In rocky times, seasoned legislators may be best suited to pushing through the difficult solutions that lie ahead.

THE QUESTIONABLE EFFECTIVENESS OF TERM LIMITS

There are questions about how effective term limits have been in states that have a long track record with them. A 2004 study by the Public Policy Institute of California, for instance, found that instead of revolutionizing the state Legislature with innovation, new members often emulated their precursors, and the policymaking process suffered. "Legislative committees screen out fewer bills, the legislative process does not encourage fiscal discipline nor link requests to spending limits," the report noted, "and committee membership and leadership continuity impacts experience and expertise crucial to effective policymaking."

In Michigan, a 12-year study by Wayne State University found that term limits have dissolved important checks and balances, and increased lobbyists' influence. Marjorie Sarbaugh-Thompson, a political science professor at the university and the study's lead author, says there is no question that the problem stems from the limited time new legislators have to understand their jobs and a lack of veteran leadership to guide them. "It's very difficult to bring new legislators up to speed," she says. "They're just barely getting a grasp of what the job consists of when they're on their way out the door."

As disenchantment with term limits echoed through several state legislative chambers, some states decided to backtrack. In 2002, the Idaho Legislature became the first state to repeal its own term limits. Whereas many other efforts to repeal have fallen short at the polls, legislatures or the courts in five other states — Massachusetts, Oregon, Utah, Washington and Wyoming — followed in Idaho's footsteps.

For states that are keeping term limits in place, the trend is toward working against the negative factors by providing new legislators with better support, communication and advanced planning. "The more time that the clerk and secretary can spend with incoming legislators," says Craig Ruff, a senior policy fellow at Public Sector Consultants, a Lansing-based policy research firm, "the faster and easier it will be for legislators to adapt to new roles." Not surprisingly, that is why Olshove, whose seat was won by state Rep. Steve Bieda, met several times with his successor to tell him what to expect.

TRANSITIONING IN THE NEW LAWMAKERS

Perhaps a perfect model of an effective orientation is the boot camp for new lawmakers based in Sacramento, Calif. For the past 12 years, the Robert M. Hertzberg Capitol Institute has provided training to new members and their employees on topics ranging from state ethics rules and computer systems to committees. Open year-round in a legislative office building, lawmakers go through an in-depth overview of processes, dissect statutes to digestible levels and receive large binders loaded with information and resources.

The program was initiated by Hertzberg, who as a freshman legislator went to a half-day of training that, he says, "didn't teach me anything about becoming a legislator." Years later, the former speaker of the Assembly decided to do something about it. He spent some time thinking about the issue and asking himself, "What do legislators need, and how do legislators learn?"

The comprehensive, intensive program that Hertzberg and former Republican Assembly Leader Bill

Leonard designed helps new members understand the need-to-know details of the job. "At the superficial level, it's about term limits, but it's more about a cultural shift," Hertzberg says. "All institutions have to modernize to deal with rapid change. We're trying to create a long-term resource."

This past November, Hertzberg headed up an initial tour for the newest class of legislators — something he tries to do every year. He herded 25 of the 28 new members who showed up to the chamber floors, the travel office, the nurse's office and other need-to-know spots. He talked about his days in state government and shared details of the Capitol's past to impart history and context.

In other states, mentor programs match freshmen with senior members, and chamber seat assignments are arranged to prevent cliques. Some states even select key legislative leaders in advance so they'll have a jump-start on critical issues. "A few states now choose the speaker designate a year ahead, and they're brought in on the budget meetings," says Thomas Little, director of curriculum development and research for the State Legislative Leaders Foundation. "They know they only have two years, so they can't afford to spend the first year trying to find out what's going on."

With the timer running, veteran lawmakers might feel inclined to keep the governing group as small as possible to maximize efficiency. But legislators can learn faster through participation, says Eric Herzik, chair of the political science department at the University of Nevada, Reno. New members, he suggests, should be identified and mentored more directly than in the pre-term limit days when they could observe from the sidelines. "The idea of a good-old boy group is harder to maintain in a time-shortened career," Herzik says. "The way around it is to bring other members into the decision-making process earlier."

There's also a movement toward providing training throughout the term. Last year, for instance, Michigan's McMillin took freshmen legislators to meet with the clerk to discuss amendments, strategies and parliamentary procedures, and he plans to hold ongoing orientations in the future. "A freshman coming in under our leadership will feel like they're part of the process and won't be overwhelmed," he says. "I want to make sure they understand the nuances."

PARTISANSHIP, INSTITUTIONAL MEMORY AND LEGISLATIVE EXCHANGES

There are other problems spawned by term limits. One is partisanship. Term-limited lawmakers have less interest in bridging the divide between parties than pushing a partisan agenda, which hampers political progress, says Sarbaugh-Thompson. "The friendships are missing," she says. "People don't know each other. The country at large has very little respect for political experience. I think they think of it as campaigning instead of governing."

There are also issues revolving around a lack of institutional memory, which some say boosts power for lobbyists: Their knowledge on certain issues gives them leverage. But in many ways, term limits also force lobbyists to start from scratch and reintroduce themselves whenever a new member enters the political arena. In that sense, veteran staffers may have more of an inside track when it comes to legislative influence. But in the chamber, who lawmakers know matters as much as — if not more than — what lawmakers know. And many will admit that they have a hard time keeping track of who's who.

"I was here before term limits, so I got to see the transition," Olshove says. "Now if I'm in a room for any event, some people may be legislators, but I don't know who they are."

In the late 1990s, a group of Michigan lawmakers set out to forge relationships through field trips called "legislative exchanges." On nonformal session days, they caravanned to various districts for excursions. Sometimes they stayed overnight in a hotel or motel, and they would meet for dinner.

"We went to each other's districts to better understand the whole state so we could work together across the aisle," says Sen. Patty Birkholz, who just termed out of the state Legislature. "When you're traveling together, it helps force relationship-building."

Since then, the legislative exchanges have been all but forgotten. In the past few years, hopes of making solid connections cracked under the weight of party pressure — and the fact that legislators come and go in a flash.

WRAPPING UP A LEGISLATIVE TERM

During one of his final days in the Legislature, Olshove looks at a picture in his office of Senate members circa 2004. "Gone, gone, gone, gone, gone," he says, moving his finger from member to member in the picture. "This is ridiculous. All these folks are gone. That's term limits for you."

One of his staff members notifies him that a class is waiting for him in the Capitol. Students from Siersma Elementary School, located in his district, visit the Capitol every November as part of the curriculum. For the past five years, Olshove has volunteered to give a tour of the Senate Chamber to the kids, "his constituents," he calls them.

Once in the building, Olshove leads a few dozen fifth-graders into the south wing of the second floor, his stomping grounds. There he breaks down the lawmaking process, using a pretend proposal: No school on Fridays. The kids cheer, and then groan when he admits that the governor probably wouldn't sign off on that bill.

Then he opens the floor for questions. The students fire away with random questions about his favorite color (he doesn't have one), what he does for fun (spends time with his children), and whether he'll ever run for governor (no). Olshove then points to one student raising her hand in the middle of the crowd.

"Do you like your job?" she asks.

The kids haven't learned about term limits in class. They have no idea that next November, a brand new senator will be here giving the tour of the Senate Chamber. But they wait with wide eyes to hear his answer.

"I do," he says. "You get to meet all sorts of people every day, and you never know what to expect. And remember, any one of you can get elected one day."

With that, the kids gather around him for a group picture. Olshove smiles for the camera and for the kids, his constituents for only a few more weeks.

15

What Legislatures Need Now

Karl Kurtz and Brian Weberg

It is clear that state legislatures need to change so they can meet the challenges of governing in the 21st century. What is less clear is how they should change.

The challenges of today's legislatures are complex. They involve questions of integrity, will, commitment and trust, and the solutions are not at all clear. The realities of today's government and politics require a new approach to strengthen legislatures. What's needed is a process that clarifies the current problems, what changes are needed and how to put those remedies into place.

In the 1970s, the Citizens Conference on State Legislatures launched a remarkable movement to strengthen our nation's legislatures by publishing "The Sometime Governments: An Evaluation of the 50 American Legislatures."

The book included sweeping recommendations for change. The guidelines were designed to give legislatures more resources of time, compensation, staff and facilities. Forty years later, that agenda for reform has been largely accomplished or is no longer as relevant.

In large measure, "The Sometime Governments" succeeded in igniting two decades of effort by legislatures in every state to build capacity—the amount of session time, the number of members, committee organization, facilities and staffing.

It provided state-specific marching orders and a battle plan to reform-minded political troops ready and able to carry out its agenda. At the time of its publication, American politics were in transition. The one-person, one-vote court decisions of the 1960s and subsequent redistricting after the 1970 census opened state legislatures to a surge of new members in the 1974 elections.

They were a generation inspired by Kennedy, but also battered by the Vietnam War and the Watergate scandal. Armed with ideas

From *State Legislatures,* July/August 2010.

set out in "The Sometimes Governments" and fueled by private foundation support, they transformed state legislatures.

For the next two decades, legislative leaders in almost every state engaged their members, the public and others concerned about legislatures in efforts to redesign and rebuild their institutions. These efforts were historic in scope and accomplishment. Legislatures became more muscular, agile, intelligent and independent than at any other time in American history.

The reform agenda of "The Sometime Governments" fell on hard times in the 1990s. There was a backlash, fueled by growing public cynicism about government, that developed against what political scientists call the "professionalization" of state legislatures. In almost all of the 24 states that allow voter initiatives, measures were placed on the ballot to limit the terms of state lawmakers. Virtually all of them passed, though some were later invalidated by courts or repealed, leaving 15 states today with term limits.

An NCSL study in 2007 showed term limits had significantly weakened state legislatures, especially in relation to the governor. Other initiatives placed limits on the tax and spending powers of legislatures in many states.

In this atmosphere of public distrust and cynicism toward government, it became difficult for legislatures to strengthen and grow in the fashion advocated by "The Sometime Governments." In the last 20 years—outside of the area of technology, which has its own momentum and societal drive—legislatures mostly have stopped taking steps such as adding staff, building more facilities or increasing the amount of time spent on the job. By the 1990s, the Citizens Conference's recommendations had run their course. They had done their job of stimulating positive change.

'The Sometime Governments'

The Citizens Conference on State Legislatures was a private nonprofit organization formed in 1964 to improve state legislatures. With a major grant from the Ford Foundation, it launched a 50-state study of legislatures in 1969 and published "The Sometime Governments: An Evaluation of the 50 American Legislatures" in 1971.

Based on criteria for "functional, accountable, informed, independent and representative" legislatures, the book evaluated state legislatures and ranked them from one to 50. The rankings caused a considerable stir among state lawmakers, and were an effective call to action: No state wanted to remain ranked in the bottom half of the list or to be below its neighbors or rivals.

The book contained both general recommendations for all states and specific recommendations for each legislature. The recommendations focused on such things as the length of the session, number of members, committee organization, facilities and staffing. They were highly prescriptive and specific.

During the study, the Citizens Conference was directed by Larry Margolis, former chief of staff to California Speaker Jesse Unruh, who led the transformation of the California Legislature into a full-time, professional body in the late 1960s. The implicit standard of "The Sometime Governments" was that all legislatures should look like California's, which, not surprisingly, came out No. 1 in the rankings.

PROBLEMS PERSIST

While some of the issues raised in "The Sometime Governments" have been resolved, new ones have emerged.

The process of legislative improvement is never-ending, requiring constant tinkering and adjustment, state by state. Partly as a result of the previous success of strengthening legislatures, they face new problems today.

In his book, "Engines of Democracy: Politics and Policy in State Legislatures," Rutgers University political scientist Alan Rosenthal identifies ailments confronting contemporary representative democracy.

- Partisanship. Strong party allegiance can organize conflict and disagreement, but in excess can lead to incivility and a lack of willingness to negotiate and compromise. Hyper-partisanship, as some have called it, undermines political trust and support for democratic institutions. Some state legislatures today, but by no means all, suffer from excessive partisanship.

- Integrity. The overwhelming number of state lawmakers behave ethically. The misdeeds of a few members, however, tar the entire institution. The public believes the majority of legislators are out to serve themselves, and they are for sale to the highest bidder.

- Deliberation. The work of standing committees, which was a major focus of the earlier legislative strengthening movement, has been undermined in many states in recent years. Partisan considerations have been a detriment to substantive study, analysis of and deliberation on all sides of an issue. Top legislative leaders and party caucuses too often bypass or downplay the committee process. Term limits have also weakened committees as they have been deprived of experience and expertise.

- Responsibility. Rosenthal is concerned about the unwillingness of some legislators to make difficult fiscal decisions because of constituent opposition, the growing tendency for committees to fail to screen out bills that lack support or merit and the practice of lawmakers not voting against someone else's bill for fear that he or she will vote against their own.

- Public cynicism. Today's excessive public mistrust of democratic institutions is harmful. Cynicism discourages qualified people from running for office, promotes a reluctance by members to address unpopular but necessary issues, encourages simplistic institutional reforms such as term limits, and increases the public's unwillingness to comply with legislative decisions.

- Institutional commitment. Rosenthal writes that lawmakers often pay little attention to the institution and distance themselves from it. "If they do not devote themselves to their institution's well-being, who can they expect to do the job for them? The responsibility is primarily theirs—and it is not being adequately shouldered."

NEW SET OF QUESTIONS

Rosenthal's list of ailments ring true and it's vital they be addressed and remedied. But it's important to emphasize that not all states have experienced all of these problems. The need for legislative improvement differs from state to state. The only problem on the Rosenthal list that is common to all the states is public cynicism, and even then there are a few states—Alaska, Idaho, North Dakota and Wyoming are examples—in which the legislature has relatively high public opinion ratings. As the Citizens Conference recognized 40 years ago, an agenda for legislative strengthening needs to be state specific.

But how can we create a state-specific agenda?

We suggest a basic set of questions that legislators, legislative staff, political scientists and interested citizens should ask and answer about the performance of their legislature. These questions are standards of a sort, expectations of what a good legislature should be.

1. Does the legislature effectively share power with the governor? Does the legislature initiate and enact its own legislation and make independent decisions about the state budget? Does the legislature provide effective oversight of executive actions?

2. Does the redistricting process for the legislature result in reasonably compact, contiguous and competitive legislative districts that do not provide an undue advantage to one party and incumbent legislators?

3. Do the members provide effective constituent service including answering requests for information, casework, local projects and public expenditures? Is the proportion of women and racial and ethnic minorities in the legislature reasonably reflective of the population of the state?

4. Does the legislature take into account interests of the state as a whole instead of the cumulative interests of districts and constituencies?

5. Is there a reasonable balance in the legislature between the need to have strong, effective leaders who guide members on procedural and policy choices and the need for internal democracy that disperses power and protects the rights of individual members?

6. Does the majority party have enough clout to get things done? Are the rights of the minority party protected?

7. Is the degree of partisanship in the legislature reasonable? Does the legislature engage in consensus-building? Are opposing sides willing to negotiate differences and find compromises to difficult problems?

8. Does the legislature have integrity? Do the members of the legislature and the capitol community behave in ethical ways?

9. Do individual citizens and organized groups with an interest in an issue have the opportunity to participate in the lawmaking process? Are all viewpoints heard and treated fairly by the legislature? Is the influence of moneyed interests that contribute to political campaigns appropriate relative to their role in the state's economy and well-being?

10. Does the legislature study and deliberate on issues effectively? Does it allow give-and-take and the open exchange of ideas at all stages of the formal and informal legislative process, especially the committee stage? Are legislative committees strong, attentive and involved in critical decision making?

11. Do the members of the legislature care about and protect the well-being of the institution? Is there adequate continuity in the membership of the legislature to promote institutional values, build up expertise, and pass on knowledge and skills? Are the leaders and members committed to educating the public about the legislative institution and defending its values?

12. Does the legislature have adequate resources—staff, time, facilities, technology—to do its job, and are those resources managed effectively? Is there an appropriate balance between partisan staff who provide strategic advice and guidance to members and nonpartisan staff who provide unbiased analysis and manage the institution?

SOLUTIONS ARE THE CHALLENGE

Each state—depending on its history, traditions and culture—will have different answers to these questions, and people within the same state will disagree. But if the answer is "no" on any set of questions, this is an area to strengthen.

Once those areas are defined, finding solutions becomes the challenge. Most 21st century problems in legislatures will not be solved by throwing more resources at them or even by structural and procedural changes. The remedies for these ailments are more likely to come through education, training and cultural changes in the institution—all of which may be difficult to bring about.

Legislators, staff, academics and committed citizens need to come together to draw up a new agenda to strengthen legislatures.

The reformers of the 1970s had a difficult task of transforming state legislatures into something more than "sometime governments." But, in retrospect, their task seems easy compared to today's work of building integrity, will, commitment and trust.

The challenges facing today's more robust legislatures are even more daunting. But that shouldn't stop them. They need to find the mechanisms and a spirit similar to those of a previous generation of dedicated people who improved America's state legislatures.

16

Legislatures Expand Training for New Members

Melissa Maynard

Winning an election and being an effective legislator are two very different jobs. This is why newly elected legislators are being sent back to school. For some it is an eye-opening and head-spinning set of lessons.

From *Stateline.org*, December 2010.

At one time, newly elected state legislators were shown to the chambers with little more than the keys to an office and a quick introduction to staff.

Those days are over in most states. The new-member orientations that many legislatures have held this year are far more involved, encompassing everything from mock committee meetings and floor debates to case studies of historical legislative accomplishments.

"My head is swimming," says Michigan state Representative-elect Deb Shaughnessy, adding that she was a legislative staffer for a decade before running for office and thought she had an adequate grasp of the job in advance. She now realizes there was more to learn. "I don't think you ever could be fully prepared," she says now.

This year's elections produced a high level of turnover in state legislatures: Roughly one in four state lawmakers in 2011 will be new. In statehouses, training programs have been ramping up over the past few weeks to educate this wave of freshmen about how to do the job they've just campaigned so hard to win. The programs, many of them established over the past decade in response to term limits, also attempt to find creative ways to transfer institutional knowledge from a dwindling number of veteran lawmakers.

The most popular sessions, says Bruce Feustel, of the National Conference of State Legislators, give new members the opportunity to learn from colleagues. Incoming legislators don't always understand what they need to know until they need to know it. So hearing from second-termers about the aspects of the job that proved challenging or surprised them is particularly helpful. "They are people who've just been through it and can speak to what they know now that they wish they knew then," Feustel says. "It's a fun session where they can share their foibles and missteps and give new legislators a sense of the humanity of it all."

BACK TO SCHOOL

A popular trend in these programs aims to prevent information overload. More legislator training is provided in chunks over longer periods of time, and regular training opportunities are made available throughout the legislative session.

For example, Wyoming stretches its training out over several weeks, so that legislators have time to digest and process the information. Wisconsin has added a day to its training and built in more opportunity for small group discussions and workshops. Trainers in Wisconsin now spend less time talking at legislators, but supplement the sessions with a 373-page textbook that the freshmen can refer back to once they are further into the details of legislating. "You just can't stand up there and talk to the members about every department of the executive branch," says Terry Anderson, director of the Wisconsin Legislative Council.

Another current trend involves paying more attention to the spouses of legislators and providing programs that specifically cater to them. The Alabama Law Institute, which oversees Alabama's orientation program, made that part of its agenda this year. The lack of staff capacity in the Alabama Legislature means that spouses sometimes end up serving as de-facto aides to their elected wives or husbands, says Robert McCurley, the law institute's director. "They can't just say 'Oh, my spouse is the legislator,'" he says. "Once the spouse jumps in the fishbowl, they are in there with them."

When the Michigan Legislature convenes next month, lawmakers will have a host of fiscal and economic ills to reckon with, including a $1.6 billion budget gap. And because of term limits and election defeats, there will be only 15 House members left with more than two years of experience. Of the 110 members of the House, 60 will be new. "I think some of them don't believe how serious the situation really is," says Mitch Bean, director of the nonpartisan House Fiscal Agency. "Some of these things are overwhelming, and I sympathize because it's not their fault. The typical person who gets elected is intelligent, works extremely hard and wants to do their best for the people of the state. The thing is, this stuff is complicated and takes a while to grasp." Bean and his staff have been involved in a range of programs for new legislators, and have come to view the training and education of junior members as a central part of their jobs.

FOSTERING BIPARTISANSHIP

In Michigan, the House orientation, focused largely on procedures, is supplemented with a more policy-focused one put on by the Michigan State University Institute for Public Policy and Social Research. That program seeks to bring legislators up to speed on the state's key problems and give them some practical guidance about the options they will have in addressing them. This year's agenda included a briefing on state and local revenue streams and tours of research organizations and businesses that represent emerging sectors in Michigan's economy. It also included a bipartisan bowling outing.

Veteran trainers in Michigan and elsewhere in the country indicate that building in time for breaks and social activities pays off as much as the best-designed study session. "Once you're sworn in, you're pulled in all sorts of different directions," says Michigan state Representative Kate Segal, who is about to begin her second term. "You never get that kind of time together again."

Camaraderie among Segal and her cohorts during 2009 training led directly to the creation of a new Bipartisan Freshman Caucus before the new class even took office. The Caucus met on a regular basis and pooled resources to search for bipartisan solutions to problems that everyone around the table agreed needed solving.

In Michigan, efforts to inspire bipartisanship actually begin before the elections take place. Michigan State has a year-long fellowship program that brings 24 aspiring office-holders to a series of 10 weekend training sessions. The training is geared toward developing leadership skills, and educating participants about how to run a campaign and how the legislature works. Fellows from opposing parties are housed together in hopes of fostering long-term friendships among future political rivals. One in ten members of the Legislature is a graduate of this program. Steve Tobocman, a state representative from 2003 to 2008, co-directs the Michigan State program. He knows first hand how term limits have created a need to educate new lawmakers in a hurry: By his fifth year on the job, he was the second-in-command of the House. "When you see almost half the Legislature turn over," Tobocman says, "the only way to maintain any level of professionalism and substance in the process is to train the people who are going to be at the helm."

Governors and Executives

There's a little old and a lot of new in governors' mansions these days. California Governor Jerry Brown won back his old job in 2010, nearly 30 years after serving two terms as chief executive in the 1970s and 1980s. Though Brown gives the Golden State a blast from the governing past, the trend in executive leadership in the states is toward new rather than familiar faces. Nearly 30 governors were elected in 2010, and many of them were holding the job for the first time.

It's not just governors. Of the 30 attorney general races on the 2010 ballot, roughly a third had no incumbent candidate. And it's not just new faces, but new offices and new challenges that characterize the executive branch of state governments in 2011 and 2012. In Rhode Island, for example, the Office of the Health Insurance Commissioner (created in 2004) has a new prominence thanks to the federal government's controversial health care reform. In most states, all executives are dealing with the grim reality that the billions in (relatively) easy dollars made available by the federal government's American Recovery and Reinvestment Act have dried up. How do you run a department, or a state, when tax revenues are down, and the federal government has turned off the tap?

All the new faces in the executive branch, and the fact that so many of them are grappling with fundamentally the same policy issue, are at least partially a product of some important differences between state and federal governments. For one thing, states differ from the federal government both in the number and in the nature of their elected executives, and all elected state executives win their jobs by popular ballot. In contrast, not a single federal executive officer is chosen by a comparable nationwide popular vote (the president is chosen by the Electoral College). No other federal executive—attorney general, secretary of state, health insurance commissioner, whatever—has even a passing relationship with a ballot box. All are appointed by the president and serve at his or her pleasure.

While the federal government has a complete absence of popularly elected executives, state governments are positively stuffed with them. All 50 governors, the chief executive officers of state government, get their jobs by winning statewide elections. Governors, though, are just the tip of the iceberg. In any given state, the heads of a wide range of executive departments—attorney general, state treasurer, the chief education bureaucrat—also get their jobs by winning elections rather than appointments from the governor.

What this means is that while the governor is technically the head of the executive branch, other key executive offices may be held by people with different partisan, ideological, and personal agendas. That can make governing hard. In many states, the executive branch resembles a collection of independent electoral fiefdoms more than a hierarchical organization with the governor at the top.

Big realigning elections such as those that occurred in many states in 2010 and 2011, then, do not simply sweep a new governor and his or her agenda into power. They can sweep in a lot of other executives, and many of them are given considerably less attention than chief executives even though their policy portfolios may be critically important.

RECENT TRENDS

The readings in this section highlight the changes and the challenges that state executives face in 2011 and 2012. The first essay by Josh Goodman highlights the implications of the gubernatorial turnover created by the 2010 elections, not just in the sense of new faces, but in the sense of the political and ideological orientation in governors' offices. One of the notable trends was the demise of the moderate governor and his or her replacement by more partisan and ideological executives. That is giving a harder edge to the policy positions of the most powerful state political offices.

The second essay by the writers at *Stateline* gives an overview of the gubernatorial policy agendas that emerged in 2011. Though these are, understandably enough, tailored to particular state contexts, there are some clear commonalities. The ambitious policy plans of the prerecession years are gone. Now it's lean and, at least according to some, just plain mean. Despite sometimes massive budget gaps, governors are pushing for tax cuts rather than tax increases. Instead, they are targeting public services and public employees.

The third essay takes a look at a group of people who arguably have the second most important and high-profile job in the executive branch of state government: attorneys general (AGs). With a Democrat in the White House, Republican attorneys general rediscovered the GOP's historical states' rights principles and began a series of high-profile and politically profitable legal skirmishes with the federal government. Are Republican AGs the new defenders of federalism and state power?

The final essay, and the second by *Governing*'s John Buntin, takes a look at the big impact of a rare state executive. Rhode Island's Christopher Koller is the only independent state health insurance commissioner in the nation. He's using that platform to take on serious reform. Rather than simply field complaints and review policy increases, Koller is comprehensively trying to address the cost of health care.

17

Goodbye Moderate Governors, Hello Partisans

Josh Goodman

The 2010 elections brought a new sort of governor. More ideological, harder-edged, and less interested in bipartisan compromise.

Kyrsten Sinema thinks her state has gone bonkers, and she isn't shy about saying so. As a Democrat in the Arizona House of Representatives, Sinema has been helpless as Republican lawmakers approve one policy after another that she thinks is nuts.

The Legislature barred ethnic studies classes in public schools. "That's crazy." Sinema says. "So now our students don't even get the option to learn about African-American history. That's just crazy." As part of conservatives' push against human cloning and stem cell research, a new law bans the creation of human-animal hybrids. "I think that people underestimate the damage that the centaurs and mermaids can do in our community," Sinema says sarcastically. Lawmakers approved a series of expansions to gun rights. "You can take guns into bars, there's no concealed carry weapon permit anymore and you can have an automatic weapon," Sinema says. "Now, I'm a supporter of the Second Amendment, but this is crazy. That's crazy. That's just crazy."

Obviously, Arizona Republicans would disagree with the way Sinema characterizes their legislation. But almost no one would disagree that her sentiments reflect what many Arizona Democrats have been feeling for the last two years. During this time, the state approved SB 1070, the landmark anti-illegal immigration bill. The Legislature has picked fights with unions, challenged the Obama administration over health-care reform and approved new restrictions on abortion. Add it all up and the last two years have been a golden age for conservative policy experimentation in Arizona.

From *Governing,* October 2010.

The main reason all of this happened is the departure of Gov. Janet Napolitano, a Democrat, who was a one-person check-and-balance on the Republican-controlled Legislature. When Napolitano joined the Obama administration, Jan Brewer, a conservative Republican, became governor. Suddenly the Legislature could do what it pleased on many topics.

Many governors like Napolitano will leave office in January, either because of term limits or because they've chosen to retire. They're Democrats in Republican states with Republican legislatures and Republicans in Democratic states with Democratic legislatures. These governors, like Napolitano, have been moderating influences on state government. They've blocked many of the more ideological impulses of their legislatures.

In the November elections, voters are likely to revert to form in many of the states with departing governors — Republicans will win in Republican states and Democrats will win in Democratic states. If that happens, Arizona's story may be repeated in states from coast to coast — and state government may end up more partisan, more ambitious and, yes, a little bit crazier.

THE MODERATE GOVERNORS OF 2002

Napolitano was a member of the class of 2002, the most topsy-turvy year for gubernatorial elections in recent memory. The 2000 presidential election established the political map of Republican red states and Democratic blue states. Two years later, the gubernatorial elections seemed to suggest that the whole red and blue thing was bunk.

Republicans won election to governor in many of the most Democratic states in the country: Connecticut, Hawaii, Maryland, Massachusetts, Minnesota, New York, Rhode Island and Vermont. When Republican Arnold Schwarzenegger won the California recall election the following year, more than half of the people in states that had voted for Al Gore in 2000 were living under Republican governors. Democrats had their own set of surprising wins in governors' races in 2002, in Kansas, Oklahoma, Tennessee and Wyoming, in addition to Arizona.

Voters have a long history of ignoring their partisan predilections in gubernatorial races. For example, Wyoming, one of the most Republican states in the country, has been

led by Democratic governors for 28 of the past 36 years. Deeply Democratic states such as Connecticut, Massachusetts and Rhode Island have equally robust recent histories of electing Republican governors. Still, what made the 2002 elections notable was that these sorts of results occurred in state after state, just when conventional wisdom said that states were becoming much more divided along partisan lines.

Much of the class of 2002 has stuck around for the last eight years. Some of these governors have been political successes, while others are failures. Some are bold partisans, while others have been cautious and conciliatory. Despite the differences, though, they played a common role.

These governors didn't just belong to a different party from most of the voters in their states. More often than not, they also belonged to a different party than most of their states' legislators. With the stroke of their veto pens, they constrained the ideological ambitions of their legislatures. In doing so, they directed state governments on a moderate, consensus-oriented approach.

In this regard, several governors set records. In 2008, Schwarzenegger vetoed 35 percent of the bills that were sent to him, the largest proportion in a single year of any California governor on record. The same year, Tim Pawlenty set Minnesota's one-year record with 34 vetoes.

In 2009, Jim Douglas became the first governor in Vermont history to veto the state budget. Thwarting the Democratic Legislature's initiatives, Douglas says, was an important part of his job. "Vermonters have sought some balance in state government," he says, "and they've chosen me to provide it."

JANET NAPOLITANO AND ARIZONA'S REPUBLICAN-CONTROLLED LEGISLATURE

In Arizona, Napolitano was a record-setter, too. She vetoed 180 bills during her six-plus years in office, easily the most by any Arizona governor. For her entire time in office, Republicans controlled both houses of the Legislature. As Democrats go, Napolitano wasn't especially liberal, but she was a loyal enough defender of her party's views to create perennial conflict on hot-button issues.

With Napolitano gone, Republican lawmakers have aggressively shrunk government, including eliminating universal all-day kindergarten, which Napolitano considered her signature achievement. These moves, though, reflect the harsh budget realities faced by Arizona as much as they reflect the Legislature's ideological preference for austerity.

The more telling pieces of legislation are the ones on social issues. Even in the middle of one of the worst economic and fiscal calamities the state has ever known, Republican lawmakers haven't shied away from restricting abortion and expanding gun rights — subjects on which Napolitano frequently issued vetoes while in office.

If there's one person who embodies the shift, it's Cathi Herrod, president of the Center for Arizona Policy, a socially conservative advocacy group. Napolitano, who is pro-choice, opposed most of Herrod's agenda. "We were not even able to get an appointment to meet with Napolitano," she says.

Today, Herrod is derided by Democrats as a secret power in the capitol, someone to whom Brewer and Republican legislators defer. She shrugs that off. "It's not about me," she says. Still, she has no trouble getting meetings — or getting results. Lawmakers have approved bills to expand private school vouchers and restrict stem cell research. The state has created a new 24-hour waiting period for abortion, restricted late-term abortions and forbidden public money from funding government employees' abortions.

Then there were legislators' forays into the hottest national issues of the day. In this regard, Arizona foreshadowed debates that would rage across the country. In June 2009, the Legislature approved a ballot measure to block requirements that everyone possess health insurance, months before that would become a source of controversy in federal health reform. Another legislatively approved ballot measure would require workers' votes on organizing unions to be conducted via secret ballots, a preemptive strike on the "card-check" legislation that is a top union priority in Congress. The state also challenged the federal government in other ways, passing a bill to bar federal gun regulations from applying to weapons that are made and sold within Arizona borders. And, of course, the state reshaped the national debate on immigration with SB 1070.

Many other states, such as Florida, Illinois, New York and Texas, are controlled by one party right now. But Arizona's activism stands out. Why?

Kirk Adams, the speaker of the Arizona House, is the best person to answer that. He notes that while Republicans lost power in many states in 2006 and 2008, Arizona Republicans actually picked up legislative seats in 2008, with Arizonan John McCain as the party's presidential nominee. When Napolitano left, the party didn't just have the opportunity to do all the things it couldn't while she was governor. It also was able to give a voice to Republicans around the country who were disconcerted by the Obama administration's policies but lacked the legislative power to do anything about them. "Arizona is becoming a leader in rebalancing the power between the states and the federal government," Adams says. "The federal government simply has usurped too much state power and continues to do so."

While Arizona's turn in the national spotlight is partially a reflection of the idiosyncrasies of the 2008 election cycle, it also reflects broader trends. Napolitano had a small group of moderate Republicans with whom she'd strike deals, especially on budget issues. Most of these moderate Republicans gradually have been swept out of office in primaries or replaced by more conservative lawmakers when they retired. That set the stage for bold conservative action once she was gone.

In this way, Arizona is following a national trend. More and more legislative elections are hinging on hot-button national issues. More partisans are demanding ideological purity from their elected officials, fueling primary challenges to incumbent lawmakers. In Arizona and other states, the end result is that more legislators are coming from the edges of the political spectrum.

That's the recipe that, combined with Brewer's ascendance, left loyal Democrats like Sinema so frustrated. "I'll be honest with you," she says, "I didn't think it was going to be this bad. I did not."

THE REPUBLICAN RESURGENCE

The question now is whether, come January, times will be just as bad for minority parties around the country. Unless several governors' races end in surprises, one-party rule is coming to more states.

The dominant theme in this year's elections is a Republican resurgence. In the races for governor, though, there's a secondary theme: a return to partisan form.

Largely as a consequence of term limits, many Republican states appear set to revert to Republican control. Many Democratic states could have Democratic governors for the first time in years.

Democratic governors are retiring in Kansas, Oklahoma, Tennessee and Wyoming. In each of those states, Republican candidates for governor are heavy favorites. It's likely that Republicans will have complete control of the legislatures in those states too, although Democrats are putting up a fight in Tennessee. If Republicans do win, they'll have total control of Tennessee government for the first time since Reconstruction and total control of Oklahoma government for the first time ever. Already lawmakers are talking about forceful conservative action, including Arizona-style immigration laws.

Given the political climate, Democratic gains look less certain. But the party is favored to win in Connecticut, Hawaii and Minnesota. Democrats have around even-money odds in California, Rhode Island and Vermont. Each of those six states has Democrats in charge of both houses of its legislature. Each has a Republican governor who's leaving office. Democratic wins in these states would provide the party with counterpoints to Arizona — places where Democrats might engage in their own ideological experimentation.

In Vermont, the shift could be particularly dramatic. As governor, Douglas has had a preference for caution and a distaste for hot-button issues. Ask about his most important accomplishments, and the first things he'll mention are his state's solid bond ratings and well stocked rainy-day fund. He'll also touch on his efforts to expand broadband access and cell phone coverage in rural, hilly Vermont. "I want everybody to know that our state motto is freedom and unity," he says, "not, 'Can you hear me now?'"

A health-care plan Douglas and Democrats agreed to in 2006 reflected these sensibilities. It provided subsidies to allow poor Vermonters to buy private insurance, but didn't include the more robust government interventions Democrats preferred. This year, the Democratic nominee for governor is Peter Shumlin, the Senate's president pro tempore. Shumlin is a forceful advocate for a single-payer health-care system, in which the state would provide health insurance to everyone. Already the Legislature has hired a Harvard economist to present the state with three health-care plans by February, including a single-payer one. A Shumlin victory could mean that Vermont becomes a proving ground for liberals' notion of health-care reform, something no state has attempted. "We're going to have to show the rest of the country," says Deb Richter, chair of Vermont Health Care for All and a Shumlin supporter. "If it can be done anywhere, it will be here."

BALANCING PARTISAN PASSIONS WITH EFFECTIVE GOVERNING

The story in Arizona reflects the possibilities for a political party in control, but it also offers a cautionary tale. Being a Democratic legislator in Arizona may have been miserable for the last two years, but being a Republican hasn't always been fun either.

Soon after she took office, Brewer proposed a temporary sales tax increase to help blunt some of the budget cuts the state had to make. Arizona's fiscally conservative Republican legislators hated the idea. Month after month the governor battled legislators from her own party, as one special session after another ended in stalemate and Democrats stood on the sidelines. "The majority has the responsibility to get the job done," says Bob Burns, Arizona's Senate president. "It's easy for the minority to sit back and take potshots." Finally this year, legislators sent the sales tax hike to voters — who overwhelmingly approved it — but the dispute almost destroyed Brewer's standing with conservatives. Only SB 1070 gave her a second political life.

Intra-party conflict like that is common. Four years ago, Deval Patrick became Massachusetts' first Democratic governor since Michael Dukakis left office in 1991, but since then he's spent much of his term feuding with the Democratic Legislature over casinos. In South Carolina, Republican legislators have clashed constantly with Gov. Mark Sanford over his quasi-libertarian philosophy. In Idaho, Gov. Butch Otter bitterly battled Republican lawmakers who opposed his gas tax hike. Long before they kicked him out of office, Democratic legislators in Illinois despised Gov. Rod Blagojevich. When a party takes complete control, it seems, all its internal divisions come to the fore. Enacting a coherent agenda isn't as easy as simply holding a majority.

Nor are all legislators motivated by partisan agendas — even in 2010. You can understand it from listening to Donald Williams.

Williams was elected to the Connecticut Senate in 1993. He's a Democrat in a state with an exclusively Democratic congressional delegation, one that has voted comfortably Democratic in every presidential election since 1992. Yet Williams, now the Senate's president pro tempore, never has served under a Democratic governor.

This year, with Gov. M. Jodi Rell retiring, there's a good chance that will change. If Democrat Dan Malloy wins, what's his big idea? Williams says his top priority will be transforming the Department of Motor Vehicles with better customer service, more online services and small kiosks close to where more people live. That's hardly the stuff of ideological warfare.

Williams isn't unique. In Kansas, eight years of Democratic governors almost certainly will come to an end. Some Republicans are eager to pursue conservative goals, but Senate President Stephen Morris isn't one of them. Instead, he says he'll focus on educating more engineers in the state. "When you have these high-pay, high-tech jobs and not enough people from Kansas to fill them," Morris says, "that hurts."

It's possible that people like Williams and Morris will end up as dutiful ideologues once they're in charge. Williams hasn't spent all his time focused on the DMV. Connecticut's Democratic legislators have battled Rell on hot-button topics such as health care and taxes.

But it's also possible that many of the ideologues are mostly engaged in bluster. Douglas wonders whether many lawmakers, even ones who are promising partisan agendas on the campaign trail this fall, will end up scaling back their ideological ambitions. With more one-party governments expected around the country, state legislators will face difficult choices balancing their partisan passions and constructive governing. "One of the best ways to make people responsible," Douglas says, "is to give them responsibilities."

18

Governors Set the Agenda for a Lean 2011

Stateline Staff

Tough times call for tough love. A new breed of governors cuts taxes, cuts the public sector and worries less about the environment as they chart a new policy course for state governments.

F or many states, 2011 is the most trying budget year of a fiscal crisis now in its fourth year. Revenues generally remain lower than what they used to be; widespread joblessness is putting unprecedented strains on safety-net programs like Medicaid; and all this is happening as federal stimulus money runs out.

In this *Stateline* look at the agendas that the nation's governors have laid out for 2011, it's clear that ambitions have been trimmed. Many of the 28 newly elected governors — 18 of them are Republicans — see that as a good thing. They see an opportunity to shrink costs associated with the public workforce, consolidate agencies and define a generally smaller role for state government.

Whether state legislatures will go along with the governors' agendas is another question. But an unusually high number of governors have the odds — or at least politics — on their side. In 20 states, Republican governors are working with a legislature controlled by their own party. Democrats enjoy that advantage in 11 states.

ENCOURAGING BUSINESSES TO HIRE WORKERS

Governors of both parties are taking aim at stubbornly high unemployment rates with ideas for creating jobs.

The most sweeping employment proposal may be the one put forward by the new Republican governor in Michigan, a state that lost more than 850,000 jobs in the past decade. Governor Rick Snyder articulated a job-creation philosophy that focuses more on "gardening," or building businesses that already exist in the state, rather than "hunting" for out-of-state businesses with tax breaks.

From *Stateline.org*, February 2011.

He said he wants to create a statewide network of "talent coordinators" responsible for connecting entrepreneurs, innovators, management talent and job seekers with established companies.

Snyder also said he would make good on his campaign promise to get rid of the Michigan Business Tax. That tax essentially is a 22 percent surcharge on gross receipts; Snyder would replace it with a flat 6 percent corporate income tax. Snyder has said the plan will reduce the corporate tax burden by $1.5 billion, putting that money "back in the hands of employers who will be able to invest in Michigan and hire unemployed workers."

Republican Brian Sandoval said he wanted to lower Nevada's 14.5 percent unemployment rate — the highest in the country — by creating a $10 million "Catalyst Fund" that he says would close business deals and finance infrastructure. Meanwhile a new $10 million "Silver State Works" program would target job-seeking assistance to veterans, welfare recipients and ex-offenders. He also would set aside $3 million to help residents in rural Nevada use broadband access to start businesses or telecommute.

In New York, Democratic Governor Andrew Cuomo used his State of the State address to outline an ambitious plan that he said would make New York more business-friendly by capping spending and property taxes. He said he would "fix" the recently enacted Excelsior Tax Credit Program that gives $5,000 for each new job created, including streamlining the application process. He also would like to set up 10 regional public-private councils across the state to create jobs and compete for $200 million in funding.

Other notable jobs ideas include New Mexico Republican Susana Martinez's pledge to encourage small businesses to hire unemployed workers by covering part of the workers' salaries for the first six months through the unemployment fund. Nebraska's Dave Heineman, a Republican, said he wants to offer angel investment credits and internships for college students at Nebraska companies. And Washington State Democrat Chris Gregoire pledged to reduce by 48 percent the amount businesses pay to fund unemployment insurance and cut the workers' compensation rate.

TAX CUTS DESPITE DEFICITS

According to a *Stateline* tally, at least 20 governors — 16 Republicans and four Democrats — have refused to raise taxes this year. They represent about half of the U.S. population. Now, some of them are pressing forward on plans to *cut* taxes at a time when revenues are just beginning to improve.

The proposals come from both parties and all parts of the country. Alaska Governor Sean Parnell, a Republican, wants to lower taxes on oil. Arkansas' Mike Beebe, a Democrat, wants to cut the grocery tax. Terry Branstad, a Republican from Iowa, wants to cut the small business tax. Maine's Paul LePage, a Republican, wants to cut income taxes. Democrat Brian Schweitzer of Montana wants to cut taxes on homeowners. Republican Chris Christie of New Jersey and Democrat Andrew Cuomo of New York are planning to cut or cap property taxes. Democrat Bev Perdue of North Carolina called for cutting the state corporate tax. And perhaps the biggest proposed tax cut of all comes from Florida, where Governor Rick Scott is facing a nearly $4 billion deficit but still proposes to cut taxes by $2 billion, including by chopping the corporate income tax rate by 45 percent before eventually phasing it out altogether.

Of course, whether any of these proposals get anywhere is another story. Economists are deeply skeptical about the wisdom of cutting taxes now, and this feeling is palpable in many of the states that are discussing it now. Beebe, for example, noted that Arkansas could afford to cut the grocery tax by only half a percent. Scott's plan in Florida is being resisted by members of his own party. And Branstad's plan in Iowa may not go anywhere in the state Senate, which is controlled by the opposite party.

There are some exceptions to the no-tax hike theme. California Governor Jerry Brown wants to raise taxes, but only if voters agree to it. Connecticut Governor Dan Malloy is pushing one of the biggest tax-hike packages in state history, affecting everything from alcohol to income. And Minnesota Governor Mark Dayton is planning to raise the state income tax rate to 13 percent for the wealthiest residents—the highest top rate in the nation.

DON'T SAY "CLIMATE CHANGE"

In 2011, governors are still among the biggest champions of alternative energy. But they're no longer talking about it in the context of what states can do to stop global warming, as was common only a few years ago.

Only Vermont's Peter Shumlin, a Democrat, has mentioned "climate change" in a State of the State speech this year. Deval Patrick of Massachussetts and Martin O'Malley of Maryland, also Democrats, referenced greenhouse gases. But when Matt Mead, Wyoming's new Republican governor, mentioned global warming, it was to declare his skepticism of its man-made origins.

Instead, governors are talking mostly about improving the economy and creating jobs when they talk about energy. For example, both Mead and Republican Haley Barbour of Mississippi touted carbon sequestration — without mentioning that the purpose of sequestering carbon is to prevent greenhouse gas emissions from entering the atmosphere. Alaska Governor Sean Parnell, a Republican, set a goal for his state to get 50 percent of its power from renewable sources by 2025. Missouri's Jay Nixon, a Democrat, called for the construction of a new nuclear power reactor. Both O'Malley and Virginia's Bob McDonnell, a Republican, touted the possibilities of off-shore wind power. New York's Andrew Cuomo, a Democrat, proposed a $100 million competitive grant program for companies that create green jobs.

Despite the caution, governors did make some provocative statements on environmental issues — mostly aimed at an Obama administration that they view as too aggressive on regulation. Utah Governor Gary Herbert condemned the federal government's reassertion of its power to designate "wild lands" as an affront to state sovereignty — a theme that has been echoed recently by other Western Republicans including Mead, Parnell and Idaho's Butch Otter. West Virginia's Earl Tomblin also pledged to continue a suit against the EPA to stop it from rejecting coal mining permits. And Republican Governor Paul LePage of Maine has proposed adopting federal air and water pollution standards, to replace Maine's more stringent standards.

STREAMLINING GOVERNMENT

Governors of both parties have launched wars on red tape. In Florida, one of Governor Rick Scott's first moves after his inauguration was to issue an executive order halting all new rules, including those currently in the pipeline. The Republican quickly learned that he had to make some exceptions, in order to keep the state lottery functioning, for example. In Wisconsin, Republican

Scott Walker wants the power to sign off on new rules. Agencies also would have to conduct economic impact statements, among other hoops, to create new rules.

In a similar vein, Democrat John Hickenlooper of Colorado wants to require regulatory impact statements to estimate the cost to businesses of proposed regulations. Governors also are establishing a number of task forces and offices to cut back on red tape, including a Mandate Relief Task Force in New York and a new "Office of the Repealer" in Kansas.

Consolidating and reorganizing agencies also is on the agenda. New York's Andrew Cuomo, a Democrat, would like to shrink the number of agencies and departments by 20 percent. Republican Brian Sandoval of Nevada and Democrat Governor Chris Gregoire of Washington State also want to chop the number of state agencies.

Some consolidation plans reach down to the local government level. Republican Rick Snyder has tasked an advisory panel with looking at opportunities for consolidating local law enforcement agencies in Michigan. Republican Mitch Daniels of Indiana used his State of the State address to revive his controversial proposal from last year to eliminate the state's 1,008 townships.

STATE WORKFORCE CUTS

2011 is looking like a contentious year for public employee unions. Republican Governors Scott Walker of Wisconsin and John Kasich of Ohio both are fast-tracking proposals that would eliminate or hamstring collective bargaining rights for most state employees. Both are proving to be controversial. Walker says he is preparing for the possibility of strikes by state workers and would not hesitate to order the National Guard in the event of labor unrest.

Many governors are looking at scaling back retirement benefits or increasing the amount that employees contribute to covering the cost of both their pensions and retiree health care. New Jersey Republican Chris Christie remains the face of this movement, but Walker is being aggressive here, too: he wants state, local and school employees to pay half the costs of their pensions and at least 12.6 percent of their health care costs — a change that he says will save the state $300 million over the next two years. Some pension proposals, including those in California, Arizona, Illinois and New Jersey, would affect current workers in addition to new hires (whose benefits are easier to change).

Governors of both parties have made dramatic proposals to reduce the size and cost of state workforces. California's Jerry Brown, a Democrat, wants to cut the pay of state workers by 10 percent. Democrat Andrew Cuomo of New York has threatened to fire close to 10,000 workers if unions don't agree to concessions that would reduce labor costs. And Iowa's Terry Branstad, a Republican, wants to begin incorporating private-sector salary data into salary decisions for state workers, as well as allowing for union workers to be dismissed when government functions are privatized.

EDUCATION REFORM DRIVE CONTINUES

Many states are preparing for the possibility of once-unthinkable cuts to K-12 education this year. But that hasn't stopped a push for classroom reforms that got a boost last year from the federal Race to the Top grant program. Republican governors in Idaho (C.L. "Butch Otter), Indiana (Mitch Daniels), Nevada (Brian Sandoval) and New Jersey (Chris Christie) are looking to do away with teacher tenure provisions and want to tie teacher salaries to performance. Daniels has been particularly vocal on the issue, pledging to take on the Indiana State Teachers' Association, a group with which he sparred last year over Indiana's Race to the Top application. In Wisconsin, where Republican Governor Scott Walker enjoys GOP majorities in both legislative houses, the union representing the state's teachers has decided to endorse the pay-for-performance model in an attempt to help craft it.

School choice is back on the agenda. New Jersey's Christie and Republican Haley Barbour of Mississippi want to create more charter schools — another idea that has found favor with the Obama administration. Sandoval, Walker, Daniels and Republican Rick Scott of Florida all have talked about creating or expanding voucher programs, although Scott has dropped his plan in light of legal questions.

In a number of states, higher education is in for big cuts, as well as administrative changes. Nevada's Sandoval would cut $162 million from higher education. Jerry Brown of California is defending a plan that would cut $1.4 billion from state colleges and universities. Arkansas' Mike Beebe, a Democrat, and Texas' Rick Perry, a Republican, are pitching incentive programs that would send more money to colleges and universities that meet certain benchmarks such as a higher graduation rate. This kind of incentive funding is gaining steam in statehouses. Republican Governor Bobby Jindal of Louisiana signed a similar measure last year and now wants to expand on that program.

SAVING MONEY ON CORRECTIONS

Governors are speaking in new ways about their criminal justice systems. Rather than striving to be "tough on crime," they are now talking about being "smart on crime," and this is true regardless of their party affiliation. Being "smart on crime" generally means that states are trying to save their costly prison beds for serious offenders, while punishing lesser offenders in the community — in halfway houses or on probation or parole, for example — at a fraction of the cost.

Arkansas Governor Mike Beebe, a Democrat, and Indiana Governor Mitch Daniels, a Republican, are among the governors for whom this kind of transformation is a top priority. Beebe told lawmakers in his State of the State speech that, "We must appropriately punish lawbreakers, but, in some instances, non-violent offenders can repay that debt to society while remaining productive for their families and their communities."

Probably the biggest and most controversial prison-related proposal from any governor is in California, where Democrat Jerry Brown wants to house tens of thousands of state prisoners at county jails instead. This is part of the governor's broader plan to shrink state government and transfer responsibilities to localities, which he thinks are better-equipped to handle certain functions. The obvious problem, however, is that many local jails in California are themselves overcrowded.

State parole boards have made a surprising appearance on the agenda in several states this year. Democratic Governor Jack Markell of Delaware and Republican Sam Brownback of Kansas want to abolish their parole boards to save money, while Democrat John Lynch of New Hampshire wants to give his parole board more power. Meanwhile, in Massachusetts, Democrat Deval Patrick is overhauling the parole board after a career criminal released on parole allegedly killed a police officer in December.

Also in the criminal justice arena, New Mexico Governor Susana Martinez, a Republican, wants to reinstate the death penalty. That plan represents a deviation from a recent trend of states abolishing it. And in Alaska, Republican Governor Sean Parenell, noting that his state leads all others in cases of domestic violence and sexual abuse, called for a crackdown on child pornography and on what he called "graphic texting."

TRANSPORTATION FALLS OFF THE RADAR

When it comes to transportation, what is most striking about governors' State of the State speeches for 2011 is what they didn't say. Only a dozen governors included prominent plans to improve their state's transportation network or other major infrastructure. That is a big drop-off from just two years ago. According to the National Governors Association, 34 governors mentioned transportation or infrastructure in their 2009 speeches. The previous year, three in four governors highlighted the area.

So it figures that the governors who did choose to mention transportation usually did so in order to highlight major new initiatives.

Michigan Governor Rick Snyder, a Republican, unveiled a novel plan that could essentially give the state a free toll bridge between Detroit and Canada — alleviating a major bottleneck — using a public-private partnership. Not only that, but the state would be able to collect federal matching funds for the $550 million that the Canadian government would pay on behalf of the state.

Another rookie Republican, Brian Sandoval of Nevada, called for high-speed rail between Las Vegas and Los Angeles — something other GOP governors have panned — as well as improved highways between Las Vegas and Phoenix. The new Democratic governor of Vermont, Peter Shumlin, said while other governors rejected federal high-speed rail money (notably in Ohio and Wisconsin), he wanted to build fast rail service between New York City and Quebec.

One ambitious proposal is already close to fruition. Virginia's Republican governor, Bob McDonnell, pitched a $4 billion transportation package to alleviate

congestion in the Washington, D.C. suburbs and the Hampton Roads metro area. "This would be an immediate infusion of funds the likes of which the Commonwealth hasn't seen in decades," he said. Virginia lawmakers are close to passing a package that gives McDonnell most of what he asked for and a major political victory.

McDonnell championed the idea of an infrastructure bank, basically a revolving fund that would pay for improvements — an idea that President Obama has called for at the national level. New Hampshire Governor John Lynch, a Democrat, also touted an infrastructure bank, while Georgia Republican Nathan Deal said he wants to loosen restrictions on his state's infrastructure bank.

CUTTING MEDICAID COSTS

As Republican efforts to get the federal health care law thrown out in court continue, governors of both parties this year have been wrestling with a challenge they all share: how to cut ballooning Medicaid costs, just as federal stimulus aid runs dry.

They don't have many options. The new health care law bars them from adopting stiffer eligibility rules for Medicaid, so cutting enrollment isn't an option in most cases. However, Arizona's Republican Governor Jan Brewer just got approval from the federal government to discontinue a special Medicaid program that covers some 250,000 childless adults. U.S. Health and Human Services Secretary Kathleen Sebelius said the Arizona program comes up for federal reauthorization in September, and the governor can simply choose not to renew it — without violating the new health care law's enrollment restrictions.

But that won't necessarily spell relief for other Republican governors who sent Sebelius a letter this month seeking a blanket reversal of the enrollment restriction. So most of the ideas governors are discussing involve making cuts in benefits and doctors' fees. For example, South Carolina is cutting hospice care and requiring nearly all Medicaid recipients to move to cost-cutting managed care programs. Colorado, Arkansas, Vermont and other states are increasing so-called provider fees paid by hospitals to raise matching funds for federal Medicaid dollars. Massachusetts will no longer pay for dentures. North Carolina has stopped covering surgery for the clinically obese.

Other notable big health care ideas:

- Vermont's new Democratic Governor, Peter Shumlin, wants to create a single-payer system in his state, an idea that proved too liberal for Democrats in Congress when they passed federal health care reform. Shumlin says the plan could save Vermonters as much as $500 million in the first year.
- In Massachusetts, Democratic Governor Deval Patrick is pushing to remove a cloak of secrecy around contracts between doctors and hospitals and insurance companies. His idea is to make those deals between these health care players public in hopes that transparency will drive down costs.
- New York's Governor Andrew Cuomo, a Democrat, established a blue-ribbon "Medicaid redesign" team charged with re-inventing New York's Medicaid program to dramatically lower costs. The project, which has an April 1 deadline, is patterned after a similar revamp in Wisconsin; former Wisconsin Medicaid director Jason Helgerson is heading it up.

19

The Rise of Attorneys General

Josh Goodman

Republican attorneys general rediscover the cause of states' rights and decide to take a legal stand against the federal government.

From *Governing,* June 2010.

When state attorneys general agreed on a landmark settlement with tobacco companies in 1997, all they needed to finish the deal was approval from Congress. But Washington, D.C.'s powerbrokers balked at taking orders from the states' chief legal officers. "Who do these people think they are?" Sen. John McCain wondered.

Over the last 13 years, it's become quite clear who state AGs think they are. The tobacco settlement, finalized in 1998 with tens of billions of dollars in payments to states, was just the beginning. State AGs continued asserting themselves on a national level as the scourges of corporate bad guys and the guardians of consumer interests. In 1997, the national influence of state AGs seemed novel. Today it doesn't.

Yet many Democrats in Washington now are asking the same question as McCain: "Who do these people think they are?" That's because the powerful people state AGs are confronting aren't just in corporate boardrooms—they're in the White House and the U.S. Capitol. In the last few months, conservative AGs have become some of the nation's most prominent opponents of federal power in general and the Obama administration specifically. They're trying to block provisions of the federal health-care reform law in court, and they're working to limit the federal government's power to regulate guns and greenhouse gas emissions.

On the surface, these actions look like another reimagining of the state AGs' role. The tobacco settlement created a model for activism for a liberal Democratic AG. Perhaps then, conservative Republican AGs, with their states' rights stands, are developing their own model as to how to affect the nation's most important policy decisions.

But it's probably more accurate to say that the Republicans are developing a new twist on older models. After all, AGs of both parties long have fought to protect state prerogatives. Nor are today's Republican AGs the first to engage in a politically charged battle with a president of the opposite party. Democrats did the same thing to George W. Bush over environmental regulation.

New model or not, one thing is clear: Almost overnight, some of the country's most important, controversial politicians are Republican AGs. They can attribute their new clout to the presence of a Democrat in the White House.

After the tobacco settlement, AGs became stars— well, some of them anyway. Connecticut's Richard Blumenthal made a name for himself as a scourge of health maintenance organizations, insurance companies and power plants. California's Bill Lockyer sued car companies for auto emissions. Most famously, New York's Eliot Spitzer cracked down on the excesses of Wall Street.

Blumenthal, Lockyer and Spitzer are all Democrats. It took two years for the first Republican AG to join Democrats in their suits against tobacco. Most of the AGs who engaged in a major anti-trust case against Microsoft in the late 1990s also were Democrats.

It's not as though Republicans completely stayed on the sidelines. Most Republican AGs eventually participated in tobacco suits. And Republicans generally have been as happy as the Democrats to become involved in consumer protection cases. But with business groups complaining that the Democratic activists were bullies who overstepped their roles as state officials, Republican AGs never quite embraced the model that Spitzer and others refined. Conservatives didn't want to be anti-business or favor excessive regulation.

In fact, some conservative AGs, led by Alabama's Bill Pryor, actively rebelled against this model. But Pryor and his ideological compatriots largely were defined by what they weren't: activists in the Spitzer mold. Most Republican AGs weren't having a national impact in the way that some of their Democratic counterparts were. They didn't seem to have a coherent, common national purpose.

In that context, it's surprising how easily Rob McKenna, Washington state's Republican AG, articulates

just such a purpose. "The role of the attorney general," McKenna says, "is to be a guardian of federalism and to protect state prerogatives."

For Republican AGs, protecting state prerogatives has meant battling the Obama administration and Democrats in Congress. In doing so, they've enjoyed instant influence.

When the Senate passed a version of health-care reform that included special Medicaid payments to Nebraska—the so-called "Cornhusker Kickback"—13 Republican AGs wrote to Congress threatening to sue, claiming their states weren't being treated equitably. Congress dropped the provision. Later, Democratic leaders in the House of Representatives considered using a procedure know as "deem-and-pass" to allow the House to give approval to the unpopular Senate version of health-care reform without a direct vote on the matter. Republican AGs threatened to sue again, arguing deem-and-pass was unconstitutional. The House dropped the strategy.

Those concessions, of course, didn't stop AGs from suing when Obama finally signed the health-care bill into law in March. The AGs argue that requiring everyone to buy health insurance is unconstitutional and that the law places an unfair burden on the states. So far, around 20 states are supporting legal action to block the law, and all but one of the participating AGs are Republicans.

Health-care reform is the most obvious example of the Republican activism, but it's not the only one. A group of Republican AGs and a few Democrats from energy-producing states also teamed up to try to prevent the federal Environmental Protection Agency (EPA) from regulating greenhouse gas emissions. Eight AGs— five Republicans and three Democrats—from conservative states are arguing in court that federal gun regulations shouldn't apply to firearms made and sold within their borders. "There is a sense now among conservative attorneys general that this position could be used creatively and aggressively to pursue conservative ends," says James Tierney, a former Maine AG who directs Columbia Law School's National State Attorneys General Program.

Among the Republican AGs, none has proven himself to be more aggressive—or more conservative—than Virginia's Ken Cuccinelli. Cuccinelli, a global warming skeptic, took the lead challenging the EPA over greenhouse gas regulations and now is challenging the EPA over new automobile fuel economy standards. Mere minutes after Obama signed the health-care reform bill, Cuccinelli filed a challenge to it that was separate from other states, arguing that a Virginia law prohibiting a health insurance mandate should supersede the federal law.

Cuccinelli also has created controversy back home. He wrote a letter to public colleges and universities telling them they couldn't bar discrimination on the basis of sexual orientation. He's demanding documents from the University of Virginia on a former faculty member's research, saying it might reveal the scientist's work on climate change to be fraudulent.

The end result is that Cuccinelli is a darling of the right and a villain to the left. He is perhaps as famous as Spitzer in his heyday. He's clearly just as polarizing. The remarkable thing: Cuccinelli took office just five months ago.

Other Republican AGs who also have been quite active, such as South Carolina's Henry McMaster and Texas' Greg Abbott, haven't become as famous. But even if they're not household names, what they're doing is national news. Democratic AGs now are the ones on the defensive. In conservative states such as Oklahoma, Arkansas and Georgia, Democrats have faced—and resisted—pressure to join the health-care suit.

While Cuccinelli is the person most closely linked to the states' rights revival, the state with the most enthusiasm for it is Utah. There, Republican Attorney General Mark Shurtleff has been an eager participant, though he hasn't completely had a choice in the matter: The Utah Legislature has demanded that he take on the federal government.

The legislature approved a resolution asserting the state's sovereignty under the Constitution's 10th Amendment. It passed a bill to opt out of federal gun regulations, setting up Shurtleff's participation in that issue. It even approved legislation directing Shurtleff to try to use eminent domain on federal lands to claim them for development.

The situation in Utah highlights one reason conservative AGs are becoming so prominent. Conservative legislators and governors are engaged in their own rebellion against the Obama administration. As states' legal officers, AGs logically are becoming some of the faces of this movement.

So is Shurtleff celebrating his brand new sense of purpose? Well, no. "This isn't new for me," he says.

Shurtleff notes that Utah long has had a fondness for fighting the federal government. He points out that early in his term, he was battling with the George W. Bush administration over federal land issues. "I said, 'I don't want to sue my new Republican president, but it's states' rights,'" Shurtleff says.

Utah isn't unique. Western states have battled Washington over federal lands for years. AGs have been the forefront of these battles—and other ones with the feds. "States and their lawyers have long been suspicious of federal power," Tierney says. "That's why we have federalism. It would be unnatural for states not to protect themselves within the federal system."

Most of these fights are bipartisan. Almost every AG supported New York as it worked to preserve states' right to enforce their own lending laws. In 2009, the Supreme Court sided with the states.

Almost every AG teamed up again to ask the Obama administration to support ending federal pre-emption of state banking regulation in this year's financial reform legislation. The White House agreed. Tom Miller, Iowa's longtime Democratic attorney general, says financial reform shows the real story—it isn't that AGs are battling the White House more; they're actually battling it less.

"My view," he says, "is that the litigation against the federal government is the exception. Overall, the attorneys general have the best relationship with the Department of Justice in decades. That includes Democrats and Republicans."

But if health-care reform is an exception, it's an awfully big one. Obama has won approval of the most far-reaching domestic legislation under any Democratic president since Lyndon Johnson. The last people standing in the way from it becoming a reality aren't in Washington, D.C.; they're attorneys general in the states.

In principle, AGs may agree on defending states against federal power, but in this case they're divided. A group of Democratic AGs plan to submit their own brief defending the constitutionality of the health-care law.

The question is whether this divide is a sign of things to come. Sure, people such as Shurtleff have been fighting the feds for a long time, but the prominence of conservative AGs in the health-care debate wasn't quite like anything that's happened previously. Over the long term, will conservative AGs become more aggressive in trying to check the grandest ambitions of the federal government?

Michael Greve, a federalism expert at the conservative American Enterprise Institute, has an interesting answer to that question: They shouldn't want to.

Greve's point is that limited government and reduced regulation—key conservative goals—aren't served by devolving power to the states. "It is a conceit and mistake on the part of Republicans to think that decentralization translates into smaller government," he says. "If you really wanted to form an effective coalition in favor of a deregulatory agenda, you'd have to oppose states that are on the pro-regulatory side."

If you look back at the role that Democratic AGs played during the Bush administration, you can see what Greve means. Liberal AGs fought for states to be allowed to set tougher auto emissions standards than the federal government. During the Bush years, more state power would have meant more stringent environmental regulation. That probably will be true again during the next Republican presidency. If conservative AGs were to fight for more state power regardless of who is in the White House, they'd end up doing so at the expense of conservative policy objectives.

But at least with regard to environmental rules, conservative AGs weren't fighting federal power under Bush. Instead, liberal AGs were. They didn't just ask to set their own emissions rules. They sued to force the Bush EPA to treat greenhouse gases as pollutants—and won before the Supreme Court.

On the policy question—whether there should be more or less environmental regulation—the two sets of AGs have been completely consistent over the last two presidencies. But on the federalism question—how much power the federal government should have to design whatever environmental policies it wants—they've flipped. Democratic AGs wanted to constrict federal power under Bush. Republican AGs want to do it now.

That's why Tierney gives a pithy answer to the question of whether conservative AGs are doing something new by fighting Obama. "It's only new," he says, "because conservatives are doing what liberals did before." Maybe Republican AGs now are so committed to fighting the feds that they'll become prominent foes of the next Republican president too, but if so, that would be something truly new.

If, instead, the precedent set in the last two presidencies continues, then the influence of Republican AGs over national policy is likely to wane the next time a Republican is elected president. With a Republican in the White House, it will be Democrats' turn to battle the federal government—and to become the new political stars.

20

The Nation's Only Health Insurance Commissioner Takes on the Health-Care System

John Buntin

State insurance commissioners usually confine themselves to reviewing policy rate increases, helping to prevent plan insolvencies and reviewing complaints. The head of the nation's only independent state health insurance commission wants to do more. Christopher Kellor wants to reform the health care system.

From *Governing*, February 2011.

If proximity were a reliable guide to power, you would think Blue Cross & Blue Shield of Rhode Island has it and that Christopher Koller, the state's health insurance commissioner, does not. Blue Cross & Blue Shield (BCBS) occupies space in a $125 million office tower that sits at the foot of Capitol Hill in Providence. Koller's offices are in Cranston, nine miles south of the capital. His desk is in a building that used to be the old state almshouse, next to what was once the state house of correction and the asylum for the incurably insane. "The joke goes," Koller says of the occupants of the Cranston buildings, "that it used to be criminals, the mentally ill and poor people — and now it's state employees."

If size were another guide to power, you'd have to give it to BCBS again. The insurance giant employs some 1,100 people in Rhode Island. Until recently, Koller had a staff of just three dedicated employees — an executive assistant, an attorney and himself — but a federal grant has allowed him to double his workforce to six.

Yet sit down with BCBS of Rhode Island CEO James Purcell, and you'll hear a very different assessment of the balance of power between Koller's office and the state's $3 billion commercial health insurance industry. "We are probably the most heavily regulated insurance industry in the country," Purcell says. And that, he adds, is largely a function of Koller's unique job: He is the nation's only health insurance commissioner.

"In the old days, when there was just an insurance commissioner," Purcell says, "he or she had a lot more to do, which from my old-school perspective was a good thing." But now, he continues, "what does Chris think about every day? He thinks about us." And in Koller's case, thought has given rise to radical action.

In the winter of 2007, Koller made a decision that took him well beyond the scope of activities common among even the most aggressive state insurance commissioners. Instead of reviewing rate increases, preventing plan insolvency and fielding the complaints of policyholders, Koller addressed the affordability of the health-care delivery system as a whole.

His admirers see his approach as nothing less than groundbreaking. "He is the person in government who can have an impact on the private delivery system," says Lt. Gov. Elizabeth Roberts, who as a state senator sponsored the legislation that created Koller's office.

But to insurers and some providers, Koller's approach has been deeply unsettling. "There is a very uneasy line between who manages Blue Cross Blue Shield," Purcell says. "That's really my job, not his." Some critics have gone even further. In late 2010, the state's most powerful hospital group, Care New England, went to court to stop Koller, charging that the health insurance commissioner had become "a rogue operator."

Surprisingly, behind these very different assessments of Koller's actions, there is an underlying agreement about what he has sought to do. Koller, says Roberts, "has tried to use it as an office that could reform the system, not just regulate it." In the process, what started as a seemingly quixotic effort may well emerge as a model for health insurance regulation, if Koller's attempt to take on two of Rhode Island's most powerful industries — hospitals and health insurers — doesn't do him in first.

THE ROLE OF STATE INSURANCE COMMISSIONERS

Insurance regulation is one of state government's oldest functions. Most states have insurance departments that date back to the late 19th century. Their purpose today is strikingly similar to what it was back then: insuring that the policies purchased by consumers are backed up by real companies with real financial assets.

"Every insurance commissioner, regardless of their political party, has a duty to ensure solvency of the marketplace and to protect consumers," says North Carolina insurance commissioner Wayne Goodwin. That means not only ensuring that the rate is not discriminatory or excessive, but also that it's adequate enough for the company to maintain solvency and not breach its policyholder obligations. Setting the right rate, says West Virginia insurance commissioner Jane Cline, is "a balancing act."

Historically, being an insurance commissioner hasn't been an unduly demanding job. Only about half of the states require commercial insurers to seek prior approval for rate increases, and until recently, insurance commissioners spent only a small portion of their time focused on health insurance. That has changed, thanks to rapidly rising health insurance premiums and to the passage of President Obama's health-care reform legislation, the Affordable Care Act.

Although rising premiums and health-care reform are often linked in the public mind, the first development preceded the passage of the second. A recent Commonwealth Fund study tells the story. Between 2003 and 2009, health insurances premiums for businesses and their employees nationwide jumped by 41 percent, while per-person deductibles rose by 77 percent. Some states have seen even more dramatic increases or proposed increases. Last spring, Anthem Blue Cross shocked California regulators by announcing plans to increase premiums for individual health insurance policies by more than 30 percent. Outside actuaries found problems with their assumptions, and Anthem retreated, but another big California insurer, Blue Shield of California, recently announced a third round of rate hikes for individual policyholders that will bring total rate increases for some individual insurance policies to 59 percent. At the current growth rates, the cost of the average family policy, which was $13,027 in 2009, will top $23,000 by 2020.

State regulators have watched these increases with mounting dismay, and several have been in the forefront of taking action to reign in rising premiums. A particular focus of concern has been health insurers' reserves, particularly the building up of surpluses beyond what is necessary to meet solvency requirements. "We are now saying," says Mike Kreidler, Washington state's insurance commissioner, "'Wait a minute. Why are they continuing to build surpluses when they are not-for-profit insurers, and I am continuing to get double-digit rate increases?'"

Kreidler's office is now working with the state Legislature to gain authority to take insurers' reserves into account when making rate approval decisions. In Maine, Insurance Superintendent Mila Kofman also has sought permission to consider health insurers' overall financial position when reviewing rate increases rather than focusing only on narrow actuarial analyses of the plans at hand.

Despite such attempts to control the rate of premium growth, even the most aggressive regulators say that there's simply not very much they can do about rising health-care costs. "Even with pretty comprehensive rate reviews, we can't do magic," Kofman says. "I don't think any insurance regulator can control medical costs. That's just the reality."

It's a sentiment most insurance commissioners agree with. But over in Rhode Island, Koller isn't one of them.

KOLLER: THE SOLE STATE HEALTH INSURANCE COMMISSIONER

Koller's unusual attitude reflects his unusual position as not just insurance commissioner, but as health insurance commissioner. No other state (with the partial exception of California, which has the Department of Managed Health Care) has broken out health insurance as the responsibility of a distinct and separate office. Rhode Island did so back in 2004. The decision to create such an office came from the realization that the state did not have the information, much less the authority, to affect — or even understand — the relationship between insurers and providers in the large- and small-group insurance markets. The legislation that Lt. Gov. Roberts sponsored as a state senator sought to change that by creating an office with broad powers to improve the health-care system's quality, accessibility and affordability. What this would mean in practice, however, remained somewhat unclear — until Koller took office in 2005.

Since then, Koller has engaged in what resembles, at least in some ways, a game of health reform "chicken," invoking his powers to demand changes while trying to avoid putting them to the test. It's a high-wire act that causes even admirers to hold their breath. "The commissioner is moving ever closer to the precipice," says William Martin, the co-chair of the Office of the Health Insurance Commissioner's advisory committee and the chief operation officer of a biotech company. "I don't know how much longer he can do that."

The first thing that strikes you about Koller is his height — he's 6' 7". The second is his wonkiness. Koller, age 49, first got interested in health-care policy as a junior at Dartmouth College. His undergraduate thesis compared and contrasted the case mix indices of for-profit and nonprofit hospitals. After graduating, Koller, a native of Rochester, N.Y., worked for a year with the Jesuit Volunteer Corps in Washington, D.C. Then it was on to Yale University to get masters degrees in management and religion. After working in various positions at an HMO in Buffalo, N.Y., Koller was offered a position as the CEO of the Providence-based Neighborhood Health Plan, a network of health clinics serving primarily low-income Rhode Islanders. By 2005, Neighborhood Health Plan had grown from 40 employees to 175; its budget was $174 million and it served 75,000 Rhode Islanders a year.

"It was a great experience," he says now. However, after nine years of running what had essentially become a Medicaid managed care plan, Koller was eager to return to the health-care policy world. So when Gov. Donald Carcieri offered him a position as the head of the newly created Office of the Health Insurance Commissioner, as well as assurances that he'd be a primary health-care adviser, he leapt at it.

Koller's early steps were fairly traditional. At first, he focused on the politically volatile issue of BCBS's $300 million-plus reserves. A study commissioned by Koller but paid for by BCBS found that the insurer was, if anything, slightly undercapitalized. Koller also pushed such modest but effective measures as requiring the state's major insurers to send proposed rate increases — and the assumptions of medical inflation and utilization that undergirded them — to his office at the same time so they could be posted online. This step has allowed policymakers to examine differences in assumptions and has created pressure among insurers to avoid being seen as proposing the highest price increases.

As satisfying as these achievements were, Koller's primary goal — promoting quality, accessibility and affordability — remained elusive. When he pushed the state's two primary insurers to report on what they were doing, he got what he describes as "a laundry list" of initiatives. Some seemed substantial. Others did not.

"I had seen at Neighborhood Health Plan how one health insurer comes in with one plan, and another comes in with another plan," Koller says. "Doctors do not want to differentiate how they provide care based on who's paying the bill. Having health plans send them different instructions was tremendously counterproductive."

So in the fall of 2007, Koller convened an advisory panel to help him develop a different approach — one that sought to define priorities for the state's commercial health insurance sector as a whole.

PUSHING FOR CHANGE IN THE HEALTH-CARE SYSTEM

Among academic researchers and health-care policy experts, there are certain areas of agreement about how the health-care delivery system could be changed and improved: A better functioning system would spend more on primary care. Care for people with diabetes and other chronic illnesses would be managed to prevent expensive and dangerous rounds of hospitalization. Providers would utilize electronic medical records to prevent redundant testing and to identify patients who need extra attention. Payment systems would move away from paying providers for the volume of services provided and instead pay for quality.

Citing the broad statutory language that created his office, Koller decided in the spring of 2009 to require insurers to do all four. Koller put forward four principles that he expected the state's three leading insurers to embrace. First, he asked insurers to increase the portion of their medical expenses that went to primary care by 1 percentage point for five consecutive years. The goal was to raise Rhode Island's primary care expenditures from a substandard 5.9 percent to something approaching such high performance systems as Pennsylvania's Geisinger Health Plan.

Koller's second requirement was that state insurers support the expansion of the Rhode Island Chronic Care Sustainability Initiative, which seeks to pair providers with case managers who can direct care for patients with chronic conditions. Providers would agree to meet a level of accreditation in keeping with the National Committee for Quality Assurance's patient-centered medical home. Insurers would agree to pay a case management fee and fund nurse-case managers.

Koller's third condition was that insurers implement meaningful incentive programs for physicians to adopt electronic medical records. Finally, he asked insurers to

commit to a serious discussion aimed at overhauling the payment system as a whole.

The reaction to Koller's demands was euphoric from certain sectors, notably primary care providers. From insurers, however, the reaction was mixed. Ultimately, insurers like BCBS's Purcell agreed that "directionally this was correct." After all, many of Koller's ideas were inspired by projects that BCBS had already begun. But there was another consideration as well. In addition to pressuring insurers, Koller was preparing to take on one of the biggest cost drivers in health care — rising hospital costs and utilization.

TACKLING THE ISSUE OF RISING COSTS

The situation in 2009 crystallized the issue. That year, the state's three major commercial health insurers filed for double-digit rate increases. As Purcell remembers it, "We were in the depths of the recession, and a number of community leaders, including the governor, asked if there was any way to skip an increase. I said, 'Governor, if I were you, I would be asking that too, but to agree to inadequate rates does nobody any favors.'" Purcell argued that if the state made BCBS rates inadequate by 5 percent, then "next year it will be whatever it is next year plus that 5 percent.'"

Rhode Island's public officials disagreed. That year, Koller approved a much smaller rate increase. His decision cost BCBS approximately $100 million dollars. However, Koller and the business community took to heart one of insurers' primary arguments — that hospital costs, primarily increases in outpatient utilization but also prices, were one of the major drivers behind rising premiums. A study of insurer contracts with hospitals produced by Koller's office in January 2010 came to a conclusion already supported by the literature: Consolidation of hospitals makes cost containment difficult. In Rhode Island, that was particularly true for insurers dealing with Care New England, a local hospital group that included Women & Infants Hospital in Providence, where 80 percent of the babies in the state are born. As Purcell notes, "It is essentially unthinkable not to have Women & Infants in your network." And that made negotiations with Women & Infants difficult.

And so in early 2010, Koller extended his delivery overhaul efforts to the state's hospitals as well. In doing so, William Martin, who chaired Koller's advisory board, knew that the health insurance commissioner would be "poking the bear a little bit." But Martin agreed that such actions were necessary, given the structure of Rhode Island's health-care system. "There is no competitive force in the marketplace," Martin says, adding that Koller's office "has to come in and put that force in through regulation."

Although Koller has no oversight authority over hospitals, he and his counsel decided that he did have the authority to present "contracting principles" that would guide insurers in their dealings with hospitals. In July 2010, he put forward six of them, among them provisions requiring quality incentives and standards for care coordination and simplicity. Perhaps the most controversial of all, however, was a provision that would cap the guaranteed rate of hospital cost increase at the level of the Medicare consumer price index, which in 2009 amounted to a mere 2.7 percent increase. In doing so, Koller was engaging in the kind of high-stakes bluffing he had perfected in dealing with insurers.

"As a regulator, you have a variety of choices about how you communicate," notes Koller. At one end are formal regulations. At the other end is oral advice. In between there can be bulletins, guidance and information sheets. "I have specifically chosen to communicate this guidance as written guidance coming from the office, not as formal regulations — although that may change going forward — with the understanding that failure to comply with this guidance will be taken into consideration during the annual rate review. So it is very important to have the rate review process in place and functioning."

But this time, Koller apparently overstepped. Care New England filed a lawsuit against Koller's office, seeking to block the insurance commissioner's new conditions, saying they were an impediment to negotiations with UnitedHealthcare of New England. In December, Koller settled part of the lawsuit — a setback for now.

The health insurance commissioner has not, however, given up on his goals. Despite all the tools and pressures he's put in place, premium increases in Rhode Island are not significantly lower than in surrounding states. All of his actions, he points out, are consistent with what it takes to keep a lid on rates of increase. "Communities that are good at this are ones that have an emphasis on primary care, payment reform and systems measure, and have delivery system leadership," Koller says. And he remains determined to ensure that Rhode Island is one of them.

VI

Courts

Most people imagine the job of a judge as something akin to being a referee; the basic gig is to honestly and objectively interpret and enforce rules. Problem is, interpreting the law can be like calling fouls. What gets you carded from one ref will be waived off by another. Similarly, the reading of the law and its application to a particular issue can vary from judge to judge. Unfortunately, on controversial issues it doesn't matter what a judge says because one side will be happy with the call, and the other will cry foul. This has always been the case. What is different is that those crying foul seem increasingly willing to believe judicial bias lies behind their legal losses, not a fair reading and application of the law. They want "fair" and "objective" jurists who will, fairly and objectively, consistently rule in their favor. As the political stakes in the courtroom can be high, partisans across the ideological divide are making judicial elections increasingly competitive . . . and nasty. The upshot is that many judges running for election are being treated less like referees and more like players, players who are asked to openly pull on one team's colors and start throwing sharp elbows into their opponents. The once sleepy backwater of state judicial elections has in many cases become a political free-for-all where anything goes.

The emergence of intensely partisan judicial elections has important implications for a broad range of policy issues. The United States is unusual in that it has dual civil and criminal judicial systems—the state system and the federal system. This parallel, two-track system is a byproduct of federalism, and, just as a governor is not subordinate to the president, neither are state courts subordinate to federal courts. Broadly speaking, the federal courts deal with issues of federal law and the U.S. Constitution. State courts deal with state law and state constitutions. The only real point of overlap between the federal and state court systems is at the very top. Sitting at the head of both systems is the U.S. Supreme Court, which has the final say on what both levels of government are empowered to do under the U.S. Constitution. What this means is that state courts have considerable independence and insulation from the federal court system. Partisans increasingly want that independence to work in their favor, and state judicial elections are increasingly becoming proxy battles for competing ideological camps.

For example, a recent state supreme court justice election in Wisconsin morphed into a referendum on Governor Scott Walker and the Republican-controlled legislature for their drive to eliminate public employee bargaining rights. Wisconsin judicial races do not list candidate party affiliation, but incumbent Justice David Prosser was seen as part of the conservative-leaning voting bloc on the bench, and his opponent Assistant Attorney General JoAnne Kloppenburg was associated with the unions.[1] Those vague left-right proclivities were enough to spark a furious ideological electoral battle in a race most had predicted would be a nonpartisan snooze. Dollars poured in from outside sources, special interest groups mobilized voters, and what would normally be an under-the-radar contest became national news as larger political coalitions did battle for "their" candidate.

Even in states where supreme court justices are appointed and affirmed rather than contested, judges are feeling the pressure of citizen policy preferences. Following the 7-0 decision to legalize same-sex marriage in Iowa, three sitting justices faced well-funded opposition to their retention and were ousted from their posts. Unseating Associate Justices David Baker and Michael Streit and Chief Justice Marsha Ternus paved the way for newly elected Republican Governor Terry Branstad to appoint replacements that may not overturn the same-sex marriage ruling but will most likely lead to more conservative future decisions. There also has been talk of impeaching the other four justices,[2] but regardless of the resulting balance of the Iowa Supreme Court gay marriage opponents sought to "send a message" to judges across the nation that citizen preferences must be taken into account in court decisions.[3]

The articles in this section focus on the changes and effects of judicial campaigns in the selection of state court judges. Emily Rock and Lawrence Baum conducted a voter-level survey of campaign effects in Ohio Supreme Court races, finding that in states that do not list candidate party affiliation on the ballot, elections with higher media coverage and campaign spending lead to more partisan voting than lower-visibility contests.

Though this spending on advertisements may lead to more informed voters, critics have warned against the increased expenditures as threatening the impartiality of the bench, as summarized in the Executive Summary of *The New Politics of Judicial Elections: 2000–2009*, published by the Brennan Center for Justice at New York University School of Law. Reformers have suggested reverting back to executive appointments or changing to public funding of elections to counter this growing problem.

Applying these trends to the most recent election, another release by the Brennan Center, a nonpartisan public policy and law institute, outlines the record spending levels, negative ads, and special interest investments in the 2010 judicial races. This evidence represents the gradual and now perhaps overwhelming shift of the judiciary from outside of the political fray right into the center, duking it out like the campaign process of the other branches.

NOTES

1. Gramlich, John. April 5, 2011. "Wisconsin Judicial Race is Test for GOP." Stateline.org. http://www.stateline.org/live/details/story?contentId=564967. Accessed April 13, 2011.

2. Lynch, James Q. March 4, 2011. "Iowa Impeachment Now 'in God's Hands.'" Easterniowagovernment.com. http://easterniowagovernment.com/2011/03/04/iowa-impeachment-now-in-gods-hands/. Accessed April 14, 2011.

3. Gramlich, John. Sept. 10, 2010. "Will Gay Marriage Decision Cost Iowa Justices Their Jobs?" Stateline.org. http://www.stateline.org/live/details/story?contentId=511967. Accessed April 14, 2011.

21

The Impact of High-Visibility Contests for U.S. State Court Judgeships: Partisan Voting in Nonpartisan Elections

Emily Rock and Lawrence Baum

The media spotlight drives up voting in judicial elections, even in traditionally low turnout non-partisan contests.

Traditionally, most judicial elections were "quiet, dignified affairs" (Caufield 2007, 36). A decade ago, however, one expert wrote that elections to judgeships "are becoming nastier, noisier, and costlier" (Schotland 1998, 150). That trend has continued, and it has important theoretical and normative implications. Not surprisingly, these changes in the character of judicial elections have attracted a great deal of attention and debate (Bonneau and Hall 2009).

This trend in judicial elections has some effects that do not relate to how voters respond to the nastier, noisier, and costlier campaigns. For instance, the influx of substantial campaign contributions into judicial elections might make judges more susceptible to influence from the interest groups providing those contributions. However, for the most part, changes in judicial elections are consequential to the extent that they change the behavior of voters. For that reason, it is important to look directly at voters' responses to what we will call high-visibility judicial contests, which have become more common in recent years.[1]

Taking advantage of a series of voter surveys, we analyze the responses of Ohio voters to a set of items pertaining to supreme court contests taking place between 1986 and 2006. Our concern is how variation in the amount of information that campaigns provide to voters affects the extent of partisan voting—that is, voting for candidates on the basis of voters' party identifications. We use that inquiry to probe the impact of changes in the character of judicial elections and to inform the ongoing debate about the most appropriate method for selecting judges in the U.S.

From *State Politics and Policy Quarterly*, 2010.

CHANGES IN THE CHARACTER OF JUDICIAL ELECTIONS

Relative to elections for the highest offices, elections to judgeships do not generally attract much attention from voters, the media, or even scholars. For voters, the general lack of information about candidates and relevant issues makes it difficult to become informed concerning the choices to be made. One study of voters in Oregon and Washington found that only 20 percent of respondents said that they had enough information to vote in state-wide judicial races (Sheldon and Lovrich 1983, 237).

These characteristics are not unique to judicial elections. They also apply to other low-visibility elections, including many contests for statewide executive-branch offices below the governorship. Nonetheless, judicial elections differ in some regards from races for other elected offices. One important difference is the presence of both formal and informal restrictions traditionally imposed on what judicial candidates can say about their positions on issues of legal policy.[2] But the evidence available from prior studies of voting behavior in judicial elections suggests that voters tend to respond to the same considerations as they do in other low-visibility contests (Dubois 1979b; Hall and Bonneau 2006; Bonneau 2007).

Occasional exceptions to the general pattern of low-visibility judicial elections have occurred in the past. There have been some contests in which the candidates, and others, provided voters with relatively large amounts of information pertinent to their choice of judicial candidates. Over the past two decades, at least at the state supreme court level, these exceptions have become quite common. More judicial candidates are spending large amounts of money, and in recent years, the growth in spending has been sharp and has involved more races than ever. For instance, "between 2000 and 2002, average candidate spending in state supreme court races increased 167 percent. From 2002 to 2004, spending increased an additional 168 percent on average" (Caufield 2007, 37).

Because judicial elections are typically low-visibility affairs, the amount of campaign money that a particular candidate spends—and thus, the amount of advertising purchased—could have a significant impact on the outcome of judicial elections. One study of low-visibility election contests suggests that "in such low information environments, even a modestly effective campaign might have substantial effects where voters have few readily available pointers on who they should support" (Schaffner, Wright, and Streb 2001, 26).

For their part, interest groups are increasingly inclined to participate in judicial campaigns, sometimes adding substantially to the candidates' own spending. Judicial candidates and interest groups both are more likely to engage in negative campaigning than they were in the past, and they are also more likely to link candidates with positions on issues of legal policy. The mass media respond to the heightened scale of campaigns, so newspapers and television news programs more frequently give judicial contests something beyond token coverage. The coverage provided tends to reflect the more negative and the more issue-oriented content of campaigns.

These changes in the roles of money and interest groups in recent judicial elections have fueled debates about the desirability of judicial elections. When low-visibility contests were dominant, those who opposed the election of judges pointed to low participation levels and the apparent lack of relevant knowledge on the part of voters. Today, some opponents of judicial elections argue that voters sometimes have *too much* information, or at least the wrong kinds of information, so that they are making their choices based on inappropriate information. While the movement led by the American Judicature Society to replace conventional judicial elections with other mechanisms has slowed considerably, it nonetheless continues. Moreover, changes in the character of judicial elections in recent years have led to a vigorous debate about how best to structure and govern those elections.

Assessments of high-visibility judicial contests generally focus on campaign activities rather than on voters responses to campaigns. As suggested earlier, while that focus is quite appropriate for some purposes, most of the questions that arise from high-visibility judicial contests relate to voters' behavior. For instance, the impact of campaign appeals that emphasize issues of judicial policy depends largely on whether voters actually choose.

The largest existing body of survey data on judicial election contests concerns elections to the Ohio Supreme Court.[3] Post-election surveys of those election contests were conducted in each non-presidential election year during the period 1986–2006, covering fourteen contested supreme court elections. We employ those survey data to undertake the first individual-level analysis of voting behavior across several years of judicial elections. Specifically, we analyze the relationship between the levels of information that campaigns provide to voters and the extent of partisan voting—that is, the extent to which voters choose candidates on the basis of their party identifications. For reasons we set forth in the next section, inquiry into this question can tell us a good deal about the impact of high-visibility judicial elections on voters.

INFORMATION AND THE VOTE IN JUDICIAL CONTESTS

In order to consider the possible effects of high-visibility contests on partisan voting, we need to think about voters' use of information. In low-visibility contests the candidates' party affiliations are a powerful cue for voters. But the advantages of incumbency counteract party for voters whose party affiliation differs from that of the incumbent. Among those voters, the ones who are moderately aware of politics (in contrast with the most and least aware) defect to the incumbent at the highest rate because they learn information that favors the incumbent more than they learn information that favors the challenger from their own party.

High-visibility (or high-intensity) contests show a similar general pattern. But voters from the challenger's party are less likely to defect from their party than in low-visibility contests, an effect that is stronger among the most aware voters. These are the voters who gather the most information favorable to their party's challenger in high-visibility contests and whose attitudes tilt most strongly in favor of the challenger in comparison with their attitudes in low-visibility contests.

Partisan voting should be lower in high-visibility partisan contests for a state supreme court than in low-visibility contests, because voters receive more information beyond candidates' partisan affiliations. This information may reinforce or counteract voters' proclivity to vote for their party's candidate, but the counteracting effect is more likely to affect the vote because it runs against the default choice of voting on a partisan basis.

The situation is more complicated in states that use a nonpartisan ballot for their judicial contests. A high proportion of the time, competing supreme court candidates are still from opposite parties, as in states with partisan judicial contests. In Ohio, the subject of our study, the use of a partisan primary election means that competing candidates are nearly always a Republican and a Democrat, but Ohio has the unusual combination of a partisan primary and a nonpartisan general election.[4] Because the general election ballot does not disclose candidates' party affiliations, voters are left with a difficult decisional task (Schaffner and Streb 2002).

Without having information on judicial candidates' party affiliations, voters in states with a nonpartisan judicial ballot frequently abstain; roll-off rates for judicial contests are considerably higher in states with nonpartisan ballots than in states that use partisan ballots (Hall 2007). Even so, significant proportions of people who turn out at the polls participate in judicial contests, as they do in even the most obscure contests for other offices.

Campaigns that provide voters with more information than is typical—what we call high-visibility contests—have the potential to enhance or reduce partisan voting in judicial elections under a nonpartisan ballot. The first issue we analyze is the overall impact of high-visibility contests on levels of partisan voting. What we know about the relationship between information and the vote suggests that these contests could enhance partisan voting in two distinct ways or reduce it via another path.

The first and more direct way that those contests might facilitate voting on the basis of party is by informing voters of the candidates' party affiliations. Larger-scale campaigns give voters a better opportunity to learn which candidate is the Democrat and which is the Republican. Having gained that knowledge, more voters can choose on a partisan basis.

A less direct source of enhancement is that high-visibility contests can provide voters with information other than the candidates' party affiliations that encourages partisan voting. For example, since the 1980s, issues of tort law have played a prominent part in some supreme court contests that attracted high levels of spending in states such as Texas and Alabama (Champagne and Cheek 2002; Ware 1999). If the Democrat is identified as pro-plaintiff and the Republican as pro-defendant, as is usually the case, voters might be encouraged to choose their own party's candidate based on shared ideological beliefs, whether or not they are aware of the candidates' party affiliations.[5]

If high-visibility contests reduce partisan voting, the source of that effect would be the other side of the effect we just described. In most nonpartisan judicial elections, the information available to voters is relatively scarce, so there might not be much to dissuade voters from making their decisions based on candidates' party affiliations, if they are aware of those affiliations. High-visibility contests provide more information about other bases for choice. As we have noted, ideological considerations tend to reinforce partisanship. But voters might also gain information that does not correlate with party, including the candidates' backgrounds and personal traits such as competence and ethical standards. To the extent that they choose on the basis of these qualities, the impact of party identification on the vote generally will decline.

It seems to us that the enhancement effect is likely to be stronger, primarily because of its more direct source. Even when judicial campaigns present a great deal of information to the voters, both their ability to reach the voters and the voters' ability to recall that information might be limited. On the whole, then, we expect the most powerful effect of higher visibility levels to be the most basic—informing voters about candidates' party affiliations. Thus, we posit that partisan voting increases with the visibility of contests.

The second issue to address is the impact of variation across voters in terms of their levels of political awareness. Do high-visibility contests have differential effects on highly aware and less aware voters? Such differential effects seem likely, but their direction is uncertain. High-visibility contests might narrow the gap between voters with more knowledge and those with less knowledge by helping the second group "catch up" with the first. Alternatively, given the extreme scarcity of information in most judicial contests, it might be that the more knowledgeable voters take more advantage of the relatively abundant information provided in high-visibility judicial contests than do less knowledgeable voters.

If more knowledgeable voters are more likely to seek out relevant information, they will make better use of the available information in high-visibility contests than will voters who are less knowledgeable. This generalization can be applied to the issue with which we are concerned, the level of partisan voting. If we are right in positing that the overall effect of high-visibility contests is to produce more partisan voting by providing more information about the candidates' party affiliations, we would then predict that this effect is accentuated for more knowledgeable voters. Thus, we posit that more visible contests enhance partisan voting to a greater extent for more knowledgeable voters.

THE STUDY

Between 1986 and 2006, survey organizations at The Ohio State University conducted post-election surveys on statewide electoral contests in Ohio in non-presidential years, when the governor and other executive-branch officials are chosen.[6] Because the seven supreme court justices hold six-year terms, in each election year, two or three seats come up for election. In the six election years in which surveys were conducted, fourteen seats came up, all of them contested by Republican and Democratic candidates.

Each of the six post-election surveys was a telephone survey of a randomly selected sample of Ohio adults.[7] The surveys differed somewhat in form and content,[8] but they were parallel in their questions about electoral participation and vote choice. Respondents who had turned out to vote in the general election were asked about their votes in most or all of the statewide contests, and the supreme court contests were always included. Questions about votes in the supreme court contests were asked in the same form in each survey, providing respondents with only the information available on the ballot, the candidates' names.[9] The comparability of surveys and of relevant questions allows us to undertake the first comparative individual-level analysis of judicial voting across several election years.

We begin our analysis by showing the bivariate relationship between levels of information available to the voters and levels of partisan voting, with the election contest as the unit of analysis.

Our measures of information reflect two channels through which campaigns can provide information to the voters. The first channel is through the candidates' activities, measured by their levels of spending.

The second channel is coverage by the news media.

FINDINGS

Table 1 shows the total expenditures by the major-party candidates and the number of news articles that referred

Table 21.1 Characteristics of Supreme Court Contests, 1986–2006

Contest	Spending	Media Coverage
1986		
Celebrezze/Moyer (CJ)	2,316,153	56
Sweeney/Holmes	447,573	16
Brown/George	277,958	15
1990		
Banks/Douglas	328,981	9
Jones/Wright	736,116	8
1994		
Haffey/Cook	424,068	7
Resnick/Harper	552,820	8
1998		
Yack Moyer(Q)	679,059	13
Sweeney/Powell	387,868	12
Suster/Feifer	485,624	10
2002		
Black/O'Connor	1,617,782	55
Burnside/Stratton	1,656,533	67
2006		
Neill/O'Donnell	440,999	11
Espy/Cupp	631,066	7
Means for two sets of contests		
High-visibility (n=3)	1,863,489	59.3
Low-visibility (n=11)	490,194	10.5

Notes: Only contests in the seven years with surveys are included.

Contest: Democratic candidates are listed first. Winners' names are in bold. Incumbents are in italics. "(CJ)" denotes contests for chief justice. Spending and media coverage figures for the three high-visibility contests are in bold.

Expenditures: Total shown is amount of money spent by both major-party candidates, adjusted to 1986 dollars (according to Bureau of Labor Statistics data), for the two reporting periods for the general election.

Media coverage: Total shown is the number of articles in the Columbus Dispatch and the Cleveland Plain Dealer between September 1 and Election Day, in which the contest or a candidate in the contest was mentioned in the headline or first paragraph.

to the candidates or contest in the headline or first paragraph in the fourteen supreme court contests analyzed in this study. While there is a wide range in the amounts of money spent as well as in the numbers of articles published about each contest, both variables can be easily grouped into the same two high and low categories. Of the fourteen races, three featured significantly greater media attention and campaign spending than the rest, the Chief Justice race between Frank Celebrezze and Thomas Moyer in 1986, and both Associate Justice races in 2002, between Tim Black and Maureen O'Connor

and between Eve Stratton and Janet Burnside. As the summary at the bottom of the table shows, the mean level of spending in those three contests was nearing four times as high as the mean in the other eleven contests, and the level of media coverage was nearly six times as high. This stark contrast facilitates the testing of our hypotheses.

As we had posited, the overall level of partisan voting was substantially higher in the three high-visibility contests than in the other eleven contests. In the high-visibility contests, the mean proportion of self-identified Democrats

Figure 21.1 Predicted Probabilities of Voting for Democratic Candidates, by Party Identification and Campaign Spending

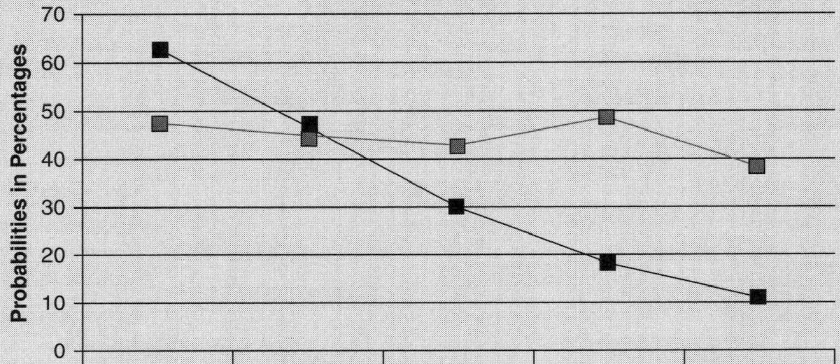

	Strong Dems	Weak Dems	Independents	Weak Reps	Strong Reps
Highest Spending	62.8	47	30.4	18.1	10.9
Lowest Spending	47.6	49.1	42.6	48.3	38.1

Note: "Weak" include; leaners..

and Republicans who voted for the candidate of their own party was 68.7 percent. In the low-visibility contests, the mean was 59.4 percent. Despite the small number of cases, the difference of means between these two sets of contests was statistically significant at the 0.01 level by a two-tailed test.

These results provide a first indication that high-visibility contests have a powerful effect in facilitating partisan voting.

The figure indicates that high-visibility contests induced partisanship in Republican voters more than they did for Democratic voters. In all likelihood, this difference reflects characteristics of the three high-visibility contests in the study period. In the two 2002 contests, Republican candidates had a moderate advantage in spending over their opponents. As a result, they had a better opportunity to make their case to voters. In the 1986 contest for chief justice, the Democratic incumbent outspent his opponent, but newspaper coverage was highly favorable to the challenger in its criticisms of the Democratic candidate.

DISCUSSION

As hypothesized, the amount of information available about a given electoral contest was related to the level of partisan voting for both the spending and media coverage variables. That is, the more information available for a race, the more likely people were to vote on a partisan basis. Campaign spending was clearly the more significant of the two information sources in this respect.

The findings on our hypothesis about differences between more and less knowledgeable voters varied across measures of knowledge. The effects of high-visibility contests on partisan voting did not differ much by voters' levels of education. However, they differed fundamentally between voters with higher and lower levels of political knowledge. Indeed, the effects of levels of campaign spending on partisan voting were concentrated heavily among voters who knew more about politics. While we should reiterate the need for care in interpreting this finding, it makes sense. Voters with greater knowledge are probably more likely to seek out and absorb available information and then use that information in their electoral choices. Beyond finding out about the candidates' party affiliations, politically aware voters might also use their own ideological positions, or their positions on political issues, as frameworks with which to analyze election information when that information is relatively abundant. In other words, the values they hold might help them retain information that leads them to partisan voting.

It is important to emphasize that the Ohio system of electing judges, despite the partisan nomination process, includes a nonpartisan general election. Because candidates' party affiliations are not listed on the ballot for judicial candidates, those affiliations are some of the first pieces of information a voter would seek out. The results of this study should not be extrapolated into partisan elections in which the party affiliations of judicial candidates would be known even to those voters who come to the polls with no outside information at all. In that case, more campaign information could have the opposite effect by offering voters reasons other than party to choose one judicial candidate over another.

However, with the appropriate caution in extrapolating from the findings of one study, our results should apply to the far more numerous states with pure nonpartisan systems for election of judges, so long as opposing candidates are a Republican and a Democrat. Indeed, the effects of high-visibility contests might be even greater in those systems than in Ohio. Because opposing candidates in pure nonpartisan systems are not automatically from different parties, voters are less accustomed to thinking about candidates in partisan terms. Further, candidates and the media might say little about the candidates' partisan affiliations. Thus, the usual level of partisan voting in nonpartisan states appears to be quite low (see Dubois 1980, 78, 89-92), and voters are likely to rely on cues provided by the ballot, such as name recognition or gender. By providing partisan information that ordinarily is scarce, high-visibility campaigns could alter voters' choices more fundamentally than they do in Ohio's semi-partisan system.

More broadly, our findings have implications for the debates over judicial selection systems. In Ohio Supreme Court elections, where parties are not listed on the ballot, increases in the information available on a given contest allow more voters to use candidates' party affiliations as bases for their choices. This finding could be viewed in different ways, depending on how one feels about partisanship in judicial elections.

Some scholars and commentators find party labels to be a useful, accurate shortcut to information about judicial candidates, providing voters with what most consider a highly relevant basis for vote choice. Studies comparing partisan and nonpartisan elections have found that elections with partisan ballots have the effects of both reducing roll-off and increasing the impact of voters' attitudes toward the parties on their choices (Dubois 1980; Schaffher, Wright, and Streb 2001). If those effects are seen as positive, high-visibility contests might seem desirable—and it might be better still for states with nonpartisan systems to adopt a partisan ballot, thereby lowering the information costs for voters who want to vote on a partisan basis.

Others, however, believe that partisanship has no place in judicial selection on the ground that the selection of judges should be free from the bias of party identification. For these observers, the results of this study might be of concern—when more information is available, more voters rely on an undesirable criterion for their choices. However, it is important to keep in mind that in the absence of partisan cues, voters could make choices based on information gleaned from the ballot that is even less meaningful than party affiliation.

The broader issue is whether judges should be selected through popular elections at all. Perhaps the most fundamental argument against judicial elections is that judges should be largely impervious to popular opinion, that their objectivity in interpreting the law ought not be tainted by the need to appeal to the public. A second argument is that even if judges ideally should be held accountable to the public, ordinary citizens are ignorant about and apathetic to judicial elections. By this logic, the disengaged and uninformed electorate is not capable of intelligently selecting state judges, so decisions should be left to those who know better, such as the governor or members of a nominating commission.

Ultimately, of course, evaluation of these findings depends on one's premises about the extent and forms of accountability to the public that are desirable for state judges. What we have learned about supreme court elections in Ohio would not reassure critics of judicial elections such as Sandra Day O'Connor. These critics typically see candidates' party affiliations as inappropriate bases for choice, and they also see as inappropriate the kinds of issues that arise in high-visibility contests such as the ones included in our study.

Further, there are other subjects for debate concerning the desirability of judicial elections. One important issue is the effect of elections on affect toward the courts. Two studies have found evidence that, all else being equal, citizens in states with partisan elections give less diffuse support to the courts than do citizens in other states (Benesh 2006; Cann and Yates 2008). A third, experimental study found that some attributes of judicial elections more prominent in high-visibility contests—campaign contributions and attack ads—reduce the legitimacy of state courts (Gibson 2008).

NOTES

The authors appreciate comments and suggestions by Herbert Weisberg, the anonymous reviewers for SPPQ, and the editors.

1. In using this term, we should emphasize that—with occasional exceptions—even these judicial contests are considerably less visible than contests for the highest offices.

2. The formal restrictions have been loosened considerably by the U.S. Supreme Court's decision in *Republican Party v. White* (2002), which struck down some state restrictions on campaign speech in judicial contests and undercut the legal basis for others. The decision required "virtually all states to abandon their existing codes of judicial conduct" (Caufield 2007, 39). Some evidence suggests that informal norms that limited the discussion of judicial policy issues in the past could be shifting in a more permissive direction as well (Dubois 1979b, 759).

3. Analyses of these survey data are discussed in Baum (2003).

4. Michigan has a similar system, although judicial nominees there are chosen at a party convention rather than a partisan primary. The only other state to have adopted such a hybrid system for supreme court elections is Arizona, which gave it up in favor of the Missouri Plan in 1974 (Dubois 1979a, 761).

5. Voters might also use the candidates' positions on particular issues as dues to their party affiliations rather than as bases for choice in themselves.

6. Surveys were conducted in only two presidential years, 1984 and 1988. Because presidential and non-presidential elections are not entirely comparable, inclusion of those two years might skew our results, and we restricted our analyses to the non-presidential years.

7. Only landline phone numbers were sampled, so the more recent surveys did not include individuals who had only cellular phones.

8. The most prominent difference was in the questions asked about topics other than the current election. There were also differences in the sets of personal attributes of respondents on which questions were asked. The total numbers of respondents to the surveys ranged from 795 to 1033.

9. In some of the years, a portion of the respondents were given additional information in order to test the impact of certain kinds of information on the vote. Those respondents were excluded from our analyses. Survey respondents as a group exaggerate their turnout, but the opposite is true of freestanding judicial elections (Adamany and Dubois 1975; Adamany and Shelley 1980). Among respondents to the Ohio surveys, reported roll-off in the supreme court contests was consistently higher than indicated by the actual election results. A study of the 1984 Ohio elections (elections not included in the current study) estimated that the exaggeration of turnout and exaggeration of roll-off in the supreme court contests approximately balanced out (Baum 1987, 364 n. 2), although that is not necessarily true of supreme court contests over the years.

REFERENCES

Adamany, David, and Philip Dubois. 1975. "The 'Forgetful' Voter and an Unreported Vote." *Public Opinion Quarterly* 39:227-31.

Adamany, David, and Mack C. Shelley. 1980. "Encore! The Forgetful Voter." *Public Opinion Quarterly* 44:234-40.

Baum, Lawrence. 1987. "Explaining the Vote in Judicial Elections: The 1984 Ohio Supreme Court Elections." *Western Political Quarterly* 40:361-71.

Baum, Lawrence. 2003. "Judicial Elections and Judicial Independence: The Voter's Perspective." *Ohio State Law Journal* 64:13-41.

Benesh, Sara C. 2006. "Understanding Public Confidence in American Courts." *The Journal of Politics* 68:697-707.

Bonneau, Chris W. 2005. "Incumbent Defeats in State Supreme Court Elections." *American Politics Research* 33:818-41.

Bonneau, Chris W. 2006. "Vacancies on the Bench: Open Seat Elections for State Supreme Courts." *Justice System Journal* 27:143-59.

Bonneau, Chris W. 2007. "The Effects of Campaign Spending in State Supreme Court Elections." *Political Research Quarterly* 60:489-99.

Bonneau, Chris W., and Melinda Gann Hall, 2009. *In Defense of Judicial Elections.* New York, NY: Routledge.

Brown, T. C. 2000. "Resnick Overcomes Attacks, Wins High Court Race," *Cleveland Plain Dealer,* November 8,1A.

Brown, T. C. 2002. "GOP Victories Alter High Court." *Cleveland Plain Dealer,* November 6, SI.

Cann, Damon M,, and Jeff Yates. 2008. "Homegrown Institutional Legitimacy: Assessing Citizens' Diffuse Support for State Courts." *American Politics Research* 36:297-329.

Caufield, Rachel P. 2007, "The Changing Tone of Judicial Election Campaigns as a Result of *White"* In *Running for Judge: The Rising Political, Financial, and Legal Stakes of Judicial Elections,* ed. Matthew J. Streb. New York, NY: New York University Press.

Champagne, Anthony, and Kyle Cheek. 2002. "The Cycle of Judicial Elections: Texas as a Case Study." *Fordham Urban Law Journal* 29:907-40.

Converse, Philip E. 1962. "Information Flow and the Stability of Partisan Attitudes." *Public Opinion Quarterly* 26:578-99.

Delli Carpini, Michael X., and Scott Keeter. 1993. "Measuring Political Knowledge: Putting First Things First." *American Journal of Political Science* 37:1179-206.

Delli Carpini, Michael X., and Scott Keeter. 1996. *What Americans Know About Politics and Why it Matters.* New Haven, CT: Yale University Press.

Dubois, Philip L. 1979a. "The Significance of Voting Cues in State Supreme Court Elections." *Law & Society Review* 13:757-79.

Dubois, Philip L. 1979b. "Voter Turnout in State Judicial Elections: An Analysis of the Tail on the Electoral Kite." *The Journal of Politics* 41:865-87.

Dubois, Philip L. 1980. *From Ballot to Bench: Judicial Elections and the Quest for Accountability.* Austin, TX: University of Texas Press.

Dubois, Philip L. 1984. "Voting Cues in Nonpartisan Trial Court Elections: A Multivariate Assessment." *Law & Society Review* 18:395-436.

Dunbar, Elizabeth. 2008. "Retired Justice Argues Against Partisan Judicial Elections." *Associated Press*, State & Local Wire, May 2,

Felice, John D., and John C. Kilwein. 1992. "Strike one, strike two...: The history of and prospect for judicial reform in Ohio." *Judicature* 75:193-200.

Frederick, Brian, and Matthew J. Streb. 2008. "Women Running for Judge: The Impact of Sex on Candidate Success in State Intermediate Appellate Court Elections." *Social Science Quarterly* 89:937-54.

Gibson, James L. 2008. "Challenges to the Impartiality of State Supreme Courts: Legitimacy Theory and 'New-Style' Judicial Campaigns." *American Political Science Review* 102:59-75.

Glaberson, William. 2000. "A Spirited Campaign for Ohio Court Puts Judges on New Terrain." *The New York Times,* July 7, Al1.

Griffin, Kenyon N., and Michael J. Horan. 1979. "Merit Retention Elections: What Influences the Voters?" *Judicature* 63:78-88.

Griffin, Kenyon N. and Michael J. Horan. 1983. "Patterns of Voting Behavior in Judicial Retention Elections for Supreme Court Justices in Wyoming." *Judicature* 67:68-77.

Hall, Melinda Gann. 2001. "State Supreme Courts in American Democracy: Probing the Myths of Judicial Reform." *American Political Science Review* 95:315-30.

Hall, Melinda Gann. 2007. "Voting in State Supreme Court Elections: Competition and Contest as Democratic Incentives." *The Journal of Politics* 69:1147-59.

Hall, Melinda Gann, and Chris W. Bonneau. 2006. "Does Quality Matter? Challengers in State Supreme Court Elections." *American Journal of Political Science* 50:20-33.

Hall, Melinda Gann, and Chris W. Bonneau. 2008. "Mobilizing Interest: The Effects of Money on Citizen Participation in State Supreme Court Elections." *American Journal of Political Science* 52:457-70.

Hinckley, Barbara, Richard Hofstetter, and John Kessel. 1974. "Information and the Vote: A Comparative Election Study." *American Politics Quarterly* 2:131-58.

Johnson, Charles A., Roger C. Schaefer, and R. Neal McKnight. 1978. "The Salience of Judicial Candidates and Elections." *Social Science Quarterly* 59:371-8.

Judicature. 1955. "How Much Do Voters Know or Care About Judicial Candidates?" 38:141-3.

King, Gary, Michael Tomz, and Jason Wittenberg. 2000. "Making the Most of Statistical Analyses: Improving Interpretation and Presentation." *American Journal of Political Science* 44:347-61.

Kritzer, Herbert M. 2007. "Law is the Mere Continuation of Politics by Different Means: American Judicial Selection in the Twenty-First Century." *DePaul Law Review* 56:423–67.

Lovrich, Nicholas P., Jr., and Charles H. Sheldon. 1983. "Voters in Contested, Nonpartisan Judicial Elections: A Responsible Electorate or a Problematic Public?" *Western Political Quarterly* 36:241-56.

McDermott, Monika L. 1997. "Voting Cues in Low-Information Elections: Candidate Gender as a Social Information Variable in Contemporary United States Elections." *American Journal of Political Science* 41:270-83.

McDermott, Monika L. 1998. "Race and Gender Cues in Low-Information Elections." *Political Research Quarterly* 51:895-918.

McDermott, Monika L. 2005, "Candidate Occupations and Voter Information Shortcuts." *The Journal of Politics* 67:201-19.

McKnight, R. Neal, Roger Schaefer, and Charles A. Johnson. 1978. "Choosing Judges: Do The Voters Know What They're Doing?" *Judicature* 62:94-9.

O'Connor, Sandra Day. 2007. "Justice for Sale." *Wall Street Journal,* November 15, A25.

Petrocik, John R. 1974. "An Analysis of Intransitivities in the Index of Party Identification." *Political Methodology* 1:31-47.

Republican Party v. White. 2002. 536 U.S. 765.

Schaffher, Brian F., and Jennifer Segal Diascro. 2007. "Judicial Elections in the News." In *Running for Judge: The Rising Political, Financial, and Legal Stakes of Judicial Elections,* ed. Matthew J. Streb. New York, NY: New York University Press.

Schaffner, Brian F., and Matthew J, Streb, 2002. "The Partisan Heuristic in Low-Information Elections." *Public Opinion Quarterly* 66:559-81.

Schaffner, Brian F., Gerald Wright, and Matthew Streb. 2001. "Teams Without Uniforms: The Nonpartisan Ballot in State and Local Elections." *Political Research Quarterly* 54:7-30.

Schotland, Roy A. 1998. "Comment." *Law and Contemporary Problems* 61(Summer): 149–55.

Sheldon, Charles H., and Nicholas P. Lovrich, Jr. 1982. "Polls: Are They Valid Tools?" *Oregon State Bar Bulletin* 42(April):10-13.

Sheldon, Charles H., and Nicholas P. Lovrich, Jr. 1983. "Knowledge and Judicial Voting: The Oregon and Washington Experience." *Judicature* 67:234-45.

Sniderman, Paul M., James M. Glaser, and Robert Griffin. 2002. "Information and Electoral Choice." In *Information and Democratic Processes,* eds. John A. Ferejohn and James H. Kuklinski. Urbana, IL: University of Illinois Press.

Squire, Peverill, and Eric R.A.N. Smith. 1988. "The Effect of Partisan Information on Voters in Nonpartisan Elections." *The Journal of Politics* 50: 169-79.

Tarr, G. Alan, and Mary Cornelia Aldis Porter. 1988. *State Supreme Courts in State and Nation.* New Haven, CT: Yale University Press.

Ware, Stephen J. 1999. "Money, Politics and Judicial Decisions: A Case Study of Arbitration Law in Alabama." *Journal of Law and Politics* 15:645-86.

Weisberg, Herbert F. 1983. "A New Scale of Partisanship." *Political Behavior* 5:363-76.

Zaller, John. 1989. "Bringing Converse Back In: Modeling Information Flow in Political Campaigns." *Political Analysis* 1:181-234.

Zaller, John R. 1992. *The Nature and Origins of Mass Opinion.* New York, NY: Cambridge University Press.

22

Executive Summary

From James Sample, Adam Skaggs, Jonathan Blitzer, Linda Casey, *The New Politics of Judicial Elections, 2000–2009: Decade of Change*

Judicial elections are attracting big money and the focused attention of special interest groups. Can judges rule impartially if getting elected means winning a partisan mudfight?

S tate judicial elections have been transformed during the past decade. The story of America's 2000—2009 high court contests—tens of millions of dollars raised by candidates from parties which may appear before them, millions more poured in by interest groups, nasty and misleading ads, and pressure on judges to signal courtroom rulings on the campaign trail—has become the new normal. For more than a decade, partisans and special interests of all stripes have been growing more organized in their efforts to use elections to tilt the scales of justice their way. Many Americans have come to fear that justice is for sale.

Unlike previous editions, which covered only the most recent election cycle, this fifth edition of this "New Politics of Judicial Elections" looks at the 2000—2009 decade as a whole. By tallying the numbers and "connecting the dots" among key players over the last five election cycles, this report offer a broad portrait of a grave and growing challenge to the impartiality of our nation's courts. These trends include:

- The explosion in judicial campaign spending, much of it poured in by "super spender" organizations seeking to sway the courts;
- The parallel surge of nasty and costly TV ads as a prerequisite to gaining a state Supreme Court seat;
- The emergence of secretive state and national campaigns to tilt state Supreme Court elections;
- Litigation about judicial campaigns, some of which could boost special-interest pressure on judges;

From *The New Politics of Judicial Elections, 2000–2009: Decade of Change,* 2010.

- Growing public concern about the threat to fair and impartial justice—and support for meaningful reforms.

THE MONEY EXPLOSION

The surge in spending is pronounced and systemic. Campaign fundraising more than doubled, from $83.3 million in 1990—1999 to $206.9 million in 2000—2009. Three of the last five Supreme Court election cycles topped $45 million. All but two of the 22 states with contestable Supreme Court elections had their costliest-ever contests in the 2000—2009 decade.

Special-interest "super spenders" played a central role in this surge. A study of 29 elections in the nation's 10 most costly election states shows the extraordinary power of super spender groups. The top five spenders in each of these elections invested an average of $473,000, while the remaining 116,000 contributors averaged $850 each. In the most widely publicized case, one coal executive spent $3 million to elect a West Virginia justice. The disparity suggests that a small number of special interests dominated judicial election spending even before the *Citizens United* case ended bans on election spending by corporations and unions.

In 2007–08, five states felt the worst blast of the super spender phenomenon. When TV spending by political parties and special-interest groups is factored in, Pennsylvania broke the $10 million barrier, while spending reached $8.5 million in Wisconsin. Texas and Alabama each topped $5 million, and Michigan, which had just under $5 million in fundraising and independent TV ads, witnessed some of the cycle's most brutal campaign commercials.

Partisan races drew the most cash, but that may be changing. Candidates in partisan Supreme Court elections raised $153.8 million nationally in 2000-09, compared with $50.9 million in nonpartisan elections (retention election candidates raised $2.2 million). But in some states, notably Wisconsin in 2007—08 and Georgia in 2006, nonpartisan races have been just as costly and nasty as their partisan counterparts.

Special-interest money sometimes comes with a cost. National business groups, often working with state affiliates, were the decade's most powerful force. But three well-funded incumbent chief justices were ousted in 2008, in part because they were tied to special-interest patrons.

The trends continued in 2009. In Pennsylvania, Wisconsin and Louisiana, candidates and independent groups spent a total of about $8.7 million on 2009 elections. And in each race, candidates accused opponents of being ethically tainted.

COURT TV: THE RISE OF COSTLY ATTACK ADS

Spending on TV ads has helped fuel the money chase. From 2000 to 2009, an estimated $93.6 million was spent on air time for high court candidate TV ads. That total includes TV spending in odd-numbered election years, which for the first time is included in the New Politics data.

New records were set in 2007 and 2008. Including costly 2007 elections in Wisconsin and Pennsylvania, the 2007–08 cycle was, at $26.6 million, the most expensive biennium ever for TV ad spending on Supreme Court races. Eight states set all-time records for spending on TV ads during the two-year period, and there were more ad airings than ever before in 2008.

Average spending on TV continues to surge. Continuing a trend seen in 2004 and 2006, in states where TV advertisements ran, an average of more than $1 million was spent on campaign ads. In 2008, in the 13 states where Supreme Court ads aired, the average was $1.5 million.

Outside groups played a critical role in the TV wars. Special-interest groups and party organizations accounted for $39.3 million, more than 40 percent of the estimated TV air time purchases in 2000—09. In 2008, special-interest groups and political parties accounted for 52 percent of all TV spending nationally—the first time that noncandidate groups outspent the candidates on the ballot.

Special-interest group ads are often harsher than candidate ads. Independent groups remain the "attack dogs" of judicial TV ads. But in 2008, Wisconsin Judge Michael Gableman's spot attacking Justice Louis Butler provoked lingering ethics and legal challenges.

WHO PLAYED? WHO WON?

Tort wars have become court wars. Judicial elections have become a multi-million-dollar duel, pitting business and conservative groups against plaintiffs' lawyers and unions. High court justices know that their decisions could trigger support or retaliation in the next election.

The two sides bring starkly different profiles. The right has brought together big-name groups like the U.S. Chamber of Commerce and National Association of Manufacturers, leaders of corporate giants such as Home Depot and AIG Insurance, and political actors like Karl Rove. Bankrollers on the left tend to be wealthy plaintiffs' lawyers, who often use state party organizations to hide the extent of their financial backing of a candidate.

Secret money dominates; players can give big sums with little publicity. In Alabama, the Montgomery law firm of Beasley Allen gave more than $600,000 to Judge Deborah Bell Paseur's unsuccessful Supreme Court campaign, without ever appearing on her contribution records. This approach has been emulated in other states, including Texas.

LITIGATION: THE BATTLE INSIDE THE COURTROOM

Federal courts have been increasingly pulled into state judicial election controversies, especially in the areas of campaign finance, candidate speech and recusal (when a judge avoids a case with potential ethical conflicts). Many of these cases are designed to strengthen or challenge rules that would insulate judges from special-interest pressure.

The U.S. Supreme Court declared that campaign spending could disqualify a judge from cases involving major supporters. The landmark *Caperton v. Massey* decision creates an incentive for every state to craft meaningful rules for when judges must step aside.

Campaign finance laws face growing litigation challenges. North Carolina's judicial public financing law was upheld by the federal courts. But a more recent Supreme Court case, *Citizens United v. Federal Election Commission,* overturned long-standing bans on election spending from corporate and union treasuries—posing a special threat in judicial elections.

> "The improper appearance created by money in judicial elections is one of the most important issues facing our judicial system today."
> —Theodore B. Olson, former U.S. Solicitor General and attorney in Caperton v. Massey case

A **2002 Supreme Court decision,** *Republican Party of Minnesota v. White,* loosened restrictions on judicial campaign speech. Interest groups are using questionnaires to pressure judges into signaling courtroom decisions on the campaign trail. Professional norms are becoming more important in helping judicial candidates steer clear of special-interest pressures and political agendas.

THE PUBLIC TAKES NOTE, DECISION-MAKERS PLAY CATCH-UP

The new politics of judicial elections has made the public fear that justice is for sale. More than seven in ten Americans believe that campaign contributions affect the outcome of courtroom decisions. *Nearly half of state judges agree.* Former Justice Sandra Day O'Connor says, "In too many states, judicial elections are becoming political prizefights where partisans and special interests seek to install judges who will answer to them instead of the law and the Constitution."

Reform efforts are making progress. After years of slow progress, reform gained steam in 2009. Wisconsin enacted public financing for court races, joining North Carolina and New Mexico, and in March 2010, West Virginia's legislature also enacted a pilot public financing program. In Michigan, the Supreme Court adopted tough new recusal rules. Polls show continued strong public support for reform measures—such as public financing of judicial races, election voter guides, recusal reform and full financial disclosure for election ads.

Merit selection has gained momentum—and more organized opposition. In a pair of 2008 county-level ballot measures, voters in Kansas and Missouri opted for appointment systems over competitive elections for judges, while Nevada lawmakers put a merit selection measure on the 2010 ballot. Meanwhile, a cadre of groups has organized to challenge merit selection systems in several states. And in a significant revisiting of its position, the U.S. Chamber of Commerce cited one model of merit selection as fair and compatible with business interests.

23

2010 Judicial Elections Increase Pressure on Courts, Reform Groups Say

Brennan Center for Justice and the Justice at Stake Campaign

The 2010 judicial contests included record levels of campaign spending that favored "populists and partisans" and ousted incumbents, following the trends of the general mid-term elections for Congress, state legislatures and governorships.

From Brennan Center for Justice and the Justice at Stake Campaign. November, 2010.

Election Day 2010 brought a new round of special interest money, nasty ads and wedge issue politics into America's courtrooms, breaking several spending records and spreading costly, ideological hardball campaigns into new states. The roar of this year's national politics—which favored populists and partisans, and tilted against incumbents and the establishment—played out in judicial elections and referenda in a number of states.

In Michigan, Supreme Court candidates were vastly outspent by political parties and an out-of-state group in a TV ad war whose cost was estimated at $5 million to $8 million. In Alabama, combined spending exceeded $3.2 million. Election costs remained modest in North Carolina, which offers public financing to qualifying appellate court candidates.

In Iowa, three Supreme Court justices were ousted after out-of-state interest groups spent nearly $700,000 to unseat them over their votes in a 2009 gay marriage case. But organized efforts to unseat high court justices failed in Illinois, Colorado, Alaska, Kansas and Florida. Non-candidate groups spent heavily on TV ads in Michigan and Ohio, while Iowa and Illinois set records for the most expensive retention elections ever in their states.

As they have done several times over the last decade, voters rejected efforts to change judicial selection systems. In Nevada, Question 1, which would have replaced competitive elections with judicial appointments and retention contests, was defeated. But in Kansas, voters in District 1 also defeated efforts to scrap a merit selection system and switch to competitive contests.

"Pressure on impartial justice is growing," said Bert Brandenburg, executive director of the Justice at Stake Campaign. "Judges are facing more demands to be accountable to interest groups and political campaigns instead of the law and the constitution."

Through Monday, Nov. 1, 2010, slightly more than $12 million was spent nationally on TV air time this year in state supreme court elections. Of that, nearly $5.1 million — 42% of total spending for the year — was spent in the week leading up to the election, between Oct. 26 and Nov. 1.

Including $4.6 million spent on TV ads in 2009, the current total for the 2009-2010 election cycle is approximately $16.6 million, about the same amount spent on judicial television advertising in the last non-presidential election cycle, 2005-2006.

"As in past years, judicial election campaigns featured substantial numbers of hardhitting, mud-slinging attack ads — many of which were as nasty as those seen in any political campaigns," said Adam Skaggs, Counsel at the Brennan Center for Justice at NYU School of Law.

Final estimates of TV ad spending, as recorded by TNS Media Intelligence/CMAG, are expected within a few days. Complete candidate fundraising data often are not fully available until weeks, and in some cases months, after the elections, meaning that total campaign cost totals tend to rise with time.

Three in four Americans believe that the special-interest money needed to finance such elections influences court decisions. From 2000 through 2009, fundraising by high-court candidates surged to $206.9 million, more than double the $83.3 million raised in the 1990s.

This year, heavy spending and angry TV ads spread to several states holding retention elections, which in 2000-2009 had accounted for barely 1 percent of spending in high court races. This year, high-court retention elections in Illinois, Iowa, Colorado and Alaska resulted in about $4.6 million in total costs—more than twice the $2.2 million raised for all retention elections nationally in 2000-2009.

In most of the 15 states where 37 justices stood in retention elections, however, campaign expenditures were far lower than in competitive election states.

Overall, 33 states held some type of election. In addition to the 15 states holding one-candidate retention elections, in which incumbents needed a "yes" vote to stay on the bench, 11 states held competitive elections for 18 seats. In seven other states, there were no challengers in elections that technically were competitive, granting automatic victory to the candidate on the ballot.

The following is a round-up of major trends in the 2009-10 judicial election campaign season, as identified by the Justice at Stake Campaign and the Brennan Center for Justice. Further information is available at the **Judicial Elections 2010** web site.

TV AD DATA

Television ads ran this year in fourteen states with elections for the state supreme court: Alabama, Alaska, Arkansas, Colorado, Idaho, Illinois, Iowa, Michigan, Montana, North Carolina, Ohio, Texas, Washington and West Virginia.

Michigan saw the highest overall spending on supreme court TV ads, with about $5.1 million spent on airtime, according to TNS Media Intelligence/CMAG; Ohio is second with more than $1.9 million in airtime spending. In both of these states, four candidates competed for two Supreme Court seats. (An additional Ohio Justice, Paul Pfeifer, ran unopposed in a vote in which no TV advertising has aired.)

The highest level of spending in a single-candidate retention race was in Illinois, where incumbent Justice Thomas Kilbride spent more than $1.6 million on TV airtime through Nov. 1.

For the year, spending on television advertising in supreme court races was evenly split between judicial candidates and non-candidate groups. Through Nov. 1, candidates spent more than $6.1 million on television advertising, while non-candidate groups — including political parties and special interests — accounted for 49% of all television airtime, spending more than $5.9 million.

Four of the top five spenders on TV airtime in supreme court elections are non-candidate groups. The Michigan Republican Party ranked first overall in TV spending (just over $2 million). Kilbride ranked second ($1.6 million); the Michigan State Democratic Party ranked third ($1.4 million); the Partnership for Ohio's Future ranked fourth (about $846,000); and the Law Enforcement Alliance of America, which spent more than $780,000 in support of two Republican candidates for the Michigan Supreme Court, ranked fifth.

"Many of the harshest ads were aired by political parties and special interest groups, which accounted for about 49% of all spending on television ads in state supreme court elections," Skaggs said.

Through Nov. 1, spending on TV airtime in states holding single-candidate retention elections has totaled approximately $2.1 million — approximately 17.5% of all TV spending during that time. This level of spending in retention contests is the greatest since the Brennan Center for Justice began compiling judicial TV ad data in 2000.

MAJOR STATES

Iowa

All three state Supreme Court justices appearing on a retention ballot were voted out, following a withering attack on a unanimous 2009 ruling that overturned a state law banning gay marriage. The margin of defeat was similar in each case, with about 55 percent voting "no" on another term. Robert Hanson, the Polk County trial judge who initially ruled in favor of gay marriage, won his retention vote.

Out-of-state groups attacking the high-court justices included the National Organization for Marriage, the American Families Association, the Family Research Council, the Campaign for Working Families and Citizens United. Along with in-state groups, reported spending to oust the three justices was about $800,000. Fair Courts for US, a group headed by former governor Robert Ray, reported spending nearly $400,000 in support of retaining the justices, raising total Iowa election costs to $1.2 million. More than half, about $700,000, came from out of state.

Iowa's supreme court had not seen a contentious retention election before this year. The election raised concerns that wedge issues could make it more difficult for courts, in Iowa and elsewhere, to rule in hot-button legal disputes.

"Under our constitutional system, courts are designed to be different from the other branches of government," Brandenburg said. "If judges in any state begin basing their decisions on political pressure and campaign spending, instead of the facts and the law, everyone loses."

Nevada

Question 1 was put on the ballot after spending on Nevada high court elections rose, and after a 2006 Los Angeles Times report unearthed questionable fundraising practices by Las Vegas trial judges. But voters, by a margin of about 58 to 42 percent, chose to keep their current system of nonpartisan competitive elections.

The election continued a trend of states preserving their existing judicial selection system, whether elective or appointive.

"The politics of 2010 made it a difficult climate to ask voters to change how they picked judges," said Bert Brandenburg, executive director of the Justice at Stake Campaign. "And yet many voters remain concerned about campaign cash in the courthouse."

Candidates for Nevada high court raised $9.8 million in 2000-2009, ranking the state eighth nationally.

Illinois

In one of the year's most extraordinary races, Justice Thomas L. Kilbride reported raising more than $2.5 million, while the Illinois Civil Justice League reported raising $648,000 to defeat him. Kilbride retained his seat with 68 percent of voters favoring another term.

Although the campaign was prompted by a business ruling, in which the Illinois court overturned legislative limits on medical malpractice awards, the league focused on Kilbride's record in crime cases, memorably running an ad in which actors playing felons savor their violent crimes and say Kilbride took their side in court.

"In Illinois, special-interest money bought one of the most tasteless TV ads ever appeared in a court election, while a sitting justice raised millions of dollars from plaintiffs' lawyers and other parties who will appear in court," Brandenburg said. "In 2004, Justice Lloyd Karmeier called Illinois election spending 'obscene,' and it's hard to see how this year did anything to restore public trust in that state's courts."

As in 2004, unions and plaintiffs' firms backed the Democrat. National business groups, including the U.S. Chamber of Commerce, American Justice Partnership, and the American Tort Reform Association, backed the opposition campaign.

Michigan

Including TV, Michigan was the nation's most expensive judicial election state in 2010.

Non-candidate groups, led by the state Republican and Democratic parties and the Virginia-based Law Enforcement Alliance of America, accounted for more than 80 percent of all TV spending.

The Brennan Center for Justice, which tracks satellite captures of major TV markets, has recorded $5.1 million in TV ads, as of Nov. 1. The Michigan Campaign Finance Network, which checks TV station ad records, placed the total at more than $8 million.

"Political parties and independent groups hijacked this election, heavily outspending the candidates, and ads on both sides were riddled with questionable claims," Brandenburg said. "Michigan remains a ground zero for negative, costly court elections."

The two incumbents reported the highest campaign fundraising. About two weeks before the election, Republican Robert Young, who won in a landslide, reported raising $776,000, while Democrat Alton Davis, who lost, raised $691,000. According to the most recent fundraising reports, total fundraising among four candidates was just over $1.8 million.

Ohio, Alabama

Ohio and Alabama, the two most expensive states for the 2000-2009 decade, showed that high court campaigns can generate big numbers in even relatively quiet years. Of the $3.2 million reportedly raised by Alabama candidates through Oct. 19, Republicans outraised Democrats four to one.

In Ohio, the most recent reports showed that candidates had raised $2.7 million, with the Republicans outraising the Democrats. In addition, the Chamber-related Partnership for Ohio's Future spent more than $840,000, according to Brennan Center data.

Colorado, Alaska, Kansas, Florida

In Colorado and Alaska, campaigns opposing the retention of sitting justices made substantial efforts but were unable to win. Alaska Justice Dana Fabe got a 53 percent yes vote, despite a campaign by social conservatives. Three Colorado justices survived a challenge by Clear the Bench Colorado that focused on tax and spending issues.

"As in Iowa, 'Vote No' campaigns showed that judges in many states must look with more concern than at the impact of single-interest protest groups," said Skaggs. "More than ever, a single vote in a single legal dispute might haunt judges at election time, and that will make it harder for many to focus on facts and the law, instead of political agendas."

Attempts by social conservatives in Kansas, and by Tea Party activists in Florida, failed to gain significant traction on announced efforts to unseat justices in their states.

# # #

The Justice at Stake Campaign is a nonpartisan national partnership working to keep our courts fair, impartial and free from special-interest and partisan agendas. In states across America, Campaign partners work to protect our courts through public education, grassroots organizing and reform. The Campaign provides strategic coordination and brings organizational, communications and research resources to the work of its partners and allies at the national, state and local levels. For information, visit www.justiceatstake.org.

The Brennan Center for Justice at New York University School of Law is a nonpartisan public policy and law institute that focuses on fundamental issues of democracy and justice. The Center works on issues including judicial independence, voting rights, campaign finance reform, racial justice in criminal law and presidential power in the fight against terrorism. Part think tank, part public interest law firm, part advocacy group, the Brennan Center combines scholarship, legislative and legal advocacy, and communications to win meaningful, measurable change in the public sector. For more information, visit www.brennancenter.org.

TV METHODOLOGY

All data on ad airings and spending on ads are calculated and prepared by TNS Media Intelligence/CMAG, which captures satellite data in that nation's largest media markets. CMAG's calculations do not reflect ad agency commissions or the costs of producing advertisements. The costs reported here therefore understate actual expenditures; the estimates are useful principally for purposes of comparison of relative spending levels across states.

For More Information:

Bert Brandenburg, Justice at Stake, 202-588-9436; bbrandenburg@justiceatstake.org

Adam Skaggs, Brennan Center for Justice, 646-292-8331; adam.skaggs@nyu.edu

Charles Hall, Justice at Stake, 202-588-9454; chall@justiceatstake.org

Jeanine Plant-Chirlin, Brennan Center for Justice, 646-292-8322; chirlinj@exchange.law.nyu.edu

Bureaucracy

Americans have always expressed skepticism about government, but they reserve a particular disdain for bureaucracy. As one scholar of bureaucracy noted, bureaucracy is generally reviled as "a sea of waste, a swamp of incompetence, a mountain of unchecked power, an endless plain of mediocrity. Our media and politicians tell us that public bureaucracy is bloated in size, inefficient compared to business, a stifling place to work, indifferent to ordinary citizens, the problem rather than the solution."[1]

Yet despite the pounding from public opinion, public bureaucracies do a lot of good. Collectively, state and local public agencies employ millions who educate children, enforce the law, and provide an astonishing range of other services ranging from public sanitation to public transportation to public recreation. Despite the popular negative image, most professional students of the bureaucracy agree that most of the time agencies do these jobs professionally and effectively.

State and local governments in many ways *are* the bureaucracy. Add up all of the legislators, elected executives, and judges, and you'd have a fraction of the number of teachers, police officers, librarians, and other professions that staff public agencies. Legislators and executives might make the law, and judges might interpret it, but the bureaucracy actually translates all these decisions into action. As such, it is the "doer" of government, the essential management tool of representative democracy.

WHAT BUREAUCRACY IS, AND WHAT BUREAUCRACY DOES

Broadly speaking, bureaucracy can be thought of as all public agencies and the programs and services they implement and manage. Most of these agencies come under the executive branches of state and local governments and run the gamut from police departments to schools, state health and welfare departments to public universities.

These agencies exist to implement and manage public programs and policies. When a legislature passes a law to, say, set maximum speed limits on state highways, it expresses the will of the state. The law, however, does not catch speeders zipping down the highway. A traffic cop does. To translate the will of the state into concrete action requires some mechanism to enforce that will, such as the state highway patrol monitoring speeders on state highways. Virtually every purposive course of action that state and local governments decide to pursue requires a similar enforcement or management mechanism. Collectively, these are public agencies and the people who work for them—the police, fire, and parks departments; schools; welfare agencies; libraries; and road crews—in short, the bureaucracy.

RECENT TRENDS

Though bureaucrats perform essential public services and positively affect many aspects of our everyday lives, these days they are not getting much thanks. Quite the opposite, in fact, as public servants have developed into a particular target of elected deficit hawks who want fewer public employees who are paid less and have fewer job-related benefits and bargaining rights. In 2010 Wisconsin Governor Scott Walker led the charge in working to reduce public employee benefits and employees' collective bargaining rights, generating a firestorm of both support and opposition across the nation. After decades of building up the wages and benefits of the public sector, the economic stress of the Great Recession has prompted a sometimes angry review of compensation for government employees. Some now view public employees as "public enemies," as Peter Harkness details in his column on the shift in American public opinion from appreciated public servants to greedy, overpaid beneficiaries of public funds.

Several newly elected Republican governors have strongly advocated this perspective of public sector workers and set their sights on cutting public employee compensation, starting with replacing the traditional pension program with 401(k) retirement plans. Stephen Fehr reports on this trend and its implications in the 2010 elections.

When reduced benefits and frozen wages aren't enough to balance the budget, local governments are looking to slash up to 500,000 public jobs over the next several years. A research brief from the U.S. Conference of Mayors, National League of Cities, and National Association of Counties warns these cuts will severely affect the quantity and quality of citizen services as well as the health of the private sector.

Finally, some municipalities are getting creative in their attempts to maintain levels of service under tight budget constraints. John Buntin reports on the use of volunteers in bureaucratic roles once filled by paid public servants.

NOTE

1. Charles Goodsell, *The Case for Bureaucracy,* 4th ed. (Washington, DC: CQ Press, 2004), 3.

24

Public Servants as Public Enemy #1

Peter Harkness

According to an increasing number of elected officials, the pay and power of public sector workers make them public enemies rather than public servants.

From *Governing*, March 2011.

One of the most disturbing legacies of the Great Recession has been its effect on the idea of public service — from the federal level to smaller localities and from elected and appointed leaders to school teachers.

We used to think of senior government employees as "public servants," and only a few years ago, we were fretting that there weren't enough qualified younger people in the pipeline to replace them as they retired. We got so worried about the quality of education that we started paying teachers more and actively recruiting the best and brightest to serve in programs like Teach for America. After the Oklahoma City bombing of a federal building 16 years ago, public employees were viewed sympathetically. And the attack on the World Trade Center almost a decade ago resulted in first responders, particularly firefighters, being heralded as cultural icons.

The death of longtime U.S. diplomat Richard Holbrooke last December was a reminder of how important an individual "public servant" can be to our national well-being. He served four presidents, and in between stints in government, he was a New York banker and best-selling author. He earned millions of dollars, yet impatiently awaited his next chance to return to a government paycheck. He undoubtedly saved tens of thousands of lives in 1995 when, through the strength of his overpowering personality, he forged the Dayton peace accords ending the war in Bosnia.

Now, as the economy has staggered, the concept of public service is being denigrated, both in Washington and out in the country. A front-page story in the Traverse City, Mich., *Record-Eagle* over the holidays seemed curiously contrived. It reported that most employees of the city and Grand Traverse County received two days off for both Christmas and New Year's, yet the paper did not document any general community disapproval. So what exactly is the story?

In Washington, disrespect for "public servants" plays out in disturbingly familiar ways. Jim Cole, a friend, was appointed by President Obama as deputy attorney general on May 24, 2010, and was approved by the Senate Judiciary Committee two months later. The nomination then languished for five months, until the Senate finally recessed at the end of last year. And yes, there were consequences. The deputy's job at the Department of Justice is somewhat unique in that he oversees the department's daily operations and those of its law enforcement agencies. For Jim, it meant cooling his heels for almost six months, waiting for a "recess appointment" so he finally could accept a significant pay cut and return to the department where he once served for 13 years.

Much of this disparagement of public service in the midst of the worst recession since the 1930s is predictable. Business, labor and government tend to suffer in public approval ratings during economic downturns, and since the majority of all union members are now in public-sector jobs, their contracts for pay, generous pensions and benefits make obvious targets.

Declining support for unions now can be seen in who is willing to cross them. After the midterm elections, Obama proposed and Congress quickly approved a two-year pay freeze for federal workers. At a recent gathering of urban leaders in Chicago, a panel of three well-known, big-city Democratic mayors sounded more like representatives of the chamber of commerce when discussing pensions and benefits. At one point, Los Angeles Mayor Antonio Villaraigosa, himself a former union organizer, blurted out, "I'm a Democrat, though I may not sound like it right now." The message from Villaraigosa and fellow mayors Richard Daley of Chicago and Michael Nutter of Philadelphia was stark: We are in such tough times that we have to rethink everything. Union leaders are in a state of denial; they think the feds or the states are just going to bail out the public pension funds, but that's unlikely. Let them go bankrupt, and then reorganize.

We're hearing much the same from the new governors. Plans to cut the workforce, freeze wages, trim benefits and limit the right to collective bargaining are proceeding not only in states like Ohio and Wisconsin, where Republicans have been elected, but also in California, New York and Connecticut, where Democrats are taking office.

If labor leaders have any political sense, which often seems doubtful, they will walk softly and play this as pragmatically as possible, not only because public opinion clearly leans against them, but because the message from the Democratic mayors and the new governors is correct—the current system of pensions and benefits is not sustainable.

"All of a sudden, we are the enemy," a veteran public school teacher from suburban Toledo, Ohio, recently told me.

Nearing the end of her career, she will be asked to take what may be a significant pay cut in the very years that determine the size of her pension. Of course she is aware that many in the private sector have suffered as much or more, but what really hurts is the sense that teachers and other public employees, most of them imbued with a sense of public service, somehow have it coming.

25

Election Adds Pressure to Change Public Pensions

Stephen C. Fehr

Newly-elected Republican governors are pushing to end traditional pension benefits for public workers. They insist this is not an attack on traditionally Democratic-leaning unions, just a matter of hard headed economics.

From *Stateline.org*, November, 2010.

S ix newly elected governors are looking favorably at some form of 401(k)-style retirement plan for public sector employees, adding to the momentum building nationally for a shift away from traditional guaranteed pensions.

Tuesday's election was in some ways the first national referendum on the future of public pensions, the cost of which has been rising in many states, counties and cities and is crowding out education and other popular programs. In addition to the gubernatorial elections, voters in eight of nine California cities and counties approved ballot measures slashing public pension benefits, and residents of more than 40 suburban Chicago communities approved a ballot question demanding that the Illinois Legislature lower benefits for future state workers, targeting public safety officers and firefighters.

"There is widespread concern about the cost of public-employee pensions," says John Pitney, Jr., a professor of American politics at Claremont McKenna College in California. "Passage of the ballot measures is another sign that voters are serious about the issue."

LOSS FOR LABOR

The election of Republican governors in Alabama, Nevada, Pennsylvania, Tennessee and Wisconsin and an independent in Rhode Island who have all embraced 401(k)-style plans was a defeat for organized labor. Public employee unions have sought to largely preserve the current system, although they have supported some benefit reductions for newly hired employees. Several other candidates for statewide offices elected Tuesday also have said they believe state employee pension plans eventually will run out of money unless new hires receive retirement benefits more in line with those of the private sector.

Pension reform already was going to be a key issue in many state legislatures in 2011; the Tuesday vote could presage tense fights between the newly elected Republicans and Democrats who received campaign cash and workers from public employee unions.

Republican governors-elect Brian Sandoval of Nevada. Robert Bentley of Alabama, Bill Haslam of Tennessee and Scott Walker of Wisconsin all say they generally back the 401(k)-style system, also called "defined contribution" plans. In that model, employees contribute to their pension fund and assume the investment risk, but are given no specified guarantee of funds upon retirement.

A fifth Republican winner, Tom Corbett of Pennsylvania, has said he would consider a hybrid that combines features of the 401(k)-like plan and fixed benefits. Independent candidate Lincoln Chafee, who was elected Rhode Island's next governor, says he would support a hybrid plan for new hires. Michigan already has a 401(k)-type defined contribution plan for state workers but newly elected Governor Rick Snyder, a Republican, has vowed to tighten public pension eligibility and increase retiree health care co-pays.

Democrats also are under pressure to trim retirement fund costs. Seven Democrats who won gubernatorial seats refrained from supporting 401(k)-style plans but said they would continue overhauling the existing public pension system to bring down costs. All had been challenged by 401(k)-supporting Republican opponents. These Democrats pledged to modify the system despite receiving campaign contributions from public employee unions.

So far, only two states — Alaska and Michigan — have adopted 401(k)-style public pension systems as their primary plan. Six states offer deined contribution benefits as an option and eight states have instituted hybrid or combined 401(k)-style and fixed benefit plans, according to the National Conference of State Legislatures. Nearly every state has discussed changing to a deined contribution plan but many have backed off because of political differences and pushback from organized labor.

Public pension plans took a severe hit from the Wall Street financial collapse in 2008; the median investment loss was 25 percent. Even before the recession, however, states were underfunding their employee pension plans. A study by the Pew Center on the States released earlier this year and based on data from before the 2008 Wall Street crisis found that there was a gap of $1 trillion between assets and liabilities of state pension funds.

LOCAL LIABILITIES

A similarly staggering gap exists in local government pension plans. In California this Tuesday, voters in Menlo Park, Carlsbad, San Jose, Redding, Riverside, Bakersfield and Pacific Grove approved ballot measures reducing public pension benefits for new hires. In San Diego, voters rejected a half-cent hike in the sales tax that would have prevented budget cuts in police and fire services. The city pension fund, in which public safety employees are included, faces a $2.1 billion deficit that is driving San Diego's budget crisis. The lone exception in the state was labor-friendly San Francisco, where voters rejected a ballot measure to boost pension contributions from city workers.

In the California governor's race, Meg Whitman, a Republican, sought to paint Democrat Jerry Brown as a tool of labor unions who would refuse to slash public pension costs. Brown, who won, said he would work with union leaders to keep the current defined-benefit plan but offer it to new employees with diminished benefits and increase contributions of current workers.

Public pensions also were a huge issue in Illinois, the state with the nation's most underfunded retirement system. By one unofficial count, 47 communities in six Chicago-area counties approved a ballot question asking the Illinois Legislature to enact additional public pension reform. Governor Pat Quinn, who held a narrow lead over Republican Bill Brady following the vote on

Tuesday, had pushed through a series of reforms earlier this year, including one raising the retirement age from 60 to 67 for new hires, establishing the highest retirement age in the country. Still, Quinn supported the existing defined-benefit plan while Brady favored defined contribution.

Analysts say the public pension funding crisis guarantees years of election debates and ballot measures similar to the ones this year. 2010 was just the start. "It's not ideology, it's arithmetic," says political scientist Pitney of Claremont College. "Money is short, and the savings have to come from somewhere."

26

Local Governments Cutting Jobs and Services

U.S. Conference of Mayors; Christopher W. Hoene, National League of Cities; and Jacqueline J. Byers, National Association of Counties

Local governments are cutting an estimated half-million people from their payrolls. The implications for public services are severe.

From Hoene, Christopher W., and Jacqueline J. Byers. "Local Governments Cutting Jobs and Services." Research Brief. The United States Conference of Mayors, National League of Cities, and National Association of Counties, July 2010.

Unemployment in America is a national crisis. It is also a local crisis. As individuals and families struggle to find work, make ends meet, and keep their homes amid an anemic economic recovery, they increasingly turn to local services for support. Local governments provide job training and assistance, transportation, support services for individuals and families in need, health care and education and afterschool programs that support working families. In many communities, local governments are also one of the primary employers.

Unfortunately, just as families are increasingly turning to local governments for support, local governments are facing their own fiscal crisis. The effects of the Great Recession on local budgets will be felt most deeply from 2010 to 2012.[1] In response, local governments are cutting services and personnel. This report from the National League of Cities (NLC), National Association of Counties (NACo), and the U.S. Conference of Mayors (USCM) reveals that local government job losses in the current and next fiscal years will approach 500,000, with public safety, public works, public health, social services and parks and recreation hardest hit by the cutbacks. Local governments are being forced to make significant cuts that will eliminate jobs, curtail essential services, and increase the number of people in need

> *Local government job losses in the current and next fiscal years will approach 500,000*

This report presents the latest survey results from local officials on job losses and service cuts. The survey results point to the urgent need for federal action to minimize layoffs and service cuts in order to help families and stabilize local economies.

THE ECONOMIC ROLE OF LOCAL GOVERNMENTS

Local governments — cities and counties — are important to the vitality of families and local economies. They provide goods and services that are important to the quality of life of families, such as public safety, parks, libraries, housing and health services, and are central to the performance of local economies.

Local budget crises lead to job losses in both the public and private sectors. The business of local governments is often conducted through the private sector — construction and maintenance, garbage collection and

> *"Mayors are holding the nation together by making impossible decisions every day, and we have made cuts to the point where only bone is left. We know from experience that investment in metropolitan economies with direct funding to cities and counties can create and save jobs and do it quickly."*
>
> —Elizabeth B. Kautz, USCM President, Mayor of Burnsville, Minnesota

> *"City cutbacks affect city employees, services to the community, and local economies. Every city employee lost means one more person in the community without work. Our communities suffer from lost services, whether it's less police on the streets or the closing of a local library. Cities are also the backbone of their regional economies, where investments in infrastructure and services provide a platform for private sector investment and growth."*
>
> —Ron Loveridge, NLC President, Mayor of Riverside, California

recycling and tree trimming are just a few examples. The Economic Policy Institute estimates that for every 100 public sector layoffs there are 30 private sector layoffs.[2] Local government investment in transportation, water, sewer and communications infrastructure also leverages significant private sector growth by reducing private sector costs and creating opportunities for additional investment. Local governments are also significant sources of employment. Local and state governments comprise one of the nation's largest employment industries, larger than the manufacturing and construction industries combined. Local governments account for seven in every 10 of these employees.[3]

Local governments across the country are now facing the combined impact of decreased tax revenues, a falloff in state and federal aid and increased demand for social services. Over the next two years, local tax bases will likely suffer from depressed property values, hard-hit household incomes and declining consumer spending.[4] Further, reported state budget shortfalls for 2010 to 2012 exceeding $400 billion will pose a signiicant threat to funding for local government programs.[5] In this current climate of fiscal distress, local governments are forced to eliminate both jobs and services.

CUTS IN LOCAL JOBS

In May and June of 2010 NLC, NACo and USCM conducted a survey of cities and counties across the country for the purpose of gauging the extent of job losses. The survey was emailed and faxed to all cities over 25,000 in population and to all counties over 100,000 in population. The survey results presented below are based on 270 responses, 214 responses from cities and 56 responses from counties.

The surveyed local governments report cutting 8.6 percent of total full-time equivalent (FTE) positions over the previous fiscal year to the next fiscal year (roughly 2009-2011). If applied to total local government employment nationwide, an 8.6 percent cut in the workforce would mean that 481,000 local government workers were, or will be, laid off over the two-year period.[6] Projected cuts for the next fiscal year will likely increase as many of the nation's local governments draft new budgets, deliberate about how to balance shortfalls and adopt new budgets.[7]

Local job losses are most heavily felt in public safety, public works, public health, social services, and parks and recreation (see Table 1). Local governments typically seek to shield direct services to residents from cuts during economic downturns and the cuts occurring in these services are indicative of the depth of the recession's impact on cities and counties.

Cities and counties almost always seek to protect public safety services — police, fire, and emergency — from cuts in personnel and funding. The need for these basic, or "core," services in terms of protecting the public against crime, fire, and disaster often increase during periods of economic downturn. The depth of the current downturn, however, means that surprising numbers of cities (63%) and counties (39%) report cuts in public safety personnel. For some communities this means fire and police stations that are

> *"U.S. cities will be forced to make gut-wrenching decisions to cut their spending in the next year. This is a story not just...of New Jersey. You're seeing it in Sacramento. You're seeing it happen in Albany and you're seeing it happen all over the U.S."*
> —Cory Booker, Mayor, Newark, N.J.
> Bloomberg BusinessWeek, July 09, 2010

closed and the potential for reduced capacity to respond to emergencies.

A majority of the surveyed cities (60%) and counties (68%) report making personnel cuts in public works. Public works services are highly visible to local residents — such as highway and road construction and maintenance and solid waste (garbage and recycling) disposal. Cuts in public works are common responses to economic downturns, but the range of local governments making these cuts in response to the current downturn is considerably higher than previously. For instance, in response to the 2001 recession, a survey conducted by NACo revealed that 26 percent of counties were delaying highway and road construction and 23 percent reported delaying highway and road maintenance.[8] Cuts in public works go beyond public jobs, with many of these services provided via contracts with private sector businesses.

Approximately half of the surveyed counties report personnel cuts in social services (52%) and public health (48%), services that are critical to local residents in need. Counties, and some cities, deliver significant services in these arenas, in many cases as extensions of state government programs. For example, many counties are the primary delivery agents for child welfare services, cash assistance payments to individuals and families in need and public health and medical services. Confronted with their own significant budget shortfalls, many states are cutting these programs. Yet, demand for these services tends to increase during periods of economic downturn. Personnel and other budget cuts will increase the already expanding pressures on case loads and the remaining personnel.

> *Survey results project that 481,000 jobs will be lost in local government services.*

Park maintenance and programs for youth, such as after-school educational and recreational activities, and seniors, such as meal delivery services, are also highly visible local services that often

Table 26.1 Percentage of Localities Reporting Personnel Cuts, by Service area

Service	Cities	Counties
Courts	NA	25%
Economic Development	27%	25%
Libraries	25%	36%
Parks and Recreation	54%	45%
Public Health	NA	48%
Public Safety	63%	39%
Public Works*	60%	68%
Social Services	26%	52%

*Includes transportation infrastructure, construction and maintenance, zoning, solid waste collection and disposal, and water and sewers.

serve as the primary point of interaction for many residents with local governments. Approximately half of cities (54%) and counties (45%) report personnel cuts in parks and recreation services.

Many local governments are also making personnel cuts in library services, resulting in closures, reduced hours and cuts in programs. Libraries often serve as centers for job searches for residents without access to computers and the Internet, or provide afterschool programs.

City- and county-run schools and school districts are also facing significant cutbacks. Economic conditions have eroded local revenue bases and, particularly in education, state budget shortfalls are resulting in significant cuts to funding for local schools. In response, teaching jobs and special programs are being eliminated, class sizes are increasing and caseloads for school aides and counselors are on the rise.

THE NEED FOR FEDERAL ACTION

While the nation's economy is slowly emerging from the worst economic downturn since the Great Depression, the consequences of the recession will be playing out in America's local communities for years to come. Since the onset of the economic downturn, local leaders have been forced to make tough choices in an effort to provide desperately needed services and to bolster their local economies while responding to large and often persistent budget shortfalls. With the nation's unemployment rate hovering around 9.5 percent and more than 8 million jobs lost since the recession began in late 2007, families are being forced to do the same.

To secure economic recovery, Congress and the Administration must act now to create jobs quickly and help stabilize local government economies. An immediate opportunity exists in the Local Jobs for America Act (H.R. 4812/S. 3500), which would provide $75 billion in targeted and temporary fiscal assistance over two years to local governments and community based organizations to save and create local jobs. Other opportunities include investing in infrastructure through targeted spending to local governments and ensuring that small businesses and local governments can obtain access to credit. Federal investment that helps save local jobs and preserve local services will help stabilize communities across the country and ensure that all of America's families are able to participate in the economic recovery.

> *"If City Hall does not have a strong financial position, if our foundation is upside down financially, we are a hindrance and a burden to other job creators, namely the private sector."*
> —Ashley Swearengin, Mayor, Fresno, Calif. Fresno Bee, July 19, 2010.

EXAMPLES

Fresno, Calif.

In two years, the city has cut its workforce by 16 percent, from 4,160 positions to 3,500. Facing a projected budget shortfall of $31 million by 2015, the city government passed a 2010 budget that includes up to 225 layoffs, reductions in the police force, reduced bus services and reduced park maintenance. Fresno's cuts will add to June's employment statistics showing that local government jobs declined by 1,300 in the San Joaquin Valley, bringing to 5,300 the reduction in local government workers over 25 months, or 30 percent of the total decline in employment in the Valley. Fresno Mayor Ashley Swearengin says the cuts are needed to keep the city's fiscal house in order. Source: Fresno Bee, July 19, 2010.

Flint, Mich.

Facing a $15 million budget deficit, Flint was forced to make cuts in public safety, eliminating 23 of 88 firefighter positions and closing two fire stations. The remaining fire stations face limitations on equipment, with crews often waiting for fire trucks to travel from other stations in responding to fires. Source: The Fiscal Times, July 19, 2010.

Brevard County, Fla.

Next year's county budget will start 14 percent below the current year — a shortfall of $125 million. As a result, the county will likely have to lay off 118 employees and will not fill 86 vacant positions. The cuts may include 31 Sheriff's deputies, eliminating a first responder emergency medical service program, closing community centers, and reduced transit service. Source: Florida Today, July 9, 2010.

> *"To fulfill their service responsibilities, county governments employ more than 2 million professional, technical, and clerical personnel. The ongoing recession has had a devastating impact on county budgets. Counties of all sizes, and in all parts of the Nation have been forced to institute layoffs, furloughs, service reductions, and fee increases. The Local Jobs for America Act comes at a very critical time, as the financial collapse has forced our states and counties to cut jobs for key people in our communities such as school teachers, police, firefighters and others."*
>
> —Judge B. Glen Whitley, NACo President, Tarrant County, Texas

> *Federal investment that helps save local jobs and preserve local services will help stabilize communities across the country and ensure that all of America's families are able to participate in the economic recovery.*

Cincinnati, Ohio

One of the ways that the city balanced a $50 million shortfall in the past year was to make cuts in public services, including the loss of 27 workers from a department that handles trash collection, snow removal and filling potholes. The cuts have reduced the department's response time in responding to requests for filling potholes and other road maintenance. Further cuts are expected in the next fiscal year as the city confronts another $50 million shortfall. Source: Cincinnati Enquirer, July 11, 2010.

Lee County, Fla.

The county's department of transportation is experiencing a 50-position reduction due to layoffs and not filling vacant positions as the county seeks to cut $48 million from its budget. The county's budget has dropped by 43 percent in recent years, from $96.5 million to $55 million, in response to the recession. Source: Naples Daily News, July 13, 2010.

Mecklenburg County, N.C.

The county recently adopted a budget that includes $71 million in cuts and could lead to layoffs of more than 300 workers. Schools, libraries and parks will all see large decreases,with major impacts on area non-profit agencies where 74 percent of county funding will disappear. For example, county veterans services will be forced to eliminate an outreach program to home-bound, elderly veterans. Source: WBTV (Charlotte), June 15, 2010.

New York, New York

The city cut a $4 million social services program aimed at helping the poor and elderly obtain health insurance, use health services, and contest denied health insurance claims. The program, which served as a model for a program at the federal level, reportedly helped 10,000 people a year, but was cut as city leaders were forced to make decisions about cuts among health services, children's services, senior centers, fire companies and libraries. Source: The New York Times, July 8, 2010.

Dallas, Texas

The city will lay off 500 employees, 4 percent of the city workforce, in an effort to solve a budget shortfall of $130 million. The city's library system is expected to see the largest reduction in positions. In addition to the layoffs, service cuts are expected in street services, libraries, recreation centers and municipal swimming pools. For example, nine of the city's 43 recreation centers will not be open a full 40 hours a week and will have less staff available. Parks cutbacks include not picking up litter and decreased mowing. The city is also delaying the purchase of new police and firefighting equipment. City Manager Mary Suhm said the cuts were necessary responses to economic conditions, "I do not think the economy will come roaring back. I do think it will come back, but I think that the slope on that line will be very slow." Source: Dallas Morning News, July 15, 2010.

San Jose, Calif.

In order to balance a $118.5 million shortfall, the city reduced employee compensation by 10 percent, eliminated 30 management-level positions and cut public services, mainly at libraries, which reduced open hours from six days to four-and-a-half days a week. Without the employee cuts and concessions, the city would have been forced to close 22 community centers. Source: The Fiscal Times, July 19, 2010.

Portland, Ore.

Portland Public Schools will eliminate 120 teaching positions, including nearly 60 special education positions, resulting in increases in class sizes and caseloads. Eliminating teacher jobs will save $13 million and was necessary after the state cut school funding by 9 percent, or $19 million in total for Portland. Portland is banking on the federal government to pass legislation that would help save teacher jobs and would cover the remaining $6 million shortfall. Without federal help, another 60 jobs will likely be eliminated. Source: The Oregonian, July 19, 2010.

AUTHORS AND ACKNOWLEDGEMENTS

The Research Brief was authored by Christopher W. Hoene and Jacqueline J. Byers. Christopher W. Hoene is the Director of the Center for Research and Innovation at the National League of Cities. Jacqueline J. Byers is the Director of Research and Outreach at the National Association of Counties. Contributions to this research were also made by Christiana McFarland, Will McGahan and Caitlin Geary at the National League of Cities and by Kathryn Murphy and Deseree Gardner at the National Association of Counties.

NLC, NACo and USCM are particularly thankful to the 214 responding cities and 56 responding counties.

NOTES

1. Hoene, Christopher W., City Budget Shortfalls and Responses: 2010-2012, National League of Cities, December 2009, http://www.nlc.org/ASSETS/01 49CE492F8C49D095160195306B6E08/Buddget ShortFalls_FINAL.pdf.

2. Pollack, Ethan, Local Government Job Losses Hurt Entire Economy, Economic Policy Institute, May 2010, http://www.epi.org/page/-/pdf/issuebrief279.pdf

3. U.S. Bureau of Labor Statistics, www.bls.gov.

4. Local fiscal conditions typically lag economic conditions, in much the same way that state fiscal conditions lag economic conditions and the unemployment rate lags overall economic recovery. For local budgets, this lag can be anywhere from one to three years, depending on the factors driving the changes in the economy and the depth of those changes. Current economic indicators suggest that the U.S. economy passed the low point of the current recession in late 2009, which means that the low point for local fiscal conditions will likely be experienced sometime in 2011. To illustrate this lag, the U.S. Census of Governments reports that local property tax collections began to decline in the first quarter of 2010, two-and-a-half years after the housing market began to decline in the summer of 2007. For more information about the lag, see City Fiscal Conditions in 2009 (NLC, Sept. 2009) at http://www.nlc.org/ASSETS/ E1BD3CEFA8094BD097A04BD10CBB785B/CityFiscalConditions_09%20(2).pdf.

5. McNichol, Elizabeth, Phil Oliff and Nicholas Johnson, Recession Continues to Batter State Budgets; State Responses Could Slow Recovery, Center on Budget and Policy Priorities, July 2010, http://www.cbpp.org/cms/index. cfm?fa=view&id=711

6. Total city and county employment statistics are drawn from the U.S. Census of Governments.

7. Not all cities and counties utilize the same fiscal year timeframes. The most common local government fiscal year runs from July 1 to June 30, which is used by 46 percent of the surveyed cities and 56 percent of the surveyed counties. Some local governments utilize a January 1 to December 31 fiscal year (28 percent cities; 21 percent counties), some use a October 1 to September 30 fiscal year (22 percent cities; 18 percent counties) and others use some alternate timeframe (4 percent cities; 1 percent counties).

8. Hayes, Harry and Richard Clark, Counties in Crisis, Carl Vinson Institute of Government, University of Georgia, July 2003.

27

Does Government Work Require Government Employees?

John Buntin

Local agencies are getting creative with personnel resources in the face of shrinking revenues and budget cuts — substitute paid public employees with community volunteers to maintain high levels of service.

"Stop! Taser, Taser, Taser!"

Triggers pull, nitrogen canisters pop and barbed darts clatter against body silhouettes taped to a wall. If the silhouettes had been people, five-second pulses of electrical current would have flowed into their bodies, toppling most of them to the ground.

"Don't aim too close to the heart," says Sgt. Jeremy Floyd. If someone's coming at you, he says, shoot for the lower abdomen.

Floyd, the training instructor at a Wednesday evening Taser recertification class in Redlands, Calif., is sharing the fine points of stun gun use with a small group of men and women, all of them outfitted in blue trousers and white shirts with police badges. The badges identify them as members of the Redlands Police Department, but things are not what they seem. For starters, Taser target practice isn't taking place at a police firing range. It's happening on the porch of the Joslyn Senior Center. And in a state where many sworn law enforcement officers retire in their 50s, most of these officers look, well, older. White hair is the norm here rather than the exception. There are other oddities, too. Police department physical fitness requirements often exclude individuals with disabilities, yet one of the men is firing from a motorized wheelchair.

That said, the men and women gathered on the porch are members of the Redlands Police Department, as their badges denote. But they are not sworn or paid officers. They're volunteers, part of the city's Citizen Volunteer Patrol (CVP) unit. And they're at the forefront of the one of the country's more ambitious efforts to integrate volunteers into the workings of local government.

At a time when most city and local governments are preparing to do less with less, officials in Redlands are taking a different approach:

From *Governing*, April 2011.

They're attempting to maintain current levels of service through other means. Ramping up the use of volunteers is one of them.

It's easy to see why. Three years ago, the police department in Redlands, a city of 71,000 people east of Los Angeles, had 98 sworn officers, 208 civilians and about two dozen volunteers. The police budget was $23.8 million, nearly half of the city's operating budget. Today, the department employs 75 sworn officers and 138 civilians and relies on 291 active volunteers, who last year contributed more than 31,000 hours of their time to the city.

The volunteers are not just answering the phones at police headquarters. They cordon off crime scenes, direct traffic, patrol the city's 14 parks, write parking tickets, assist with animal control and provide crowd control at special events. They are also trained to check in parolees, assist with records processing, help staff DUI checkpoints, take reports on routine property crimes, serve as the liaison with the local San Bernardino County district attorney's office, provide counseling to crime victims and monitor sex offenders remotely. In addition, they serve more traditional functions as volunteer reserve officers. Two volunteer reserve officers even conduct investigations alongside the city's detectives. One has his own caseload. Some of the volunteers—those who go through the special training session—are allowed to carry Taser guns for their own protection.

It isn't just the police department that's assigned volunteers to important duties. Eighteen months ago, when Les Jolly took over the city's Quality of Life Department, he started to develop a program that will soon field volunteer code inspectors. "Our staff was cut by over 10 percent this fiscal year," Jolly says. "If you don't think of creative ways to supplement what you do, then you are going to fail." Redlands also employs a part-time volunteer coordinator, Tabetha Johnson, who routinely works with local civic clubs to mobilize hundreds of volunteers for events such as Redlands' annual professional bicycle race.

"We have fewer resources," says City Manager N. Enrique Martinez. "We had to cut staff. My challenge is to maintain the same service level if not better. The public is not interested in whether you have 15 fewer people than before or not."

Nor should they be. At least that's the argument Police Chief Jim Bueermann makes. "The fallback position for most local government bureaucrats like me," he says, "is that it's so much easier to say, 'We have $3 million less so you are going to get fewer services.' But there are multiple ways to get to the outcomes that taxpayers expect their police department is going to deliver." Prominent among them are a greater reliance on technology and a greater use of volunteers. Call it do-it-yourself government. But can volunteers really put in the hours and perform sensitive, highly skilled jobs that take more than a friendly smile? Can they enable a government to do more with less? A close look at Redlands' experience suggests that under some circumstances, the answer just might be yes — although that might not translate into taxpayer support.

Jim Bueermann took command of the Redlands Police Department in 1998. A lifelong resident of the city and a 20-year veteran of the force, he knew his community well—the rough neighborhoods as well as the affluent enclaves where, starting in 1870, wealthy visitors from the Midwest and the East found an ideal retreat in Redlands' fragrant orange groves and snow-capped San Bernardino Mountains. Over the years, the visitors endowed their new community with such gifts as a symphony, a magnificent Moorish-style library, and perhaps most importantly, the University of Redlands. The city soon became known as "The Jewel of the Inland Empire."

That phrase is not heard much anymore. Today, the Inland Empire is defined more by foreclosures than orange groves. The problems of neighboring communities, such as gang-plagued San Bernardino, with which Redlands shares a border, have crept in. And, despite its relative affluence, Redlands has suffered through three years of declining revenues, which have resulted in budget cuts to city departments, including the police.

When the police department's workforce fell by a third, Bueermann turned to a city tradition: volunteerism. He accelerated volunteer-recruitment efforts and hired a volunteer coordinator to oversee his department's initiatives. In the process, Bueermann discovered something surprising. Volunteers are not deterred by requirements that are demanding and responsibilities that are real. They are attracted to them.

Veteran police officers discovered something too. When the volunteer program was starting out, says Lt. Chris Catren, "we were filling the gaps with volunteers." But as police came to realize that volunteers could do many of the routine tasks that had once constituted a significant part of their workdays—directing traffic, taking reports, delivering evidence to the district attorney's office, providing crime-scene control— they came to depend on them. "They are," Catren says, "as much a part of our service delivery model as the person in a black-and-white uniform with a badge and a gun."

The department has used volunteer officers to take on specific, new tasks, such as patrolling parks, municipal orange groves and desert areas that stretch across the 40-square-mile city. One such area is the Santa Ana river basin, known locally as "the wash."

The Santa Ana River, Southern California's largest, begins in the San Bernardino Mountains and ends in the Pacific Ocean at Huntington Beach. Once upon a time, mountain storms would send deluges of water coursing through the river's channel and into the sea. Today, subdivisions in Orange County occupy many of those floodplains, and the Seven Oaks Dam holds back the waters that would otherwise sweep those subdivisions away. But dams silt up. To maintain them, authorities must occasionally release water into the wash. That poses a problem because the wash also serves as home for the homeless.

In the past, police officers alerted encampments of the homeless to the coming water release so they could move to safer grounds. Now, the city relies on a group of volunteers known as the Citizen Volunteer Park Rangers to make sure the homeless are out of harm's way.

On a recent Friday afternoon, two uniformed rangers, Lee Haag, a retired Air Force officer, and Sherli Leonard, the executive director of the Redlands Conservancy, descend on their horses into the wash. A few weeks earlier, they had distributed fliers warning of the water release at two recently spotted encampments— one north of the Redlands Municipal Airport, the other in the lee of the Orange Street Bridge. Now they're checking the encampment near the bridge. As they approach, it is deserted except for a stray dog. As the horses climb out of the wash, the rangers encounter a woman out for a walk. She stops to pat the horses. Knowing that rangers are out patrolling the wash, she says, has made her day.

The creation of the Volunteer Park Rangers says a lot about how the city interacts with its volunteers. The ranger program started almost accidentally. Three years ago, retired audiologist Brad Billings read an interview in

the local paper in which Police Chief Bueermann expressed a desire to organize a volunteer patrol to tackle problems of graffiti and disorder in the city's parks. Billings e-mailed the chief and two hours later got an e-mail back inviting him to a meeting. Their discussion was brief.

"Brad, it's yours," Bueermann told him. "Go for it." Bueermann appointed a sergeant to supervise the program but left it to Billings to organize, raise funds and run the initiative, which now numbers more than two dozen volunteers. Like the Citizen Volunteer Patrol, rangers received training, uniforms, iPhones (to mark the location of graffiti and other problems) and access to city equipment. Sending volunteer rangers into the wash is something many cities wouldn't do—even if the volunteers were trained and well equipped. Bueermann says such risk-taking is essential. "Too often we accept a lack of money as a reason not to do things," he says. "There are so many ways to get around that if we just accept a level of ambiguity, develop a tolerance for risk-taking and realize that sometimes failure is about learning."

As for Haag and Leonard, they say they have never felt unsafe.

Redlands is unusual for the depth and breadth of its volunteer activities, but it isn't alone. Confronted with the challenges of the Great Recession, cities across the country have begun to reconsider what can be done with volunteers. In December 2009, New York City Mayor Michael Bloomberg assembled 15 mayors to announce the launch of a new initiative, Cities of Service. Underwritten by both Bloomberg Philanthropies and the Rockefeller Foundation, the initiative provides cities with $200,000 grants to hire "chief service officers" to identify local priorities and develop plans to address them, using volunteers.

One of the mayors who appeared with Bloomberg was Nashville's Karl Dean. In January 2010, Nashville received one of the first $200,000 Cities of Service grants. Dean tapped Laurel Creech to run the program. Her first day of work last May coincided with the 100-year flood that submerged parts of downtown Nashville as well as several residential neighborhoods. From the city emergency command center, Creech worked with a local volunteer group, Hands On Nashville, to text thousands of volunteers with a request for help sandbagging downtown against the rising Cumberland River.

Within three hours, more than a thousand volunteers were on hand.

Since then, Creech has developed a service plan that focuses on two issues — education and the environment. According to Creech, working with the heads of city agencies has been challenging. Although quite a few departments utilize volunteers in many ways, a lot of them don't use volunteers as effectively as they could or, she says, they "don't really know what suitable volunteer programs are and what volunteers can do and can't do. The challenge is getting them to recognize that there are opportunities for improvement."

Still, Nashville's chief service officer believes that volunteers will take on more and more tasks once performed by government employees.

In Redlands, that moment has already arrived. When budget cuts nixed the Redlands Police Department's plans to lease a helicopter from the county (at a cost of $500,000 a month plus operating costs) to provide air support, the department used drug forfeiture funds to purchase a 1967 Cessna 172, which it then kitted out with a $30,000 video camera that could be operated by a laptop in the back of the plane. To operate the plane, the department turned to volunteer pilots like Bill Cheeseman, age 70.

Cheeseman is a retired engineer who describes himself as "a gentleman acrobatic flier." On a recent sunny afternoon, he takes the plane up for a patrol shift. A police officer, Sgt. Shawn Ryan, sits in the back, along with his electronic equipment: image-stabilized binoculars, a laptop to monitor the police dispatcher and operate the video camera, as well as a LoJack system for detecting stolen cars. As the plane lifts off the runway of the Redlands Municipal Airport, a police dispatcher reports a recurring alarm in a neighborhood of mansions between Caroline Park and the Redlands Country Club. Two patrol cars arrive at the scene just minutes before the Cessna, which circles overhead.

Two officers from the patrol car have entered the house. They have silenced their radio. If there's a burglar inside, they don't want its squawk to announce their presence. Two thousand feet overhead, Ryan focuses on the house. "If someone runs out," he says, "we'll see them."

No one makes a run for it. The officers on the ground report that the wind was opening and closing an unlocked door. But even when the plane responds to a false alarm, it serves a useful purpose. One of Bueermann's first and most controversial actions as chief was to disband a "beat" system that assigned police officers to various sectors of the city, with little regard for actual crime rates. Needless to say, affluent low-crime neighborhoods were unhappy with the change. By putting a plane in the air — and highly visible police vehicles on the ground (albeit ones often driven by volunteers) — he's been able to assuage their concerns and free up his officers for the proactive police work of targeting gangs, guns and violence in the most dangerous parts of town.

It's the kind of creative problem-solving that has allowed the city to cut personnel by 16 percent without damaging city services, says Redlands City Manager Martinez. Last spring, San Bernardino County and the city of Redlands commissioned a polling firm to gauge public satisfaction with city services. Even though citywide staffing and funding have been cut and cut again since 2007, 81 percent of respondents said services were at least satisfactory — and 30 percent of that 81 percent actually rated services as better than satisfactory.

To Martinez, it was a testament to the creativity of city staff and the partnerships they have been able to build. "Less is not less," he says. "The way services have been delivered for the past 20 years is very labor intensive."

But the city's approach may also have lulled the citizens of Redlands into thinking that city leaders have solved the problem of doing more with less and that the city doesn't need more money to keep providing a top-notch level of service. Last November, when a measure to impose a half-cent sales tax surcharge to shore up city services went before the voters, it failed. In Redlands, the voters have spoken. Do-it-yourself government is here for good.

VIII

Local Government

Like their state counterparts, local governments are dealing with grim budget forecasts and are staving off insolvency with a painful mixture of cuts in services, hikes in taxes and fees, and billions of dollars in federal aid. Though restricted by state-level decisions, the tactical mix of raising revenue and/or spending cuts varies across local governments and may be dependent on local political culture. The implications of the tough choices at this lowest level of federalism can only be truly appreciated with a general understanding of what local governments are and what they do.

WHAT LOCAL GOVERNMENTS ARE

Local governments come in three basic forms: counties, municipalities, and special districts. Counties originated as, and to a considerable extent still are, local outposts of state government. For governing purposes, states historically subdivided themselves into smaller political jurisdictions called counties, and turned over to these units basic local functions, such as road maintenance and law enforcement.

Municipalities are public corporations, created to provide basic governance to defined geographic jurisdictions, and include familiar political entities such as towns, villages, and cities. The local entities differ from counties in that they tend to be more compact geographically, are more urban, and legally exist as independent corporations, rather than being the local offices of state governments.

Special districts are a miscellaneous category that includes everything else, and with local government there is a lot of everything else. The most obvious difference between counties, municipalities, and special districts is that the first two are general governance units. Counties and municipalities provide a broad range of programs and services while special districts provide a specific program or service. School districts are the most common form of special district—they exist solely to provide public education. Other examples include water treatment and sewage management districts.

Despite that distinction, these definitions are fairly loose. State law sets the definition of a town, village, or city, and the powers and policy responsibilities of these different categories of municipality may vary considerably. Municipalities, counties, and special districts are not even clearly separated by geography, but piled on top of each other, which can be confusing to citizens and create coordination and control problems for public officials. A county may be almost completely covered by a municipality, or a series of municipalities. There may be several school districts crossing over county and city boundaries. Crisscrossing these jurisdictions may be other special districts. Local governments fit together like some sort of three-dimensional jigsaw puzzle with some pieces missing. Given this patchwork, it should not be surprising that local governments sometimes get into arguments about who should be doing what.

Though local governments seem to be a confusing jumble from a big-picture perspective, there is a fairly clear difference between the vast majority of local governments and state government. Generally speaking, state governments are sovereign governments, and local governments are not. What this means is that state governments get their powers and legal authority directly from citizens—this power and authority is codified in the state constitution.

Most local governments, however, get their power from state government, not directly from citizens. Their powers and legal authority are mostly set by state law, which is to say the state legislature. And what the legislature gives it can take away. So unlike the relationship between the federal and state governments, which at least in theory is a relationship of equals, the relationship between state governments and local governments is legally a superior-subordinate relationship. Some states

grant local governments broad powers; others reserve much of these powers to themselves and delegate comparatively little. Even in the states that grant local government considerable independence, however, the state technically is still the sovereign government, while the local government is not.

This hierarchy is codified legally in what is known as Dillon's Rule, which is the legal principle that local governments can only exercise the powers granted to them by state government. The independence and power of local governments thus vary enormously not just from state to state, but from locality to locality within states. Some municipalities are virtual city-states, powerful political jurisdictions with a high degree of self-rule. Others are little more than local extensions of state governments.

RECENT TRENDS

The readings in this section highlight a difficult set of challenges that are forcing change on local governments whether they like it or not. The most obvious of these, of course, is the immediate problem of keeping local governments solvent and providing key public services. In the first article, Alan Greenblatt highlights one of the major challenges of local government submission to state authority: unfunded mandates. States are devolving more and more services and programs to the local level, while cutting aid and continuing to restrict local taxing authority. This leaves city and county governments to provide required services with diminishing revenue.

A response to this challenge and others brought on by the recent recession is to consolidate efforts. Benedict Jimenez and Rebecca Hendrick discuss the trade-offs between fewer, consolidated and several, smaller governments in the areas of service delivery, spatial segregation, and urban sprawl. Though the results from empirical tests are mostly mixed due to measurement differences, this review of the research highlights an important debate regarding the benefits and limits of public choice in governing.

Another approach to doing more with less is to just do less. In the libertarian-spirited city of Colorado Springs, Colorado, home of nationally low property taxes, street medians are going unmowed, public pools are closed, and some traffic lights have been turned off.

A property tax increase referendum was defeated in 2009, signaling to municipal officials that citizens would rather do without, or rely on volunteers, than pay more to maintain services.

While most local governments are struggling with the status quo or actively cutting services and programs, there are some cities exhibiting a pioneering spirit in policy and service innovation. As Greenblatt notes, Mayor Michael Bloomberg's New York City has become the new "California" of policy laboratories with its health and urban planning programs providing national exemplars of what cities can do.

28

States Handing Off More Responsibilities to Cities

Alan Greenblatt

States are requiring municipalities to shoulder more policy responsibilities even as they cut municipal aid. For many cities already struggling with state-mandated limits on their ability to raise revenue, this is creating some tough choices.

Jerry Brown is dusting off one of the oldest plays in his book. Back in 1975, during his first term as governor, Brown had appeared before the California State Association of Counties (CSAC) to talk about realignment—the term of art in California for devolution, or changing the way responsibilities are split between the state and localities.

Now that he's back in the governor's office, Brown is putting some of those ideas into action. He returned to CSAC on his first full day in office to promote a realignment package that would make counties responsible for running a much larger share of public safety and social service programs. Proposition 13 the property tax law that passed during Brown's first term— "took away the power of counties to tax, for the most part," Brown said at CSAC in January. "It sent the decisions up to Sacramento. So we want to redistribute all that."

County officials are welcoming the chance to take charge of certain programs, while expressing great concern about handling others. Unsurprisingly, the big question is money whether the state will send enough cash to localities to fund the missions it expects them to carry out. "There's a lot of anxiety," says Jean Kinney Hurst, a legislative representative with CSAC. "We're talking about $6 billion worth of programs, many of which counties have never done before."

Similar anxieties are being expressed elsewhere around the country. Other states may not be holding the same overt policy debate about whether localities should take on a larger load, but the question is nonetheless being posed in the form of budget cuts that leave localities more on their own. "There's a potential," says Ellis

From *Governing,* April 2011.

134

Hankins, executive director of the North Carolina League of Municipalities, "for local elected officials to have to pick up more of the burden and increase the taxes to pay for more public services."

There's nothing new in this. States always cut aid to local governments in recessions. During the ongoing state budget crunch, the cuts have grown so deep that many officials at the local level are complaining that states are doing to them what Washington does to the states — passing on more mandates even while cutting funding.

"We want to make sure that, at a minimum, states don't try to balance their budgets on the backs of cities by mandating that local governments do what historically has been done by states," says Don Borut, executive director of the National League of Cities. "And we don't want the states preempting or putting restraints on how cities can raise money."

Devolution by budget cut is happening all over the country. Very few states still have a line item called "aid to localities." But program responsibilities—and finances—are all mixed up between the state and local levels across a broad range of program areas, including health, public safety and the big cost driver of education.

States have slashed billions over the past couple of years that otherwise would have gone to local governments. In Massachusetts, for example, Gov. Deval Patrick has proposed cutting direct municipal aid for the fourth year in a row. His package would bring the total cut to more than $481 million, or 37 percent. Beverly, Mass., Mayor William Scanlon says such cuts are "really painful," because state aid is the second largest share of his city's revenue. But cuts in total state aid to localities — education has been better protected than municipal aid — aren't out of line with levels of Massachusetts' spending cuts overall. Scanlon says he recognizes that the governor and legislators have had little choice in the matter. "The state's revenues have fallen off the table," Scanlon says. "If I was in their shoes, I'm afraid I would do what they've done."

What Scanlon and other mayors object to, however, is the state backing out on prior promises — failing to return what are really local revenues. Massachusetts established a program back in the 1970s to encourage police officers to continue their education by increasing their salaries when they receive degrees in higher education. The state promised localities it would pick up 50 percent

of the tab. Under that formula, the state's share for the coming year stands at nearly $60 million, but Patrick's budget only provides $5 million. Court decisions suggest that localities may be on the hook for the rest.

Similar stories can be told all over. North Carolina Gov. Bev Perdue wants to slash the local share of lottery proceeds from 40 percent to 10 percent. And her budget would shift the $57 million cost of school bus replacements onto counties, a responsibility they have never had before. In all, the overall cost shift to counties is $345 million. In Michigan, where much local taxing authority was taken away decades ago in favor of a local share of state sales taxes, the state over the past decade has cut $4 billion that, by statute, should go to local governments.

Michigan Gov. Rick Snyder not only wants to cut remaining revenue sharing by a third this year, but wants to make localities earn the money. State aid, under his proposal, would be contingent on their putting in place measures to save money, including consolidation of services and winning concessions on wages and benefits from their workers.

Last month, Snyder pushed a bill that would make it easier for the state to intervene in municipal and school district finances by creating "emergency fiscal managers" with broad authority. Snyder said he didn't want the state to have to take over local budgets but that his legislation would create an early-warning system when localities are getting in trouble.

It has become a common tack. Governors promise more flexibility on certain rules or help with pensions or employee health costs in exchange for less money overall, and demand that localities change workforce rules and consolidate certain services — or merge with their neighbors altogether. Governors haven't gotten far over the past decade with most of their proposals that local governments consolidate, but they are now wielding a much bigger financial stick. "The fiscal constraints are now coming to bear on localities," says John Krauss, director of the Indiana University Public Policy Institute, who helped run a local government reform commission for Gov. Mitch Daniels.

"Resources are becoming scarce, things change and you can't do it the same way," Krauss continues. "Localities are now seeing that it is probably wise to have merger and intergovernmental agreements. Those are taking off."

Krauss argues that consolidation at the local level is "logical," and notes that many of the ideas his commission recommended echo back to a governmental reorganization report from 1932. But local officials are understandably wary of reorganization that is pushed from above. They naturally worry about having to pick up any financial difference, particularly where they are operating under constraints — often imposed by their states — in terms of their own ability to increase taxes.

But they also worry about equity issues. Some local governments are better off financially than others. As more and more responsibility falls primarily or wholly on local governments, states may be abdicating their role in seeing that a certain level of service is made available to all residents, regardless of the jurisdiction in which they reside. For some services, such as education, states are required to see that disparities based on ZIP code are not too wide.

That's certainly the case in California, which is a pioneer state when it comes to school-equity lawsuits. Because of a 1988 ballot initiative, the state is required to spend at least 40 percent of its general fund revenues on K-12 education. A lot of the money the state spends on education comes out of locally collected property taxes, which the state vacuums up and then redistributes.

Education is just one way state and local finances are hopelessly entangled in California. There are dozens of others. A discussion solely about how revenues from vehicle license fees are shared between Sacramento and localities could go on for many long and tedious hours. Even local officials who are nervous about Brown's proposals give him credit for trying to sort through the mess. There's a lot to be said for citizens' being able to know who's responsible for raising the money and spending which funds for which programs. But given the convoluted nature of the way money is taxed at one level of government—and then chopped up and redistributed to other levels of government — it's often impossible to know who to thank and who to blame. "One of the reasons why California got so screwed up," says former California Assembly Speaker Robert Hertzberg, "is the unintended consequences of the jury-rigged attempts to get money to the locals."

Hertzberg is a strong backer of Brown's realignment proposal. He recognizes, however, that the word "realignment" is code to local governments that they will have to pick up more responsibilities without getting more money to pay for them. Brown initially proposed offering localities funding to cover their new responsibilities for five years, but has since said he will find a way to provide more permanent funding. "It's a long discussion that starts with, 'There better be enough money,'" says David Finigan, a Del Norte County, Calif., supervisor.

Finigan has reason to be wary. Brown's whole idea is predicated on the hope that voters will approve a tax package to pay for it in a special election in June. And past realignment debates in Sacramento haven't all come through with the kind of money that Brown is promising. A 1991 realignment of social services left counties about a billion dollars short.

Cities are already livid that Brown wants to eliminate nearly $2 billion in local redevelopment funds. The state of California has long been notorious for dipping into local coffers, either by using sticky fingers to hold on to tax dollars the state is supposed to hand down, or by "borrowing" local revenues. Local officials in California have twice succeeded in recent years in convincing voters to pass propositions designed to block such behavior on the part of the state. "There has been a long-standing history of distrust in the relationship between the state and local governments in California," says CSAC's Hurst. "Unless you put things in the constitution, you can't rely on anyone's word or handshake agreement."

Los Angeles District Attorney Steve Cooley warns that Brown's proposed realignment will "wreak havoc" and be a "public safety nightmare." He notes that jails in his county are already at or near capacity limits imposed by federal courts. County supervision of paroled rapists and murderers, he says, would mean some convicted felons will serve little or no time in custody due to insufficient bed space.

But many other local officials in California aren't opposed to the idea of realignment—in principle. Just as states have long argued that they can run programs more efficiently than the feds if given adequate support and flexibility, Finigan says that localities can handle most of the programs Brown has put on the table "better and cheaper" than the state.

Hertzberg now co-chairs California Forward, a policy group that has advocated better alignment of services and level of government. He says it's unfortunate that the idea has been distorted by the unending arguments in

California about how revenue streams flow up and down and diverge between the state and localities. He recognizes that money has to follow program responsibility in order for realignment to work, but argues that realignment is a necessity in order for localities and regions within the state to operate in a more responsive way.

It's possible that Brown's ideas—ambitious as they are represent only a first step in this regard. It will be challenging enough to put counties in charge of parole, for instance. But the current debate about public safety and social services may only be the opening of a long discussion that will eventually incorporate even bigger issues such as education and the tax code.

If it's done right—and isn't just a cost-cutting maneuver many local officials in California believe they can offer more efficient coordination of services. As things stand now, though, counties struggle to knit together closely related programs that nonetheless are funded through separate state revenue streams, each with its own set of mandates.

Some counties have figured out how to do this already. Kids who are at risk of being removed from their homes, for instance, might fall under the purview of any of three different agencies, depending on whether the problem is parental abuse, drug use or involvement in crime. Each of these programs comes with its own set of state money that goes to either the county health, human services or probation department. Quite often, the problems of at-risk kids are intertwined. But this has often led to situations where local agency officials point fingers at one another and argue, "This kid belongs to you, it's a substance abuse issue," or "No, the primary problem is the criminal activity." Taking kids out of their homes is an expensive proposition and no one wants to be stuck with the bill.

About a decade ago, officials in San Mateo County, Calif., decided it was pointless to try to shift responsibility between departments. Officials from different agencies began meeting on a weekly basis, getting to know the kids and their problems, and trying to coordinate the whole panoply of services that they might need. It didn't always go smoothly at first, but over time the agencies learned to work together. The result has been a 50 percent reduction in the number of kids removed from their homes. "Kids who stay in their homes, so long as they get the right services, do a whole lot better in the long run," says County Health System Chief Jean Fraser.

Fraser recognizes that her county has resources others might not be able to draw on. The county is made up largely of affluent suburbs just south of San Francisco and has 700,000 residents as many as the state of Vermont. But she argues that it's even more important for poorer counties to have greater flexibility in expending the limited resources at their disposal.

Already facing budget shortfalls of their own, it's difficult for local officials to contemplate the prospect of taking on further program responsibilities. Many of the programs Brown is expecting them to take over come laden with mandates from either the state or federal level or both. And in many other states, localities are being asked to do more without seeing real help in terms of delivery on promises of greater flexibility, or even serious debate about what responsibilities best lie with which level of government.

The issue, of course, is whether California will remain committed to funding the responsibilities Brown hopes to pass down an ever-present source of anxiety for local officials in California, as it is for their counterparts in other states. If the commitment is there, Fraser sees real promise in the notion of freeing counties to design programs in ways that best meet the needs of their own residents. "From our perspective, the idea of having more flexibility about what we do is really exciting," she says. "We're raring to go."

29

Is Government Consolidation the Answer?

Benedict S. Jimenez and Rebecca Hendrick

It's an age-old argument. Is it better to have a larger, one-stop-shop local government, or lots of smaller governments doing their own thing? Two academics take a look at the tradeoffs between big and small government.

INTRODUCTION

Through economic boom or bust, nothing, it seemed, could slow down the growth of local governments in the United States. Within a period of two decades, the total number of governments grew by 7.6 percent. From 1987 to 2007, some 8,141 new governments were created, the majority of which were special districts. These local governments—counties, municipalities, boroughs, townships, school districts, and special districts—play a crucial role in delivering public services to citizens. In 2007, the 89,476 local governments generated over $831 billion in revenues from own sources, and spent $1.29 trillion for a wide array of functions from basic services such as police, fire protection, and education, to lesser known services such as mosquito abatement.

The Great Recession that started in late 2007 is threatening to alter the local government landscape in the United States. With the steep decline in property and sales taxes, as well as deep cuts in state aid, many local governments now face great difficulty maintaining pre-recession service levels (Hoene and Pagano 2009). Not surprisingly, a number of state governments are now reviewing how their local government systems can be restructured to improve service delivery from the standpoint of efficiency. Many local governments also are exploring new governance structures that involve combining operations or even consolidating units of government to maintain core services during this downturn.

For more than a century now, scholars from two camps—the advocacy of regional versus multiple centers of local government—have proposed contrasting visions of how the local public sector

From *State and Local Government Review,* 2010.

should be organized. Earlier studies from both camps focused on the effects of local government fragmentation on service delivery. Regionalists, also called metropolitan government reformers (Ostrom 1972), claim that greater efficiency and responsiveness in service delivery can be achieved with the consolidation of numerous governments in metropolitan areas (Rusk 1993). Localists from the public choice school counter that only a fragmented system is capable of bringing marketlike forces to bear on the production of public goods and services, insuring a more efficient and responsive local public sector (Tiebout 1956; Ostrom, Tiebout, and Warren 1961; Ostrom 1973, 1983; Ostrom, Bish, and Ostrom 1988).

Beyond service delivery, more recent studies have linked local government fragmentation to issues such as racial and social class segregation and the unsustainable expansion of urban areas or urban sprawl (Howell-Moroney 2008). The presence of numerous local governments may provide incentives for citizens to pursue certain lifestyle choices such as the desire to live in socially and racially homogenous communities, resulting in the spatial separation of races and social classes in metropolitan regions (Weiher 1991; Lowery 2000). Moreover, by facilitating the formation of new communities, and ensuring that such communities would be served by newly created local governments, fragmented systems can facilitate urban sprawl (Carruthers 2003; Dye and McGuire 2000).

This essay discusses the different arguments for local government fragmentation versus consolidation and reviews the empirical evidence. It focuses on the impacts of the local public sector structure on service delivery, spatial segregation, and urban sprawl. This discussion is particularly important for state and local governments as they debate how to respond to the Great Recession. It is tempting to assume that fewer larger governments are more efficient than many small ones, but research shows this is not always the case. State and local governments must also be aware of the trade-offs in costs and benefits associated with fragmented and consolidated system, as each system has positive and negative aspects. Finally, the essay identifies future areas of research that will better inform debates about the advantages and disadvantages of different systems of local governance.

SERVICE DELIVERY
The Arguments

Efficiency in service delivery is often the focus of many arguments at the state level about whether to limit the proliferation of new local governments and create incentives for local consolidation. Both regionalists and localists claim that their preferred vision of the local urban government system will lead to more efficient service delivery. Before dissecting these claims, it is useful to distinguish what are often considered the two distinct components of efficiency—allocative and technical efficiency (see Dowding and Mergoupis 2003). Allocative efficiency is about government responsiveness, that is, the extent to which government supplies the goods and services preferred by local residents. Technical efficiency, on the other hand, involves producing a higher level of output given the same level of input, thereby reducing the cost of public services.

The metropolitan reform tradition established its roots and gained prominence in the first half of the twentieth century with contributions from scholars such as Maxey (1922), Studenski (1930), Jones (1942), Gullick (1962), and others (see Stephens and Wikstrom 2000, for review of literature). These reformers pointed out that fragmentation leads to unequal level of services as a consequence of the unequal capacity of jurisdictions to generate internal fiscal resources. The absence of a region-wide government hinders the formulation of policies to address this problem and others at a regional level. Additionally, metropolitan fragmentation increases the cost of local government. Smaller governments are unable to realize economies of scale from expanded production, leading to higher average per unit price of a service. These governments also do not share service inputs (e.g., administrative staff) leading to duplicated efforts in delivering services and diseconomies of scope (see Boyne 1992a; Oakerson 1999; Foster 1997).

By the second half of the last century, scholars from the public choice approach to the study of urban government set in motion a vigorous defense of the fragmented structure of the local public sector. In his seminal work on the theory of public expenditures, Tiebout (1956) argued that fragmentation of local governments creates a market place where residents shop for political jurisdictions that offer different bundles of taxes and services.

Those who prefer different types of goods and are willing to pay for them can "vote with their feet" and relocate to the jurisdiction which offers the tax and service package that best satisfied their preferences. Tiebout, thus, contradicted the metropolitan reformers' assumption that residents in metropolitan areas want the same types or levels of services.

Oates (1972) approached the issue of government responsiveness in fragmented systems from the perspective of fiscal federalism. He argued that for services not characterized by diseconomies of scale and significant negative externalities (spillover of problems across jurisdictions), allocative efficiency is enhanced when lower tiers of government determine the level of public outputs within their jurisdictions. Given decision-making autonomy and better information about local preferences, decentralized local governing systems are better able to tailor goods and services according to the needs and demands of residents compared to centralized systems.

Subsequent scholars have extended Tiebout's arguments and proposed that the competition created by local government fragmentation also lowers public service costs. As local governments compete for tax-paying households and business firms in the public sector marketplace, they are forced to operate more efficiently (Ostrom, Tiebout, and Warren 1961). Local government growth is controlled in this case from the threat of exit by residents and businesses to relocate to other local jurisdictions with better services and lower taxes. Competition also limits the success of local bureaucrats who, for reasons of self-interest, desire bigger budgets (Niskanen 1975; Schneider 1986, 1989). In the Leviathan hypothesis, Brennan and Buchanan (1980) argue that the natural tendency of governments is to grow by exploiting taxpayers' lack of information about the true level of revenues local government collects and the costs of services. Decentralizing services ensures that residents and businesses will be better informed about the true price of public services.

Localists also responded to the regionalist argument that fragmentation leads to diseconomies of scale and scope. Ostrom, Tiebout, and Warren (1961) pointed out that local government performs two basic functions—production and provision. Production is the transformation of inputs into specific goods or services, while provision includes decisions about revenues, spending,

and the regulation of private activity for public purposes (see Oakerson 1999). The separation of these two functions means that local governments need not produce all the services demanded by residents. They can contract out production of public services to other organizations in the private sector and even to other local governments. This arrangement allows them to realize cost savings from economies of scope and scale, while retaining control over important policy decisions such as expenditures for a particular service (Bish and Ostrom 1973).

The Evidence

Much of the research on the impact of fragmentation has focused on establishing the relationship between governing structure and technical efficiency rather than allocative efficiency primarily because of the ease of measuring the former relative to the latter and the availability of data. Most of these studies measure technical efficiency as government spending or use another indicator of government size such as revenues or the number of employees.

There is also general agreement in the literature that fragmentation of general-purpose governments leads to lower spending, but fragmentation of special-purpose governments produces the opposite effect (see Nelson 1986; Zax 1989; Stansel 2006; Berry 2008; Eberts and Gronberg 1988; Craw 2008; Schneider 1986, 1989, among others). There is likely to be greater competition among multipurpose governments that offer different bundles of services, compared to special-purpose governments that offer single types of services (Eberts and Gronberg 1988; Boyne 1992a; Stansel 2006; Foster 1997). Also, since many single-purpose governments are created to provide capital-intensive services to a large population or area (e.g., water provision or reclamation), their fragmentation creates diseconomies of scale (Zax 1989; Dowding and Mergoupis 2003).

There are relatively few studies assessing the impact of the local public sector on allocative efficiency. Extant research focuses almost exclusively on citizen satisfaction using survey methodology (Dowding and Mergoupis 2003). In their study of police services, Ostrom and her colleagues found that residents of smaller jurisdictions expressed greater satisfaction with law enforcement compared to residents of bigger communities (Ostrom 1976; Ostrom and Smith 1976; Ostrom, Parks, and Whitaker 1978). However, DeHoog, Lowery, and Lyons (1990) argued that some of these studies only confirmed that city size affected citizen satisfaction with police services. Because the studies compared large and small jurisdictions within the same metropolitan area, no inferences could be made about the impact of local governing structure. DeHoog, Lowery, and Lyons (1990) assessed the effects of governing structure more specifically using survey data from five matched pairs of neighborhoods in consolidated versus fragmented metropolitan areas in Kentucky. They found that overall citizen satisfaction did not vary systematically between these two governmental settings.

SOCIAL CLASS AND RACIAL SEGREGATION

The Arguments

By the 1960s, regionalists added segregation as another negative consequence of government fragmentation (Hamilton, Miller, and Paytas 2004). In the social stratification-government inequality thesis (SSGI), Hill (1974) and Neiman(1976) suggested that local government fragmentation promotes and protects racial segregation and income inequality in metropolitan areas. With respect to social stratification, Hill (1974, 1557) argued that "political incorporation by class and status into municipal enclaves is an important institutional mechanism for creating and perpetuating inequalities among residents in metropolitan communities."

The original version of the thesis focused on the exclusionary powers of political jurisdictions, specifically, the use of zoning laws and other land use regulations to keep the poor, Blacks, and other ethnic minorities away from richer, White suburban communities (Hill 1974; Savitch and Vogel 2000; Lyons, Lowery, and DeHoog 1992; Burns 1994). Later revisions focused on the role of household residential choices in promoting segregation. Weiher (1991) and Lowery (2000), for example, argued that the presence of numerous governments not only creates a competitive market for public goods as argued by Tiebout (1956) but allows citizens to pursue preferred lifestyle choices, including the desire to live in a socially and racially homogenous community. Weiher (1991) noted that local governments often recruit mobile households by advertising the racial and socioeconomic characteristics of their own community compared to others.

With respect to government inequality, the SSGI thesis predicts that segregation by race and social class will lead to the mismatch of fiscal capacity and service needs. The sorting out process of residents and businesses in a region leaves central cities and many older suburbs with a disproportionate share of needy populations, but fewer fiscal resources to meet rising demand for public services (Hill 1974; Ihlan-feldt 1999). The resulting fiscal disparity exacerbates inequity in the distribution of services across the metropolitan region due to the separation of needs and resources (Lyons, Lowery, and DeHoog 1992). Lowery (2000) also argued that lower spending in highly fragmented regions is likely to be caused, not by increased government competition but by extreme concentrations of poverty.

Public choice scholars take a different view of the problem of segregation in metropolitan areas and propose that government fragmentation may actually empower poor and racial minorities. With few barriers to fragmentation, Blacks and the poor can organize their own autonomous communities, receive services they prefer for lower costs, and have greater access to community decision-making processes (Ostrom 1983; Ostrom, Bish, and Ostrom 1988; and Bish and Ostrom 1973). Consolidation is not the answer to spatial racial segregation because the inclusion of predominantly White suburban areas will dilute Black voting strength in central cities, and services would be more likely designed to meet White residents' demands (Zimmerman 1970).

One solution to the problem of fiscal disparities among local jurisdictions is to transfer more fiscal resources to poor governments through intergovernmental grants or interlocal resource sharing (Ostrom 1972; Oakerson 1999; Parks and Oakerson 2000). Other public choice scholars, however, have negative views of fiscal transfer because it violates the principle of fiscal equivalence. Fiscal equivalence means that citizens get what they pay for and must pay for what they get (Oakerson 1999). Brennan and Buchanan (1980) argued that this principle is violated when governments receive high levels of intergovernmental aid in which the costs of public services are not entirely borne by local residents. This situation creates the illusion that the tax price of the service is lower than what it actually is, which results in residents demanding more of that service thereby inducing government growth. Other scholars also point out that fiscal transfers that shift resources from wealthy to poor jurisdictions are not likely to be agreed voluntarily by all jurisdictions affected by this arrangement (Oliver 2001).

The Evidence

There seems to be greater agreement in the literature that a large number of local governments contributes to racial segregation at both the neighborhood and city levels (see Morgan and Morescal 1999; Weiher 1991; Rusk 1993; Burns 1994; Altshuler et al. 1999), but whether or not government fragmentation leads to economic segregation needs additional empirical testing as the evidence is quite mixed. In his qualitative study of Los Angeles metropolitan area, Miller (1981) observed that the creation of new suburbs facilitated sorting by both race and income over time. Also, research by Weiher (1991) showed that segregation by race, income, and education from 1960 to 1980 occurred increasingly at the city level compared to the neighborhood level. However, other studies that focused on city-suburb income differentials failed to find any statistically significant relationship between measures of fragmentation and income differences among residents (see Logan and Schneider 1982; Bollens 1986; Morgan and Morescal, 1999). Stein (1987) found that fragmentation of municipal governments increased residential sorting by education only, as sorting by race and income was not statistically significant in his study of 224 metropolitan areas in forty-one states. But his study may have underestimated the degree of income and racial homogeneity in metropolitan areas because of the exclusion of cities with population under 5,000 which are likely to be more homogeneous than larger municipalities.

Other studies of the SSGI thesis focused on the mismatch of service needs and fiscal capacity, especially between central cities and suburbs. Ladd and Yinger (1989) provided evidence that expenditure needs of large cities indeed grew faster than their revenue-raising capacities in the 1980s. Bahl (1994) and Oakland (1994) also concluded that population sorting had left central cities with a disproportionate share of needy populations, but it is unclear if these findings can be attributed to excessive government fragmentation. Morgan and Morescal (1999), for example, found no statistically significant relationship between the number of cities in a metropolitan area and the fiscal health of the central city. Interestingly, they also found that the higher the central-city share of metropolitan population (greater consolidation), the worse the financial condition of the central city. They argued this event occurs because smaller, central cities are more fiscally vibrant due to competition from surrounding jurisdictions. But one can also argue that smaller cities have lower spending needs and, therefore, lower risk of fiscal stress.

URBAN SPRAWL

The Arguments

Over the last forty years, the public choice case for fragmentation has been the orthodoxy in both academic and policy discourses on metropolitan government organization. Compared to regionalists, localists have contributed considerably more to the literature on the relationship between local governing structure and urban service delivery (Hendrick, Jimenez, and Lal 2008). On the policy front, the regionalists' prescription for local government consolidation has been consistently rejected by voters (Pagano 1999). Nevertheless, by the 1990s, a new case for regionalism8 was made that moved beyond service delivery concerns. These arguments emphasized not only equity issues but also the perceived inability of fragmented governments to deal with metropolitan-wide issues such as urban sprawl.

Controlling urban sprawl has been the primary issue in many local elections. But Downs (1994) argued that growth-related problems are regional in nature rather than local. They represent problems that spillover from one jurisdiction to others, and their resolution provides region-wide and individual benefits. But because of their scope, these problems cannot be addressed solely by individual local governments.

Fragmentation has been blamed for making it difficult to formulate a coordinated response to urban sprawl and also for causing sprawl itself (Carruthers 2003; Carruthers and Ulfarsson 2002; Dye and McGuire 2000). Fragmentation can lead to urban sprawl through different mechanisms. First, fragmentation divides land use authority, allowing municipalities to implement low-density zoning to limit growth within their boundaries and control fiscally undesirable land uses such as multi-family residences and public housing (Carruthers 2003;

Downs 1994). Residential and commercial demands in the region are then accommodated through the development of less expensive land in the urban fringes where there are fewer constraints on land use. Second, fragmentation intensifies competition for the property tax base, and local governments are likely to encourage development of land in outlying areas to capture the tax gains (Dye and McGuire 2000). Third, regional special districts that provide infrastructure to areas with poorer economies of scale, and which are subsidized by taxpayers from across the region, facilitate new commercial and housing developments in outlying areas (Carruthers and Ulfarsson 2002).

Some observers argue that urban sprawl influences government expenditures for public services (see Frank 1989; Burchell et al. 1998, for literature review). Low-density and spatially expansive development patterns require large investments to extend roadways and other types of infrastructure-related services over long distances to reach communities in the urban fringes (Ladd 1998; Burchell 1998). Additionally, urban sprawl can lead to diseconomies of scale in consumption for services such as police protection and public education as it lowers the density of individual consumers (Carruthers and Ulfarsson 2002).

Localists have yet to launch a vigorous response to the regionalist argument that fragmentation has become an institutional barrier to addressing metropolitan-wide issues. According to Lowery (2000, 2001), public choice scholars recognize that these problems exist, but they question whether the solutions offered by regionalists are the only viable alternatives. Localists prefer a greater role for state governments and also emphasize the role of voluntary cooperative agreements (institutional collective action) among local governments to resolve common-pool problems (see Oakerson 1999; Ostrom 1990; Feiock 2009; Feiock and Sholz 2009).

The Evidence

The majority of the evidence linking governing structure and sprawl demonstrates a positive relationship. In a study of 822 metropolitan counties, Caruthers (2003) found that fragmentation of municipal and special district governments increased growth outside of incorporated areas. Focusing on more than 100 of the largest metropolitan areas in the United States, Dye and McGuire

(2000) concluded that municipal fragmentation increased urbanized land areas and the share of population in collar counties. Carruthers and Ulfarsson (2002) provided empirical evidence that fragmentation of general- and special-purpose governments had a two-way relationship with urban sprawl. Tiebout sorting facilitated the formation of new communities in unincorporated areas, which in turn, led to the creation of new local governments to insure provision of services. Razin and Rosentraub's (2000) analysis had different results. They found that residential sprawl had significant positive effects on fragmentation, but fragmentation did not predict sprawl.

There also is growing empirical evidence that sprawl increases government spending. Burchell's (1997) study of South Carolina concluded that sprawl would cost taxpayers $56 billion over two decades for statewide infrastructures. Modeling the impact of urban form on service expenditures as a linear relationship, Carruthers and Ulfarsson (2003) found that per capita total direct expenditures and spending for specific services such as capital facilities, roadways, police protection, libraries, and education had an inverse relationship with density and a direct correlation with the spatial extent of urbanized land. Other studies arrived at a different conclusion.

For example, Ladd (1998) found that the relationship between density and spending was U-shaped with expenditures declining with an increase in urban density but then increasing sharply in very dense areas. Ladd (1998) argued that as development becomes more compact, congestion problems such as increased crime rates or traffic are likely to arise necessitating a larger budget to support the delivery of services. As development becomes more scattered, extending the reach of infrastructure services and diseconomies of scale in consumption eventually lead to higher government expenditures.

FUTURE RESEARCH

The century-old debate between regionalists and localists has generated a considerable body of theoretical and empirical literature from which state governments can draw as they consider the most effective way of organizing their local governments. The literature has identified certain trends regarding the effects of the local public sector structure on service delivery, segregation, and urban sprawl, but more studies are needed to clarify a number of issues that are relevant to both state and local governments.

From the urban service delivery literature, we know that the fragmentation of multipurpose governments leads to lower public sector spending. It is a mistake, however, to equate lower government spending with improved technical efficiency. As Boyne (1992a, 343) correctly pointed out, "Inferences on efficiency can be drawn directly from evidence on expenditure only if it is assumed that variations in output quantity and quality are not related to variations in spending." For example, the government in a more fragmented system may be spending less because it has implemented cuts in the level of services or may be providing the same level of service but has sacrificed quality (Dowding, John, and Biggs 1994). Clearly, researchers need to employ better measures of technical efficiency.

Additionally, although the finding that bigger jurisdictions spend more compared to smaller ones may mean that they are operating inefficiently, there are other equally plausible explanations. In particular, bigger jurisdictions may be undertaking redistributive policies to compensate for the under provision of support programs by smaller governments that fear attracting the mobile poor (Oates 1985; Dowding, John, and Biggs 1994). Future research needs to carefully explore the underlying mechanisms that explain higher spending in more consolidated systems.

The empirical evidence on the effects of government fragmentation or consolidation on citizen satisfaction with services also is not conclusive. One issue is that individual studies often focus on different types of services. Because satisfaction and other impacts may vary by type of service, it is difficult to draw broad conclusions from this research. Other than police services, we know very little about the effects of government structure on citizen satisfaction with other public services. Stronger research designs, such as that used by DeHoog, Lowery, and Lyons (1990), will help clearly establish the effects of governing structure in this area more clearly.

The unfortunate consequences of government fragmentation on racial distribution in metropolitan areas have been well documented in the literature. More work needs to be done to ascertain if fragmentation leads to income-based spatial segregation in metropolitan areas that, in turn, causes a mismatch of population

services needs and the fiscal capacity of jurisdictions to provide necessary services. Specifically, few scholars have focused on the effects of government fragmentation on the capacity of suburban communities to finance services from own-source revenues. Does fragmentation result in unequal level of services, which in turn leads to conditions among subsets of the suburban population that threaten the health and safety of these citizens? Do jurisdictions with very poor fiscal opportunities face conditions they cannot improve without intervention and financial subsidy? Answers to such questions are most relevant to state governments as they make decisions about whether to lower or even eliminate local grants and shared revenue to resolve their own financial crises.

More and more researchers are focusing on the relationship between the regional governing structure and urban development patterns, and evidence is mounting that fragmentation of both municipal and special district governments contributes to urban sprawl. The problem for local governments in regions with a lot of sprawl is that it generates additional costs associated with traffic congestion and pollution (Ewing, Pendall, and Chen 2002), environmental degradation, and the loss of open space (Howell-Moroney 2008). More recently, studies have shown that sprawl can also lead to higher government expenditures for certain public services (Carruthers and Ulfarsson 2003), especially public infrastructure (Burchell 1997; also see Burchell et al. 1998).

Efforts to understand how excessive urban sprawl and its associated costs can be addressed will surely benefit from more contributions by scholars in the public choice tradition. In particular, the emphasis of localists on governance (which focuses on voluntary, self-regulating, and cooperative action), rather than government (which emphasizes hierarchy and formal authority) to address metropolitan-wide issues needs further empirical testing. Assuming voluntary, cooperative action is possible, will it be effective in addressing problems such as urban sprawl or will it be limited to solving easy problems with fewer conflicting interests and outcomes? What conditions or institutions will promote voluntary collaborative arrangements to solve regional problems, yet maintain the advantages of decentralized and independent local governance? Answers to these questions will be of most interest to local governments, as they consider more ways of collaborating to deliver services in response to the Great Recession.

REFERENCES

Altshuler, Alan, William Morrill, Harold Wolman, and Faith Mitchell, eds. 1999. *Governance and opportunity in metropolitan America.* Washington, DC: National Academy Press.

Bahl, Roy W. 1994. Metropolitan fiscal disparities. *Cityscape: A Journal of Policy Development and Research* 1:293-306.

Berry, Christopher. 2008. Piling on: The fiscal effects of jurisdictional overlap. *American Journal of Political Science* 52:802-20.

Bish, Robert L., and Vincent Ostrom. 1973. *Understanding urban government: Metropolitan reform reconsidered.* Washington, DC: American Enterprise Institute.

Bollens, Scott A. 1986. A political-ecological analysis of income inequality in the metropolitan area. *Urban Affairs Quarterly* 22:221-41.

Boyne, George A. 1992a. Local government structure and performance: Lessons from America. *Public Administration* 70:333-57.

Boyne, George A. 1992b. Is there a relationship between fragmentation and local government cost? *Urban Affairs Quarterly* 28:317-22.

Brennan, Geoffrey, and James Buchanan. 1980. *The power to tax: Analytical foundations of a fiscal constitution.* Cambridge, UK: Cambridge University Press.

Burchell, Robert W. 1997. *South Carolina infrastructure study: Projection of statewide infrastructure costs 1995-2015.* New Brunswick, NJ: Center for Urban Policy Research, Rutgers University.

Burchell, Robert W., Naveed A. Shad, David Listokin, Hilary Phillips, Anthony Downs, Samuel Seskin, Judy S. Davis, Terry Moore, David Helton, and Michelle Gall. 1998. *The costs of sprawl revisited.* Transportation Cooperative Research Program Report 39. Washington, DC: National Academy Press.

Burns, Nancy. 1994. *The formation of American local governments: Private values in public institutions.* New York: Oxford University Press.

Campbell, Rebecca J. 2004. Leviathan and fiscal illusion in local government overlapping jurisdictions. *Public Choice* 120:301-29.

Carruthers, John I. 2003. Growth at the fringe: The impact of political fragmentation in United States metropolitan areas. *Papers in Regional Science* 82:475-99.

Carruthers, John I., and Gudmundur F. Ulfarsson. 2002. Fragmentation and sprawl: Evidence from interregional analysis. *Growth and Change* 33:312-40.

Carruthers, John I., and Gudmundur F. Ulfarsson. 2003. Urban sprawl and the cost of public services. *Environment and Planning B: Planning and Design* 30:503-22.

Craw, Michael. 2008. Taming the local leviathan: Institutional and economic constraints on municipal budgets. *Urban Affairs Review* 43: 663-90.

DeHoog, Ruth Hoogland, David Lowery, and William E. Lyons. 1990. Citizen satisfaction with local governance: A test of individual, jurisdictional, and city specific explanations. *Journal of Politics* 52:807-37.

Dolan, Drew E. 1990. Local government fragmentation: Does it drive up the cost of government. *Urban Affairs Quarterly* 26:28-45.

Dowding, Keith, Peter John, and Stephen Biggs. 1994. Tiebout: A survey of the empirical literature. *Urban Studies* 31:767-97.

Dowding, Keith, and Thanos Mergoupis. 2003. Fragmentation, fiscal mobility, and efficiency. *Journal of Politics* 65:1190-207.

Downs, Anthony. 1994. *New visions for metropolitan America.* Washington, DC: Brookings Institution.

Dye, Richard F., and Therese J. McGuire. 2000. Property taxes, schools, and sprawl. *State Tax Notes* 29: 1899-908.

Eberts, Randall W., and Timothy J. Gronberg. 1988. Can competition among local governments constrain government spending? *Federal Reserve Bank of Cleveland Economic Review* 1:2-9.

Ewing, Reid, Rolf Pendall, and Don Chen. 2002. *Measuring sprawl and its impact.* Washington, DC: Smart Growth America.

Feiock, Richard, ed. 2004. *Metropolitan governance: Conflict, competition, and cooperation.* Washington, DC: Georgetown University Press.

Feiock, Richard. 2009. Metropolitan governance and institutional collective action. *Urban Affairs Review* 44:356-77.

Feiock, Richard C., and John T. Sholz. 2009. *Self-organizing federalism: Collaborative mechanisms to mitigate institutional collective action dilemmas.* London: Cambridge University Press.

Forbes, Kevin F., and Ernest M. Zampelli. 1989. Is Leviathan a mythical beast? *American Economic Review* 79:568-77.

Foster, Kathryn A. 1997. *The political economy of special purpose governments.* Washington, DC: Georgetown University Press.

Frank, James. 1989. *The costs of alternative development patterns: A review of the literature.* Washington, DC: The Urban Land Institute.

Gullick, Luther Halsey. 1962. *The metropolitan problem and American ideas.* New York, NY: Alfred H. Knopf.

Hamilton, David, David Miller, and Jerry Paytas. 2004. Exploring the horizontal and vertical dimensions of the governing of metropolitan regions. *Urban Affairs Review* 40:147-18.

Hendrick, Rebecca, Benedict Jimenez, and Kamna Lal. 2008. Does local government fragmentation affect local spending? Paper presented at the Association for Budgeting and Financial Management (ABFM) Annual Conference, Chicago, Illinois, October 23-25.

Hill, Richard Child. 1974. Separate and unequal: Governmental inequality in the metropolis. *American Political Science Review* 68:1557-68.

Hoene, and Michael A. Pagano. 2009. City fiscal conditions 2009. *Research Brief on America's Cities* 2:1-11.

Howell-Moroney, Michael. 2008. The Tiebout hypothesis 50 years later: Lessons and lingering challenges for metropolitan governance in the 21st century. *Public Administration Review* 68:97-109.

Ihlanfeldt, Keith R. 1999. The geography of economic and social opportunity in metropolitan areas. In *Governance and opportunity in metropolitan America,* eds. A. Altshuler, W. Morrill, H. Wolman, and F. Mitchell, 213-52. Washington, DC: National Academy Press.

Jones, Victor. 1942. *Metropolitan government.* Chicago: University of Chicago Press.

Ladd, Helen F. 1998. Land use regulation as a fiscal tool. In *Local government tax and land use policies in the United States: Understanding the links,* eds. H Ladd, 55-74. Cambridge, MA: Lincoln Institute of Land Policy.

Ladd, Helen F., and J. Milton Yinger. 1989. *America's ailing cities: Fiscal health and the design of urban policy.* Baltimore, MD: John Hopkins University.

Logan, John. R., and Mark Schneider. 1982. Governmental organizations and city/suburb income inequality, 1960-1970. *Urban Affairs Quarterly* 17:303-18.

Lowery, David. 2000. A transactions costs model of metropolitan governance: Allocation versus redistribution in urban America. *Journal of Public Administration Research and Theory* 10:49-78.

Lowery, David. 2001. Metropolitan governance structures from a neoprogressive perspective. *Swiss Political Science Review* 7:130-6.

Lyons, William E., David Lowery, and Ruth Hoogland DeHoog. 1992. *The politics of dissatisfaction: Citizens, services, and urban institutions.* New York: M.E. Sharpe.

Maxey, Chester. 1922. The political integration of metropolitan communities. *National Municipal Review* 11:229-53.

Miller, Garry J. 1981. *Cities by contract.* Cambridge, MA: MIT Press.

Morgan, David R., and Patrice Mareschal. 1999. Central-city/suburban inequality and metropolitan political fragmentation. *Urban Affairs Review* 34:578-95.

Neiman, Mark. 1976. Communication: Social stratification and government inequality. *American Political Science Review* 70:149-80.

Nelson, Michael A. 1986. An empirical analysis of state and local tax structure in the context of the leviathan model of government. *Public Choice* 49:283-94.

Niskanen, William A. 1971. *Bureaucracy and representative government.* Chicago: Aldine-Atherton.

Niskanen, William A. 1975. Bureaucrats and politicians. *Journal of Law and Economics* 18:617-59.

Oakerson, Ronald. 1999. *Governing local public economies: Creating the civic metropolis.* Oakland, CA: Institute of Contemporary Studies Press.

Oakland, William. 1994. Recognizing and correcting for fiscal disparities: A critical analysis. In *Fiscal equalization for state and local government finance,* eds. John Anderson, 1-19. Westport, CT: Praeger.

Oates, Wallace. 1972. *Fiscal federalism.* NewYork: Hardcourt, Brace, Jovanovich Inc. Oates, Wallace. 1985. Searching for leviathan: An empirical study. *American Economic Review* 75:748-57.

Oliver, Eric J. 2001. *Democracy in suburbia.* Princeton: Princeton University Press.

Ostrom, Elinor. 1972. Metropolitan reform: Propositions derived from two traditions. *Social Science Quarterly* 53:474-93. Reprinted in *Readings from the workshop in political theory and policy analysis*, ed. M. McGinnis. 1999, 139-62. AnnArbor, MI: University of Michigan Press.

Ostrom, Elinor. 1976. *The delivery of urban services.* Beverly Hills, CA: Sage.

Ostrom, Elinor. 1983. The social stratification-government inequality thesis explored. *Urban Affairs Quarterly* 19:91-112.

Ostrom, Elinor. 1990. *Governing the commons: The evolution of institutions for collective action.* Cambridge, UK: Cambridge University Press.

Ostrom, Elinor, and Dennis Smith. 1976. On the fate of 'Lilliputs' in metropolitan policing. *Public Administration Review* 36:192-99.

Ostrom, Elinor, Robert B. Parks, and Gordon P. Whitaker. 1978. *Patterns of metropolitan policing.* Cambridge, MA: Ballinger Publishing Company.

Ostrom, Vincent. 1973. *The intellectual crisis in American public administration.* Tuscaloosa, AL: University of Alabama Press.

Ostrom, Vincent, Charles Tiebout, and Robert Warren. 1961. The organization of government in metropolitan areas: A theoretical inquiry. *American Political Science Review* 55:831-42.

Ostrom, Vincent, Robert Bish, and Elinor Ostrom. 1988. *Local government in the United States.* San Francisco, CA: Institute for Contemporary Studies.

Parks, Roger, and Ronald Oakerson. 2000. Regionalism, localism, and metropolitan governance: Suggestions from the research program on local public economies. *State and Local Government Review* 32:169-79.

Pagano, Michael A. 1999. Metropolitan limits: Intrametropolitan disparities and governance in US laboratories of democracy. In *Governance and opportunity in metropolitan America*, eds. A. Altshuler, W.

Morrill, H. Wolman, and F. Mitchell, 253-95. Washington, DC: National Academy Press.

Razin, Eran, and Mark Rosentraub. 2000. Are fragmentation and sprawl interlinked? North American evidence. *Urban Affairs Review* 35:821-36.

Rusk, David. 1993. *Cities without suburbs.* Washington DC: Woodrow Wilson Press. Savitch, H. V., and Ronald K. Vogel. 2000. Paths to new regionalism. *State and Local Government Review* 32:158-68.

Schneider, Mark. 1986. Fragmentation and the growth of local government. *Public Choice* 48:255.

Schneider, Mark. 1989. *The competitive city: The political economy of suburbia.* Pittsburgh, PA: University of Pittsburgh Press.

Stansel, Dean. 2006. Interjurisdictional competition and local government spending in U.S. metropolitan areas. *Public Finance Review* 34: 173-94.

Stephens, G. Ross, and Nelson Wikstrom. 2000. *Metropolitan government and governance: Theoretical perspectives, empirical analysis, and the future.* New York: Oxford University Press.

Stein, Robert. M. 1987. Tiebout's sorting hypothesis. *Urban Affairs Quarterly* 23:140-66.

Studenski, Paul. 1930. *The government of metropolitan areas in the United States.* New York: National Municipal League.

Tiebout, Charles. 1956. A pure theory of local expenditures. *Journal of Political Economy* 44:416-24.

Turnbull, Geoffrey K., and Salpie S. Djoundourian. 1993. Overlapping jurisdictions: Substitutes or complements? *Public Choice* 75:231-45.

Weiher, Gregory R. 1991. *The fractured metropolis: Political fragmentation and metropolitan segregation.* Albany, NY: SUNY Press.

Zax, Jeffrey S. 1989. Is there a leviathan in your neighborhood? *American Economic Review* 79:560-67.

Zimmerman, Joseph F. 1970. Metropolitan reform in the U.S.: An overview. *Public Administration Review* 30:531-43.

30

Colorado Springs' Do-It-Yourself Government

Zach Patton

Property taxes did not go up in Colorado Springs. As a result, pools are closed, street medians are not mowed and traffic lights have been turned off. With no money, public services have become a do-it-yourself project.

O n a hot afternoon in late summer, the city pool at Monument Valley Park in Colorado Springs, Colo., usually would be teeming with children and families—the kids splashing, swimming and soaking up the August sun. But this year, the pool stayed quiet. Budget cuts forced the city to close all its swimming facilities. A few of them were taken over by a private swim club, but the ones that couldn't find a backer, like Monument Valley, remained shuttered.

"This place ought to be packed," says Kim King, administration manager of the Parks, Recreation and Cultural Services Department, as she stands outside the fenced-off pool in Monument Valley Park. "This should be crawling with kids. But there's nobody here."

Nearby, King points to a set of public restrooms housed in a small Spanish-style building clad in yellow stucco. Those are closed too, with signs on the door: "NOTICE: Due to budget reductions, this facility is closed indefinitely." Opposite that building is a moderate-sized pond with a small island in the middle. Today, the pond stands empty. The city can't afford to maintain it, and the water's been reduced to a stagnant, scummy puddle.

Times are tough in the Springs, as veteran residents call it. Like cities throughout the country, this town has been hit hard by the recession. But its fiscal problems are especially severe. The city is famously right-wing, and property taxes here are some of the lowest in the nation—in 2008, the per capita property tax was about $55. City revenue instead comes mostly from local sales taxes. As a consequence, Colorado Springs is feeling the downturn's effects faster and more sharply than other cities. At the close of 2009, the city found itself facing a nearly $40 million revenue gap for this year.

From *Governing,* September 2010.

So the Springs slashed its budget and enacted a series of severe service cuts to save money. One-third of the city's streetlights were turned off to reduce electricity costs. The city stopped mowing the medians in the streets. (At one point earlier this summer, the medians were so overgrown with weeds that the city was in violation of its own code for property maintenance.)

The parks department was hit especially hard its budget was gutted from $17 million in 2009 to just $3 million this year. In addition to closing the pools and restroom facilities, the city pulled out all the trash cans from its parks, since it could no longer afford to collect the garbage. Four community centers and three museums were put on the chopping block, although private donations and some emergency public funds are keeping them open for the rest of the year. With maintenance money wiped out, the vast majority of the city's parks were left to wither and brown in the summer heat. Former flower beds downtown are now just messy tangles of weeds.

And it's not just aesthetics. As money has gotten tighter over the past two years, the city has cut some 550 employees from its work force by eliminating positions or through outright layoffs. Of the 1,600 municipal employees left, 1,200 are police officers or firefighters. Municipal bus service has been reduced by 100,000 hours, meaning buses no longer run in the evenings or on weekends a problem in a place where the vast majority of transit riders have no alternative way to get to work. The police department auctioned its three helicopters on the Internet. Spending on infrastructure projects has essentially ceased, and the city faces a $700 million backlog in capital needs.

It's a crisis, to be sure. But in this politically conservative, tax-averse town, it's also something of an experiment. After the impending cuts were announced in fall 2009, the city put a property tax increase on the November ballot. The measure was soundly defeated. Thanks to Colorado Springs' Taxpayer Bill of Rights (TABOR), which actually predates the state of Colorado's TABOR by a year, any proposed tax increase must be voted on by the citizens. With their vote, residents made it clear they'd rather suffer service cuts than see their taxes raised.

As a result, other cities are watching, waiting to see if this exercise in stripped-down government might actually serve as a model during tough economic times. City Councilmember Sean Paige is one person who thinks scaling back government's role in the Springs is a good

thing. "People in this city want government sticking to the fundamentals," he says. "There's a crybaby contention in town that says, 'We need to raise taxes and we need to get rid of TABOR.' But I think the citizens have made it clear that this is the government people are willing to pay for right now. So let's make it work."

VOLUNTEER EFFORTS REPLACE LOST SERVICES

Colorado Springs' service cuts made national headlines when they were rolled out this past spring and summer. After reading the media stories, one half-expects the city to look like some urban dystopia: fallen trees in the streets, boarded-up buildings, roads left dark by switched-off streetlights, drivers swerving around giant, unfilled potholes.

But when actually walking around Colorado Springs, things don't look that bad. The city is hemmed in to the west by Pikes Peak and other spires of the Front Range (the original "purple mountain majesties" in *America the Beautiful,* which was written here in 1893). Take away the mountains, though, and Colorado Springs could be any mid-sized American city. Downtown consists of a clutch of dun- and clay-colored mid-rises along broad, flat avenues. There's a small, walkable strip of bars and outdoor cafes.

This city of about 420,000 residents also has something of an earthy, hippie side: Acacia Park, a leafy square at the north end of downtown, is ringed by art galleries, an indie music store, a Tibetan imports place, a hookah bar and an Afghan kabob joint. There's even a feeling of progressive urban planning that belies the town's Libertarian reputation. More than 70 miles of on-street bicycle lanes thread their way across the city, and the city manages another 100 miles of urban trails for jogging and hiking. Green spaces downtown are filled with eclectic sculptures by local artists.

In fact, it's easy to walk around the place and wonder what all the fuss is about. So what if there are a few weeds in the medians? Or if some of the streetlights have been turned off? Is that such a price to pay for low taxes and limited government?

Colorado Springs may have gained a reputation as a bastion of right-wing values and small-government ideals, but the city hasn't always been quite so conservative. Thanks to several military bases nearby, as well as the United States Air Force Academy, there's long been a Republican bent to the area. But it wasn't until about 20 years ago that the Springs began to shift to the Christian right. In the 1980s, in a bid to diversify the area's economy, the city began actively courting non-profit organizations to relocate to Colorado Springs. Dozens of groups moved in, especially religious ones.

At one point, Colorado Springs was home to the national headquarters of more than 80 religious organizations, including, most famously, the socially conservative Focus on the Family, which relocated there in 1991. By 1993, Focus on the Family ran a 45-acre campus on the north side of town, with 1,200 employees. Other, similar groups followed, earning Colorado Springs the nickname of "the Evangelical Vatican."

As local politics have swung to the right, Colorado Springs has become more virulently opposed to taxes: Since 1990, the local property tax rate has plunged 41 percent. The local TABOR law, implemented in 1991, imposes an inflation-based cap on the amount of revenue the city can collect. Any revenue over that limit must be returned to taxpayers. That's kept the city government lean and small, even before the recent round of cuts.

The proliferation of non-profit groups has had another effect—a strong current of can-do volunteerism in the community. As the government has scaled back its services, private organizations have, in many cases, stepped in. In addition to the citizen groups that have taken over some of the pools and one of the city's community centers, companies and non-profit foundations have helped raise funds for visitors' centers and other facilities. At the Phantom Canyon Brewing Company in the center of town, the front of the menu implores diners to "Save the Fountain!" by purchasing a new signature ale—some of the proceeds go to keeping the water turned on at The Continuum - Julie Penrose Fountain, a giant metal loop that rains water down on kids in America the Beautiful Park. The city cut funding for the fountain a couple years ago.

As the cuts worsened this year, the city has increasingly relied on these volunteers' efforts. By lining up residents to "adopt a trash can," the city's been able to return about one-third of the rubbish bins that were removed from municipal parks. Citizens can "adopt a street light" on their block and have it turned back on by paying a donation — between $100 to $240, depending on the type of light. The city has even discussed an "adopt a median" program, recruiting residents to trim the medians with their own lawnmowers.

"This city has really stepped up, and I'm proud of it," Paige says. "It's almost like we're moving to a do-it-yourself model."

But that's a concern for some, including Paige's fellow City Councilmember Jan Martin, who authored last fall's proposed tax increase that would have covered this year's shortfall and prevented the service cuts. "Right now, in this crisis, we've sort of lost the sense of the common good," she says. "There's a real sense of, 'I'll take care of mine. You take care of yours.'"

Look a few years down the road, she says, and the city's rich areas will prosper while the poorer sections of town will suffer. "The parts of the community that can't afford services will continue to deteriorate," Martin says. "And the neighborhoods that can afford to pay for street lights, parks, trash removal and medians will continue to prosper and be beautiful. I worry we're creating a city of haves and have-nots."

BUDGET CUTS AND PUBLIC SAFETY IMPLICATIONS

For now, the outpouring of volunteer support has mitigated some of the most visible impacts of Colorado Springs' budget cuts. But there are bigger, longer-term issues, says Interim City Manager Steve Cox. "We get a lot of attention for the trash cans and the street lights, but that's just scratching the surface. There are deeper problems than that."

One of those problems is public safety. Everyone agrees that the police and fire departments should be last on the list of cuts. Still, those departments have had to reduce services as well. In addition to selling off helicopters, the police department has slashed its ranks, says Chief Richard Myers. Property detectives have been cut by one-third, and the department has completely wiped out some units, including its fugitive-investigation group. "We've eliminated entire street teams out of our regional drug unit. In 2011, we're significantly shrinking the number of school resource officers. Our specialty units are just imploding."

All in all, the department is down about 80 officers, from a high of 689 a few years ago. That's a significant cut, but what's worse is that the force already was stretched thin. "Most police departments in comparable cities would have 750, 800, maybe 900 police officers," Myers says. "Now we're down in the low 600s, and the city isn't shrinking." Even more challenging, Myers says, is that Colorado

Springs covers such a large area of land. Geographically, the city is huge: Boston, Miami, Minneapolis and San Francisco could all fit within its borders.

With a dwindling number of cops serving a growing population across a vast tract of land, residents are feeling the cuts. Officers no longer can respond to as many incidents in person — if someone breaks into a car or steals a kid's bike, the police just take the crime report over the phone. And it's unlikely they'll have the resources to follow up on it, Myers says. "We're struggling with the fact that so many people can be victimized by property crimes and have it treated more as an insurance report and a cursory tick mark on the tote board, rather than us helping them try to solve their crime."

Technology is a problem, too. The police department already was lagging in technology before the latest cuts. Investing in them now would be impossible. For example, Myers points to in-car video cameras, a tech upgrade he implemented at his previous two posts as police chief in other cities. "That's standard in police departments; it's a routine tool in law enforcement," he says. "We don't have a single one in a squad car here."

Despite all the reductions, Myers says he can't point to an uptick in crime. But he worries about the longer-term implications of a bare-bones force. Myers says he firmly believes that a proactive, decentralized style of policing, as it was proven in the 1990s, reduces crime, increases the public's confidence in the police and increases the collaborative kind of policing where citizens and police work together for long-term solutions. "And to now see us moving more and more and more to almost a completely reactive style of policing is just difficult for me to tolerate."

Still, he says he recognizes that tough times call for tough measures, and if this is the police department Colorado Springs is willing to pay for, so be it. "My mourning period is over, and the focus now is on redefining the new norm. We're past doing more with less," he says. "We're doing less with less."

A NEW MODEL OF GOVERNMENT?

Colorado Springs' fiscal day of reckoning has arrived. But the reason other cities are watching the Springs is because what happens here isn't necessarily just an extreme experiment in do-it-yourself government — it could be the future.

Thanks to the city's heavy reliance on sales taxes, the revenue crisis was brought to bear last year. In other municipalities, where revenues rely more on property taxes, the problems may only be beginning. "Cities are really going to be hard hit at least through 2011," says Christiana McFarland, director of finance and economic development programming for the National League of Cities (NLC). Because property taxes are based on periodic assessments, there's an 18-to-24-month lag before the city feels the full effect of the downturn. "We're anticipating property tax revenues will take a huge hit this coming year."

And cities already have been making cuts, according to NLC surveys. More than two-thirds have delayed investments in infrastructure or capital improvements. Another 22 percent have made cuts in public safety; 27 percent have reduced their spending in human services; and a full 71 percent have already been forced to make cuts in personnel. "With the budgets already cut down to the bone," McFarland says, "they're going to start digging into the marrow."

The big question is whether the cuts are part of a crunch-time crisis, or whether they represent a new era in smaller government. For her part, McFarland says she doesn't think the Colorado Springs model can be a long-term solution. "Cities need to get back to a basic level of delivering services, particularly in public safety."

Meanwhile in Colorado Springs, the crisis is spawning broader conversations about what citizens expect government to be. "It really brings you to some fundamental questions that elected representatives should be asking themselves," Martin says. "It forces you to prioritize and decide, what is the role of government? And what services should the city be providing?"

One thing seems certain in the Springs: The service cuts are here to stay. Thanks to TABOR, it could be years before the city is even able to return to 2009 spending levels. The pools may reopen and the medians may get mowed, but those services will likely be performed by the private sector. As public funds start to trickle back in — and local sales tax revenues have been on the uptick so far this year — they'll go toward rebuilding the police department and adding back some of the bus routes. And for many, that's just the way things should be. "I think we're plowing fertile new ground here," Paige says. "And I think we can make it work."

31

The Big Apple: Urban Incubator

Alan Greenblatt

From increased bike lanes to restricting salt intake, New York City has been an innovative leader of municipal policy during a time where other local governments are cutting services and freezing new programming.

Michael Bloomberg wants you to cut down on your salt. The mayor of New York City doesn't really plan to control how much salt you shake onto your fries; instead, his National Salt Reduction Initiative targets packaged and restaurant foods that account for nearly 80 percent of the average American's sodium intake. It may seem like overreaching for a municipal leader to try to dictate terms to giant food companies, but since Bloomberg's health officials launched the initiative early this year, he has enlisted the support of two dozen other local and state health departments. The group has won commitments from 16 companies to cut back on the salt in selected products, but the goal is clearly to push the Food and Drug Administration to set industry-wide standards. "Obviously, it has to be done nationally if it's to be done at all," says Linda Gibbs, New York City's deputy mayor for health and human services.

No one in the food industry discounts Bloomberg's chances of getting that done. Former members of his team are sprinkled throughout the Obama administration, including in the major health agencies, and the Big Apple has already demonstrated that it can change the national terms of debate when it comes to public health.

A comprehensive smoking ban enacted there in 2003 has spread to jurisdictions all over the country. After a dozen cities and states, encompassing about 20 percent of the U.S. population, essentially copied New York's legislation banning transfat, some restaurant chains replaced their old recipes with healthier ones. Likewise, after New York City began requiring restaurants to post

From *National Journal*, July 10, 2010.

calorie counts for their menu items, many other cities embraced variations of the concept. The National Restaurant Association—whose New York state branch sued twice, unsuccessfully, to block Bloomberg's law— eventually endorsed similar national requirements to avoid confronting a patchwork of regulations in different parts of the country. Congress included them in the health care overhaul legislation that it enacted in March.

"New York City has been extraordinary in the public health world," says Michael Jacobson, the executive director of the Center for Science in the Public Interest, a nutrition advocacy group. "On those issues, numerous other cities and states have followed New York's lead."

The city has made its mark in many other policy matters as well. From education and the environment to housing, public safety, and poverty programs, it has arguably emerged as the "new California"—where policy innovations are born and then widely copied by many other jurisdictions, including the federal government.

"New York City is just the world's largest laboratory," Memphis Mayor AC Wharton Jr. says.

Wall Street may not be as robust as it was a few years ago, and some of Bloomberg's economic development programs have yet to pay major dividends in the recession's wake. But at a time when innovation in governance seems to be happening in cities such as Youngstown, Ohio, and Detroit—places that are "in the process of managing decline," as Patrick Phillips, the CEO of the Urban Land Institute, puts it—the Bloomberg administration is thinking about how New York can enhance its reputation as the nation's most vibrant city.

Thinking Big

- From education and the environment to housing, public safety, and health, Mayor Michael Bloomberg has made his city a testing ground for policy innovation.
- "New York City is just the world's largest laboratory."
- Critics say that Bloomberg hasn't addressed problems such as poverty, inequality, inadequate revenues, and Wall Street's decline.

A WHOLE SYSTEM OF CHANGE

Bloomberg's formal blueprint for the city of 2030 is New York's first long-term planning document in 40 years. No one can yet say if the plan will succeed in nurturing the city's growth and livability, but Philadelphia, San Francisco, and other cities are already closely imitating Bloomberg's vision. What's more, his core notion of linking what have traditionally been considered separate, if not conflicting, issues in a mayoral portfolio— economic growth, environmental sustainability, and quality of life—is having a broad impact. "In some ways, mayors are just starting to realize the whole set of things going on in New York," says Carol Coletta, the president of CEOs for Cities, a Chicago-based nonprofit. "You can pick up one idea, but it's the whole system of changes in New York that makes it so exciting."

The Bloomberg administration, which won election in 2001 and is now in its third term, seeks what Phillips calls an "integrated perspective": Instead of thinking about individual projects, City Hall is developing policies that address large, underlying problems. The city has to deal with the costs of obesity and chronic diseases, so it has targeted such root causes as smoking and salt. Where the city needs more housing, rather than seeking a one-off deal to foster an apartment block, it looks for a way to reshape an entire area through job creation and transit and all of the other elements of a thriving neighborhood. "It's difficult to get mayors to focus less on brick-and-mortar projects and more on the kinds of decisions you have to make to attract that investment," Phillips says, but "that influence is now percolating across the country in small cities and big cities."

It's also showing up in the Obama administration. Bloomberg's former housing commissioner, Shaun Donovan, is putting these ideas into play as President Obama's Housing and Urban Development secretary. Donovan has been perhaps the lead convener in formulating Obama's nascent urban policy, working with the Environmental Protection Agency, the Transportation and Energy departments, and other agencies to wed programs together at the local level. The idea is to plan with a "place-based" focus, which means considering how programs such as worker training, housing, and environmental cleanup can operate symbiotically within a locale. The programs that address multiple priorities ought to be the ones that move forward, replacing the old paradigm of isolated projects funded by separate agencies.

Many disparate players have influenced the programs that Donovan and the White House Office of Urban Affairs are pursuing. The Brookings Institution's Metropolitan Policy Program holds a lot of sway among local officials and the administration; and other mayors, including Chicago's Richard M. Daley and Denver's John Hickenlooper, can claim considerable credit for the new approach.

Clearly, though, Bloomberg has had an impact. "Donovan comes from Bloomberg," says MarySue Barrett, president of Chicago's Metropolitan Planning Council. "It's not like these federal officials dreamed this up in a vacuum. It's actually what metropolitan places have come to on our own."

BIKE LANES AND BUDGETS

People tend to hold their mayors to task for trash pickup, public safety, and fiscal stability rather than for their ability to persuade other cities—or even Cabinet secretaries—to imitate their initiatives. Bloomberg, moreover, hasn't had an unerring Midas touch as mayor. He has chased his share of urban get-rich-quick schemes, such as a failed stadium deal and a hapless Olympics bid. The state rejected one of his signature ideas, a congestion pricing fee for people who drive their cars into Manhattan during peak traffic hours. "I don't think he's solved the basic problems of New York City, which are job creation and income inequality," says Joel Kotkin, an author and scholar in urban futures at Chapman University in California.

Bloomberg's large and highly engaged public-relations and political teams have unquestionably hyped many of his success stories. And critics say that some of his celebrated ideas, such as turning Times Square into a pedestrian plaza and opening up miles of bike lanes, don't count for much in a city that is facing a $5 billion deficit. "The health innovations, I basically support, but are they essential to the city's future? Not remotely," says Fred Siegel, a senior fellow at the Manhattan Institute. "Much of what he's doing is creating a platform for himself, presenting himself as a national and international figure."

Even Bloomberg's critics concede, however, that the city's look and feel have improved on his watch. Putting aside congestion pricing, his administration has succeeded in "calming" and improving transportation throughout the city. It has "upzoned" abandoned brownfields and unlocked long-abandoned stretches of property for development. The city has encouraged high-density housing around subway stations and added 500 acres of parkland—notably along the Manhattan Waterfront Greenway.

This spring, Coney Island opened its first amusement park in 50 years. "New York hadn't been thought of as a waterfront city since Marlon Brando," says Kathryn Wylde, president of the Partnership for New York City, the local chamber of commerce. "That was a long time ago and a different sort of waterfront."

Given its size and prominence, New York has always been a center of urban innovation. Central Park was the first landscaped public park in the country. Thomas Brophy, a city fire marshal in the early 20th century, practically invented the science of arson investigation. During the Depression, Mayor Fiorello La Guardia pursued a policy of slum clearance and construction of low-cost public housing that would serve as a national model until Robert Moses, the city's "master builder" of the 1960s, took it to extremes.

Mayor Rudy Giuliani lowered the city's crime rates during his two terms from 1994 to 2001, largely through aggressive precinct-by-precinct statistical analysis that other cities have widely imitated. In certain ways, Bloomberg has continued Giuliani's attack on crime, but the two mayors' managerial approaches are starkly different. Giuliani was a notorious micromanager and attention-grabber. When his police commissioner, William Bratton, began getting attention for the crime reduction—he made the cover of *Time* in 1996—Giuliani fired him rather than share the spotlight.

Bloomberg, by contrast, has given his police commissioner, Ray Kelly, plenty of latitude. The mayor generally delegates authority freely and has allowed other city officials to emerge as the public faces of prominent initiatives such as the transfat ban or the push to promote charter schools. He has been widely praised for hiring talented people from outside his inner circle and from outside government altogether.

Making a Difference

Not every policy idea that Michael Bloomberg has promoted as mayor has worked to perfection, and not all the ideas he's tried were his own. Bloomberg has borrowed freely from other U.S. cities and from London, Sao Paulo, Brazil, and Tokyo.

It is fair to say, however, that many of the ideas conceived, or at least tested, in New York have spread to other cities. Bloomberg's administration has left some mark on just about every issue of concern to urban officials, particularly transportation, housing, and public health.

Poverty. Bloomberg, "someone who could, frankly, be totally aloof from poverty, has such an intimate grasp of poverty and its effects," says Memphis Mayor AC Wharton Jr. Wharton, like other mayors, has consulted with Bloomberg on poverty issues. A delegation from San Antonio recently visited Manhattan to study New York's methods for helping poor households and communities gain better access to banking.

One anti-poverty idea that Bloomberg borrowed from overseas didn't work out so well. In March, the city announced that it would discontinue its conditional cash-transfer program, called Opportunity NYC, which gave poor families money for taking steps such as getting vaccinations and health checkups for children, and making sure they attend school. The program was begun as a pilot project supported by private funds (including money from Bloomberg's own foundation), but it showed few results. That same month, however, the U.S. Commerce Department adopted a method that New York City had developed for measuring poverty—examining expenses such as taxes, child care, and housing, as well as government assistance, rather than using the standard method of comparing income with only the cost of food.

Public safety. It is fair to say that, aside from his performance after the terrorist attacks of September 11, 2001, the greatest legacy of Bloomberg's predecessor, Rudy Giuliani, was making New Yorkers feel secure again. It became the safest big city in the country, according to the FBI. Smarter community policing, better use of statistics, and low tolerance for minor infractions—along with a drop in the drug trade—helped bring down New York's crime rate by 57 percent.

Bloomberg has successfully followed the same path. Overall crime in 2009 was down by 35 percent from 2001, Giuliani's last year in office, and the murder rate

was the lowest it's been since the city began compiling comparable statistics in the 1960s. Bloomberg has also given the NYPD important new responsibilities—1,000 officers, including a dozen stationed in trouble spots around the world, devote their time to intelligence and counterterrorism.

His pet initiative, Mayors Against Illegal Guns, which he guides in tandem with Boston Mayor Thomas Menino, has had difficulty gaining traction in an era that favors gun owners' rights. Their campaign suffered a big setback on June 28 when the Supreme Court ruled that localities cannot ban handguns. But New York has made a splash by running undercover investigations at out-of-state gun shows.

Environment. Over the past five years, many cities have tried to outdo one another with promises to combat climate change by reducing their carbon footprint. Many of their pledges have proved to be more symbolic than effective. New York, however, has been widely credited with taking some important steps.

Bloomberg's proposed $8 congestion pricing charge for cars entering Manhattan went nowhere in Albany. And he can't match Chicago Mayor Richard M. Daley's record in promoting green roofs. But New York is outpacing other cities when it comes to keeping its promise to plant 1 million trees. Aside from his emphasis on open space and the city's expansion of parkland, Bloomberg has set in place one of the strictest "green building" codes in the nation.

In December, the City Council approved legislation requiring New York's biggest buildings to reduce their energy consumption and to pay for energy audits and better lighting. Two months later, a panel of experts convened by the city released a list of 100 recommendations to make the city's building code even more rigorous on energy use. "We are the first major city to enact a green building code providing real incentives and ultimately mandates for retrofitting," says Kathryn Wylde, president of the Partnership for New York City. Bloomberg has been pushing regulations and incentives to convert the city's taxi fleet to hybrid vehicles.

In May, the New York Academy of Sciences issued a report praising the Bloomberg administration's attention to climate change, but its long list of recommendations suggested that the city still has a lot of work to do.

(Continued)

Education. Mayoral control of schools is something that Bloomberg's predecessors sought for decades. Since the state Legislature granted school control to Bloomberg in 2002, he and his chancellor, Joel Klein, have aggressively tried numerous strategies for improvement. "It would be hard to think of any big policy issues in education where Klein hasn't played an important role," says Michael Petrilli, vice president for national programs and policy at the Fordham Institute, a conservative education think tank.

Klein has had a "multiplier effect by getting people excited about reform," Petrilli says, because when his employees move to other places, they take the ideas with them. Baltimore's schools chief, Andres Alonso, for instance, had served as Klein's chief of staff and deputy chancellor. Klein's ideas—and the NYPD's ideas as well—have also traveled to many other cities.

New York has been at the forefront in promoting many fashionable education policies, including making schools smaller; incorporating formerly spurned charter schools as part of the district's overall strategy; and recruiting teachers who don't come from a traditional education-school background. New York's method of grading schools and using the grades in closure decisions has become a common approach for states in their applications for federal Race to the Top grants. Its "mutual consent" teacher-hiring provision morphed into a highly touted tenure evaluation law that

Colorado enacted in April, as well as a closely watched new contract that Washington, D.C., teachers ratified on June 2.

"Joel Klein has given a lot of cover for changes that have happened elsewhere," says Andrew Rotherham, a prominent education consultant. "The aggressiveness with which they're doing things would be notable in any case, but the fact that it's New York, which is so large and is such a cultural touchstone, gives it additional resonance."

Like a lot of other big-city superintendents, Klein has tried out many ideas and has clearly improved school performance. The question is, how much? Sol Stern, a senior fellow at the Manhattan Institute, says that New York City's results on state test scores "are completely inflated." Results of the National Assessment of Educational Progress tests came out in May. They showed that New York's fourth-graders are reading better than they were when Bloomberg and Klein took control, but eighth-graders show little improvement. "No doubt, New York City did better than Detroit and Chicago," Stern says, "but to me, that doesn't show fantastic achievement."

Julia Vitullo-Martin, a scholar of New York issues and a former city official, says that the proof of Klein's success lies in growing enrollments. "The big problem in New York—and this is something nobody could have predicted 20 years ago—is the tremendous increase in the demand for public schools."

—A.G.

Bloomberg's financial information-and-media company landed him at No. 8 on Forbes magazine's list of the richest Americans last year. Many people speculate that his ability to finance his own campaigns means that he has not racked up political obligations to reward supporters with plum jobs. "He hires people more for their professional credentials than their loyalties to him," says Thomas Wright, the executive director of the Regional Plan Association, an independent research group covering the New York City metropolitan area, "and then he has them working on reforms and institutionalizing them."

Bloomberg's commissioners and deputy mayors are pretty much required not only to manage existing programs but also to contribute innovative ideas, Wright

says. The mayor has fostered a sense of healthy competition at City Hall and among the agencies that they need to create the next new thing to improve life in the city. "He's been a huge supporter of ideas, many of which were called political suicide when they came up," Deputy Mayor Gibbs says. "As a commissioner, you really value that the important thing is to try, even if that means you have failures. If you don't fail, you're not trying."

That may sound like so much buttering up of the boss, but it is a strikingly unusual sentiment in the generally risk-averse culture of local government. Bloomberg often makes the same point. He retains the contrarian instincts that served him well as an entrepreneur, and he keeps looking for ways to learn not just from failures but also from apparent success.

Even after what is still probably viewed as his most heroic moment—his performance in informing and calming the city during the 2003 blackout—Bloomberg immediately sought input from inside and outside city government about what had gone wrong. He took the findings about breakdowns in communication and transportation and announced them himself to reporters, earning some rotten headlines but learning a lot in the bargain.

Not surprisingly for a man who amassed one of the world's great fortunes by moving information around rapidly, he is obsessed with data. He came into a City Hall where paper notebooks abounded and BlackBerrys were practically unknown—a picture he quickly changed. Today, "there is a data-driven culture in New York that has been adapted to various degrees elsewhere in the best-run cities," says the Urban Land Institute's Phillips. "Not only has it changed local government decision-making, but anybody who does business with local government has to be able to defend their position using metrics, to defend the impact of their project."

When Bloomberg's subordinates develop an idea, they must show the mayor that they've done their homework—the specific ways the initiative will save money or otherwise improve the city. Turning Times Square into a pedestrian plaza "was not just a decision to do something because it would be cool," says Jeff Kay, director of operations for the mayor's office. The controversial move grew out of extensive research about transportation speeds and the potential impact of the change on small business.

In a city that has been challenged by declining revenue throughout much of Bloomberg's administration—despite his willingness to impose hefty tax increases—the mayor's team has consistently looked for ways to make government more efficient. New York was not the first city to set up a 311 citizen complaint hotline, but it has used the data drawn from the calls to identify the gaps in government performance. An uptick in complaints about graffiti led to the realization that six agencies shared responsibility for cleanup. Bloomberg reduced that number to two. "The measurement of things that matter to citizens and the transparency of those measurements all combine to make this administration in New York very special indeed," says Coletta of CEOs for Cities.

IT'S THE MONEY

The most common complaint about Bloomberg is that he has been able to buy off critics because of his wealth and his willingness to use it. He has also spent public money freely to appease doubters. He used a 43 percent pay increase, for example, to sweeten an education contract that included changes in hiring practices and other policies that the teachers union wasn't crazy about.

Both Bloomberg's personal foundation and the Mayor's Fund to Advance New York City have helped pay for items on his official agenda. In his first term, Bloomberg spent $7 million of his money backing an unsuccessful ballot initiative to institute nonpartisan local elections. "Traditionally, interest groups buy mayors," says Siegel, the Manhattan Institute fellow and a historian at Cooper Union. "He's reversed the flow. He's bought the interest groups."

With a huge budget deficit to deal with and the prospect of worse to come, money is uppermost on the minds of Bloomberg's officials. In place of bold new initiatives, agencies are talking about ways to save money by sharing such services as fleet management and information technology.

But City Hall also hopes to extend the ethos of customer service that has made it easy for residents to call 311 when they have a problem. In effect, officials want to provide businesses a similar one-stop-shopping way of interacting with city government. As a headquarters city, New York has long been dominated by corporate priorities, but the Bloomberg administration is focusing increasing attention on the 80 percent of the city's businesses that are not behemoths. Officials recognize that they need to nurture these essential small businesses if New York is to move beyond its longstanding reliance on Wall Street as its main cash cow.

Bloomberg has established a Small Business Services Department and has changed tax laws to reduce costs for independent contractors and freelancers. His economic development team is setting up business incubators in a variety of fields—the biosciences, the arts, media, fashion, and food production—linking entrepreneurs with universities, and even making deals with landlords who are willing to rent surplus space at discounted rates. The city has put up money for seed grants, and some of the initiatives are starting to attract venture funding.

There's a saying in New York that government skims the cream off of Wall Street while Wall Street skims the cream off the rest of the country. That model looks to be broken, or at least in need of serious repair. If Wall Street doesn't generate the kind of profits that it has in recent years, the city will have to develop a economy in which people can get things done at a reasonable cost. So far, Bloomberg has not been able to bring the cost of doing business in New York down to reasonable levels, and that is perhaps the mayor's greatest ongoing challenge.

"Bloomberg still has the problem, like all New York mayors, of fiscal issues," says Vincent Cannato, a historian at the University of Massachusetts and the author of a biography of former New York City Mayor John Lindsay. "It's becoming even more than in the past what Bloomberg called a luxury city, of the very wealthy, of immigrants, and the poor. It's a city that middle-class people are still leaving."

Budgets and Taxes

For the past several years, budgets and taxes have been *the* story of state and local governments. Historically, the three primary sources of state and local government revenue are income, sales, and property taxes, and all three have been squeezed by the tough economy. Property values plummeted with the bursting of the housing bubble, high unemployment limited income tax collections, and debt-laden consumers watching pennies meant sales taxes took a hit too. As income shrank, demand for public services—read demand for more government expenditure—increased. Unlike their federal counterparts, state and local governments cannot run up huge deficits or print money. That means tough choices, years of tough choices with no end in sight.

With traditional revenue streams slowing to a trickle, for the past couple of years state and local governments have been kept in the black by the federal government. In 2009 the feds passed the American Recovery and Reinvestment Act (ARRA), a massive stimulus bill that funneled billions of dollars toward state and local treasuries. Yet even with the federal government stepping up to become the largest single source of revenue for state and local governments, it has not been an easy ride for many states and localities. Many have faced repeated budget falls with painful decisions about slashing spending, raising taxes, or some combination of both. Those choices are not getting any easier because the federal government's stimulus funds were a temporary stopgap, and subnational governments are now trying to figure out how to function on their much reduced traditional revenue sources. As the readings in this section highlight, states are getting creative in the ways they try to deliver services to their citizens and foot the bill.

RAISING AND SPENDING MONEY

According to the most recent estimates, state and local government expenditures total more than $2 trillion.[1] That's a lot of money. Where does it all come from?

As already mentioned, historically speaking the big three revenue sources have been sales, property, and income taxes, which traditionally account for roughly half of state and local government revenue. In 2009 and 2010, however, the big three were, well, not so big. Well into 2011 the single biggest source of revenue for state and local governments has been the federal government. Even before the economic crisis, state and local governments got approximately $380 billion from the federal government. ARRA piled hundreds of billions of dollars more on top of that figure; it was a rescue package so massive that state and local bureaucracies strained simply to digest the new diet of federal dollars. Simply the data processing—keeping up with what money was being spent, where, and on what—was an accountant's version of scaling Mount Everest (you can see the results of all the mind-boggling bean counting at a centralized website set up by the federal government: www.recovery.gov).

State and local governments do not rely solely on the federal government and sales, income, and property taxes for their revenue. Estate taxes; license fees to hunt, fish, or marry; lotteries; and even interest earned on bank deposits help fill public treasuries. There is enormous variation from state to state—and even locality to locality—in what mix of revenue sources governments use. In the current economic climate, states and localities are casting a broad net to expand and broaden their revenue streams.

Balancing the books, though, does not just mean raising money. These days it also means cutting services. States and localities have reduced staff and cut the budgets of everything from welfare programs to university systems. These decisions are painful, but there's little choice. Unlike the federal government, most state governments are legally obligated to produce balanced budgets, and where the revenue cannot keep pace with expenditures, expenditures must get cut.

RECENT TRENDS

The readings in this section begin with Corina Eckl's "Deep Holes, Few Options," describing how the end of federal stimulus money and the continued recession may make 2012 "the worst budget year yet." Most state budget gaps are due to revenue shortfalls, but others are struggling as spending growth outpaces revenue increases. In the face of these challenges, the basic options are finding new sources of revenue, cutting spending, and finding ways to deliver government more efficiently.

Tim Weldon reports on recent initiatives in South Carolina and Georgia to provide a comprehensive review of state tax codes in attempts to eliminate certain exemptions as well as create a more equitable distribution of taxes and fees. These efforts may not raise more revenue but instead create a more "business-friendly" atmosphere that will hopefully stimulate the economy.

Raising taxes in an economic recession and the current political climate is not a viable option for most state and local governments. More and more states have turned to lotteries as potential alternative revenue sources, but as Zach Patton reports, lottery and gambling programs are not exempt from the effects of the economic downturn, and services tied to these revenue sources are in jeopardy.

As mentioned in past chapters of this volume, cutting employees and services and freezing open positions and new services are more common tactics to address budget gaps. Another popular approach, at least publicly, is to trim the fat off government processes, streamlining services and hopefully saving money. Mikel Chavers recounts state-level efforts to centralize something as basic as paying the bills to a paperless, efficient system that saved on employee overtime, postage, and other costs. Other states are increasing audits to uncover tax evaders and integrate tax systems to collect back taxes.

NOTES

1. U.S. Census Bureau, *Statistical Abstract of the United States*, 2010, Table 418, http://www.census.gov/compendia/statab/2010/tables/10s0418.pdf. Accessed May 3, 2010.

32

Deep Holes, Few Options

Corina Eckl

The end of federal stimulus money and the continued recession may make 2012 "the worst budget year yet." Most state budget gaps are due to revenue shortfalls, but others are struggling as spending growth outpaces revenue increases, leaving few options for correcting the budget imbalance.

From *State Legislatures,* February 2011.

Hit with the deepest recession since the Great Depression, state lawmakers in the past three years have confronted ballooning budget gaps triggered by steep revenue declines.

For the first time in a long time, however, there is some good news: FY 2011 state revenues are widely expected to exceed last year's collections. And while the return to pre-reces-sion levels is expected to be painfully slow and uneven across states, at least revenues are on the road to recovery.

So much for the good news.

Two factors overshadow the positive trend. Foremost on lawmakers' minds is the virtual end of federal stimulus money that was included in the American Recovery and Reinvestment Act of 2009. This extra money was critical to shoring up state budgets. But the money is running out soon. Today's budget lexicon features a new and widely used term—"the ARRA cliff"—that aptly describes how state policymakers view the end of the stimulus money.

Swelling spending pressure also is troubling lawmakers. Recessions always generate new spending demands because more people become eligible for safety net programs such as Medicaid and Temporary Assistance to Needy Families. But that's not all. Some programs have been cut so deeply that agencies are seeking supplemental appropriations. Indeed, within the first few months of this fiscal year, half the states reported that spending was outpacing budgeted levels. Medicaid and other health care programs were most likely to be over budget.

These two developments—the end of ARRA funds and rising expenses—represent enormous challenges for state lawmakers as they begin work on their FY 2012 budgets. Even with state revenues starting to improve, the uptick won't be enough to make up for those two factors.

> *"We may be a decade away from the good times."*
> —John Kavanagh

Some lawmakers may look back nostalgically to FY 2011—when there was still stimulus money and revenues were improving—as the year before the next, and possibly worst, fiscal storm strikes.

Arizona Representative John Kavanagh, chair of the House Appropriations Committee, put it bluntly. "We may be a decade away from the good times."

MISERY HAS COMPANY

Deep budget problems have plagued state lawmakers for several years now, with every state except North Dakota falling into the deficit vortex. Going back to FY 2008, when the shortfalls attributable to the latest recession began appearing, states have faced, and largely closed, a cumulative budget gap of nearly $414 billion. The FY 2011 imbalance already has hit $110 billion. With several months remaining before this year's books are closed, the number could rise.

Many of the new imbalances in FY 2011 have an interesting source: the federal government.

One provision of the American Recovery and Reinvestment Act was a temporary increase in the Federal Medical Assistance Percentage or FMAP, the share of total Medicaid costs the federal government pays. The enhanced rate originally was scheduled to expire on Dec. 31, 2010.

Earlier last year, Congress appeared on the verge of extending the enhanced FMAP through June 30, 2011, which is the end of FY 2011 for 46 states. Many state lawmakers, believing the extension was close to a done deal, based their budgets on

> *"The hole is so deep and the options so few, that even if tax collections tick up a bit, it's probably like drowning in 5,000 feet of water instead of 5,050 feet—you don't really feel much difference."*
> —Jack hailey, director of california's senate committee on human services.

receiving the more favorable federal rate. Ultimately, Congress did provide a six-month extension, but at a lower rate than expected. This action created gaps in states where the enacted budget assumed the higher FMAP rate, though it generated a windfall in states that did not count on an extension.

Anemic revenues are contributing to new shortfalls, too. Nearly $58 million of Colorado's $249 million gap is the result of lower than expected revenue. About $206 million of Arizona's $825 million gap stems from a revenue shortfall as well as another $469 million traced to the Nov. 2 defeat of ballot measures prohibiting fund transfers to the general fund.

Some of the gaps are mind boggling. Consider Illinois. The gap there has snowballed to $13 billion or about 47 percent of the state's general fund budget. To make matters worse, about 23 percent of this year's revenues are needed to cover delayed payments for last year's bills. The state comptroller reported late last year that the structural imbalance, coupled with higher debt service costs and the loss of federal stimulus funds, "creates the very real possibility that the governor and General Assembly will face a working deficit of $15 billion or more when the fiscal year 2012 budget is crafted." Illinois lawmakers are working on that budget right now.

California faces a similar, though not nearly as severe, multi-year problem. Officials there project the state will end FY 2011 with a deficit of $6.1 billion, with an additional gap of $19.2 billion—18.7 percent—for FY 2012.

"The hole is so deep and the options so few that, even if tax collections tick up a bit, it's probably like drowning in 5,000 feet of water instead of 5,050 feet—you don't really feel much difference," says Jack Hailey, longtime director of California's Senate Committee on Human Services.

Top Fiscal Issues

Legislative fiscal directors are keenly attuned to the pressures confronting their states, which is why NCSL asked them to identify the top fiscal issues their states expect to address in the 2011 legislative sessions. It is not surprising that budgets are expected to top legislative agendas in nearly two-thirds of the states. Concerns about Medicaid, education, taxes and pensions also loom large for what could be a very difficult budget year ahead.

The following are the top fiscal issues facing states.

- Overwhelmingly, states expect the budget to be the top fiscal priority in 2011 sessions. Addressing budget shortfalls and structural gaps, replacing diminishing federal stimulus funds and other one-time budget balancing solutions are expected to capture the most attention.
- Medicaid and health care costs will receive priority attention. Issues to be addressed include growth in enrollment and use of services, and the reduction in the Federal Medical Assistance Percentage the amount of Medicaid costs picked up by the federal government.

- Education will be another priority in many states. Discussions will center on adequate funding levels, school finance formulas and increased student enrollment.
- A number of states expect tax and revenue discussions to dominate legislative agendas. The focus for most will not be tax increases, but an examination of existing tax and revenue structures.
- Also garnering top attention are state pension and retirement issues. Addressing unfunded liabilities and enacting significant reforms may lie in the year ahead for state lawmakers.
- Other commonly cited top fiscal issues include state employee benefits and compensation, unemployment trust funds, transportation and other infrastructure projects, and rainy day funds.

All these issues underscore an unfortunate fact: Lawmakers' endurance to resolve extraordinary fiscal problems will be tested yet again this year.

—*Todd Haggerty, NCSL*

GAPS IN 2012 AND BEYOND

Illinois and California are just two of the 35 states, along with Puerto Rico, that project imbalances in their FY 2012 budgets. The aggregate estimate so far is $82.1 billion, but since not all states were able to assign a figure to the projected gap, that number will rise.

One of the biggest concerns about the FY 2012 gaps is their sheer size, which comes on the heels of several consecutive years of big budget gaps. Of the 31 states reporting estimates to an NCSL survey, 28 expect gaps above 5 percent of their general fund budget, with 21 of these expecting gaps above 10 percent. Illinois, Nevada, New Jersey and North Carolina forecast imbalances above 20 percent, with the Illinois gap possibly at 50 percent.

If that wasn't enough, 24 states and Puerto Rico expect gaps in FY 2013, too. The preliminary tally is $66 billion. Both the number of states and gap tallies are expected to rise as more information becomes available.

The end of state fiscal problems is not expected even in FY 2013. Twenty-nine states and Puerto Rico have

structural budget gaps, which occur when ongoing revenue growth is inadequate to cover ongoing spending growth. For instance, gaps can develop when K-12 student enrollment increases, health care costs spike and the number of people eligible for programs such as Medicaid increase. Many states report structural imbalances extending to FY 2014 and beyond.

RUNNING OUT OF OPTIONS

Budget gaps are always hard to close, but they become more challenging when they are large or recur year after year. It's simple to explain, but the options available to lawmakers shrink with each successive shortfall.

Some actions, such as using money from other state accounts or delaying a payment into the next fiscal year, can be used only once. Other options, such as tapping rainy day funds, are available only if the fund still has money in it. This recession has been so long and deep that many states have exhausted their rainy day funds. Other alternatives, such as raising taxes or fees, can be politically risky or economically ill-advised. Even so, many states have boosted taxes or fees, and

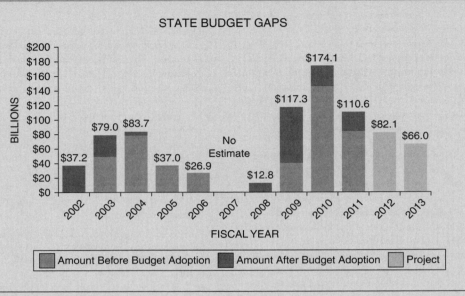

Figure 32.1 State Budget Gaps

STATE BUDGET GAPS

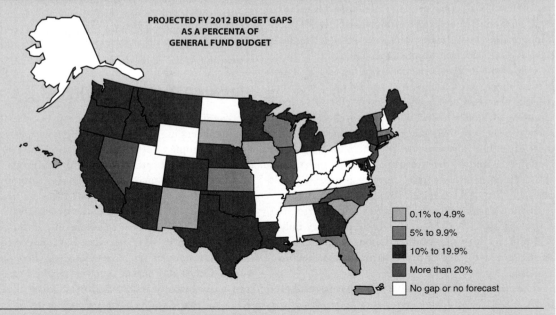

Figure 32.2 Projected Fy 2012 Budget Gaps as a Percentage of General Fund Budget

PROJECTED FY 2012 BUDGET GAPS
AS A PERCENTA OF
GENERAL FUND BUDGET

0.1% to 4.9%
5% to 9.9%
10% to 19.9%
More than 20%
No gap or no forecast

lawmakers may be reluctant to go down that path again. That leaves budget cuts—or in this instance—further budget cuts.

"It's a choice between the disastrous and the unpalatable," says Utah Senator Dan Liljenquist, vice chair of the Executive Appropriations Committee.

Many legislative fiscal directors see FY 2012 as possibly the most difficult budget year yet. At an NCSL meeting of legislators and staff in December, participants were asked to dispute this contention. Not a single one did.

33

Bringing State Tax Systems Into the 21st Century

Tim Weldon

Recent initiatives in South Carolina and Georgia have provided a comprehensive review of state tax codes in attempts to eliminate certain exemptions as well as create a more equitable distribution of taxes and fees.

I
n 2000, 50 percent of all retail sales in South Carolina were taxable; this year, that percentage is down to 38 percent.

The State Tax Realignment Commission, appointed by Gov. Mark Sanford and the leadership of the state legislature, wants to see that changed. The commission is recommending discarding sales and use tax exemptions on dozens of items, including resurrecting a 2.95 percent tax on groceries the South Carolina legislature eliminated in 2007. If legislators approve that recommendation, South Carolina will become one of just 15 states that tax groceries.

Chairman Burnet Maybank said the tax commission is trying to create some balance in South Carolina's tax code, which he calls one of extremes.

"We have the lowest property taxes on residences in urban areas," he said. "We have the highest taxes in the country on manufacturing."

A NEW LOOK AT TAXES

As states pull themselves out of recession, many state legislatures this year will have to grapple with taxes. Some believe tax commissions can take the politics out of the issue in their non-elected advisory role.

South Carolina and Georgia have created commissions to examine the tax codes with the goal of overhauling antiquated tax systems to make them more balanced, equitable and efficient.

That doesn't mean the new taxes will raise new revenue.

In fact, the South Carolina Tax Commission's recommendations are revenue neutral, according to commission member Kenneth

From *Capitol Ideas,* January/February 2011.

Cosgrove. But supporters have hailed the tax changes as a way to make the Palmetto State more business-friendly.

"This is not a revenue grab to fix the recession," Cosgrove said. "We want South Carolina to be competitive, and we want it to be a great place to live and work."

Because the state's sales and use tax accounts for 42 percent of total General Fund revenue—the largest single component of the General Fund—it has been one of the commission's major focus areas.

The commission reviewed more than 100 sales and use tax exemptions, exclusions and minimum sales taxes, estimated to cost the state $2.7 billion per year.

"There's more (sales and use tax) exempted than there is collected," Maybank said.

At the same time the commission wants to remove some sales and use tax exemptions—including eliminating exemptions on groceries, utilities and prescription drugs—it is recommending reducing the overall sales tax rate from 6 percent to 5 percent.

The commission also wants the 2011 legislature to consider two options for a fuel tax: a general 5-cent increase or one that adjusts with the cost of fuel. The draft plan also proposes a sales tax on manufactured homes, which make up 20 percent of the homes sold in South Carolina.

Cosgrove said the commission is attempting to fix an archaic tax code that is riddled with inconsistent exemptions and deductions.

"Over 70 or 80 years of tax policy, we've added a little bit here and a little bit there. ... It's just been piecemeal over time, and I'm not sure that's the most effective way," he said.

REACTIONS MIXED

But some of the recommendations have resulted in a firestorm of controversy.

Rep. Bill Sandifer complains the commission's proposals "have been represented as if they are a done deal." He said he has seen a wave of confusion in his district among constituents who believe the commission was given power to implement the tax changes.

"In reality, they must be debated and voted upon by the General Assembly," he said.

Sandifer reserved his strongest criticism for the proposal to tax what he terms "necessities, not frills."

"Too many households in our state are already in desperate shape, and (the commission's) proposals hit them where it hurts most," he said.

The commission's recommendations would make South Carolina more business-friendly, according to some. They would retain tax exemptions for manufacturing, agricultural and other business "inputs," but not the finished product. For example, newsprint used for newspapers would be exempt from sales and use taxes, but the retail sale of the newspaper itself would be taxed.

Lewis Gossett, president of the South Carolina Manufacturer's Alliance, however, points out manufacturing accounts for 20 percent of the jobs in South Carolina. He argues a 2006 law placed the lion's share of paying for K–12 education on business and industry, and he calls the state's tax structure broken.

"Shifting the tax burden onto our members will not result in a better deal for taxpayers in the end. ... No one should forget that higher tax burdens make (manufacturing) plants less competitive, and in this global economy the tolerance for high taxes simply no longer exists," Gossett said in a statement from the Coalition Against Unlimited Spending.

The legislature will consider changes to the state's tax structure when it meets in January.

Maybank, for his part, is not counting on South Carolina legislators taking action on his commission's recommendations this year. He believes they will address tax reform sometime, even if it's two or three years away. And when they do, he believes his commission's report will be dusted off and be influential in redesigning a new tax structure for South Carolina.

GEORGIA ALSO LOOKING AT REFORM

South Carolina isn't the only state looking to tax commissions for recommendations.

In June 2010, the Georgia legislature enacted House Bill 1405, which created the Special Council on Tax Reform and Fairness for Georgians. It has been studying the state's tax laws and was expected to issue a report in

December to the General Assembly that could substantially realign the state's tax structure.

"This legislation sets up a framework that will allow for a serious examination of our tax code and ensure that it works for Georgians," Gov. Sonny Perdue said after signing the bill into law.

As with neighboring South Carolina, Georgia's Special Council has been looking at more than 100 sales tax exemptions and dozens of income tax credits available to businesses.

Unlike South Carolina, however, the process used by Georgia's council—comprised of Perdue, economists and business leaders—does not allow legislators to cherry-pick the components of tax reform they like. Georgia's legislation requires the council's report be sent to the Special Joint Committee on Georgia Revenue Structure, which will write a bill from the report. The Georgia General Assembly will consider the bill in a strict up or down vote, without amendments.

34

Lottery Revenues Not a Sure Bet

Zach Patton

Though a popular alternative revenue source, lottery and gambling programs are not exempt from the effects of the economic downturn, putting services tied to these revenue sources in jeopardy.

From *Governing*, April 2011.

O ver the past few decades, states increasingly have turned to lotteries and other types of gambling as potential new sources of revenue. But the recent economic crisis suggests that gaming endeavors may not be the predictable cash cows they once were.

Forty-three states and the District of Columbia have legalized lotteries to help raise revenue. For most of the past 20 years, state lotteries have shown phenomenal growth, more than doubling from $8.8 billion in 1993 to $17.7 billion in 2007.

Two years ago, the math changed. In 2009, state revenues from lotteries dipped by 2.3 percent—the first major decline in the past three decades, according to a report from the Nelson A. Rockefeller Institute of Government. That's a problem, the report says, because states frequently earmark lottery revenues for specific spending in areas like education. "Expenditures on education and other programs will generally grow more rapidly over time," the report says. "Thus, new gambling operations that are intended to pay for normal increases in general state spending may add to, rather than ease, long-term budget imbalances."

Since 2009, lottery revenues have rebounded, but not by much, says Lucy Dadayan, a senior policy analyst at the Rockefeller Institute and a co-author of the report. For fiscal 2010, she says, lotteries nationwide saw a revenue increase of 2.7 percent. "That's much weaker compared to previous years," Dadayan says.

Georgia, for example, is facing a $1.2 billion revenue gap for lottery-funded programs, and slower ticket sales mean the state must find alternative ways to fund education expenditures. Gov. Nathan Deal last month approved deep cuts to the state's popular HOPE scholarship program, which is funded by lottery proceeds. Florida and West Virginia have made similar cuts to their lottery-backed scholarship programs.

The overall lesson, says Dadayan? "No matter how many different games states come up with, they cannot count on it as a dependable source of revenue."

35

Efficiency in State Government

Mikel Chavers

States are leveraging the power of technology to streamline bill payment processes and tax collection, leading to substantial savings and increases in revenue.

The Comptroller's office in Pennsylvania was spread out over eight separate locations. Inundated with paper bills and other paper documents, the office was known as more of a place where things got stalled, not a model of government efficiency.

That negative stereotype was something the office had to fight. The battle was further complicated because in uncertain economic times, the state was expected to do more with less money, according to Anna Maria Kiehl, deputy secretary for the Office of Comptroller Operations in Pennsylvania's Office of the Budget.

"Pennsylvania is no different than any other state. We've been struggling with this economy, and budget cuts and program cuts have just become a way of life," said Pennsylvania Secretary of the Budget Mary Soderberg.

The budget office is operating with 7.5 percent less funding than the 2002–03 fiscal year and about 30 percent less people.

Paper invoices were coming in to all the different locations and all the different agencies, and then coming into the respective comptroller's offices. There was such a backlog of bills and invoices, according to Soderberg.

In fact, just one utility company the state did business with would send about 10,000 paper invoices a year—all going to different locations, including state hospitals, state police barracks, prisons and the state department of transportation warehouses, according to Soderberg.

Bills could be paid late, incurring late charges if just one of thousands of invoices was lost on someone's desk. So officials completely revamped the organization of the office and streamlined operations

From *Capitol Ideas,* January/February 2011.

with the latest technology. All offices were consolidated into one and everything went paperless.

"So we've flattened the organization," Kiehl said, "which goes against the grain when it comes to state governments and hierarchies."

The new system centralized all invoice receipts from vendors.

The result was a complete streamline of perhaps one of the most basic functions of state government: paying bills and paying employees. Another result? "Vendors are no longer being paid late," Kiehl said.

And that's helping state government funds to stretch even further, bringing a new level of efficiency. The new system and organization led to a 47 percent reduction in overtime costs, a 63 percent reduction in travel expenditures (because with only one office, staff weren't traveling throughout the state) and a 35 percent reduction in office postage, according to Soderberg.

That's especially important in tough times.

"The more that we can save on the administrative side of the budget, the more that we will have to invest in significant programs like education, health care or the cost of running our prisons," Soderberg said. "Unfortunately, because of the economy and because of the current environment, there is no appetite to increase taxes. This has given us more visibility about where we're spending the money."

In fact, in 2009 the system proved its very important worth. When the budget was late for 101 days because of political reasons, state government in Pennsylvania basically came to a standstill. Almost no invoices could be paid until a final budget was passed.

When the budget was finally signed, the office had a mere two weeks to play catch-up with bills and invoices. In that two weeks, the office processed $4 billion in payments, Soderberg said. That level of efficiency hadn't been seen before in comptroller operations.

"We could not afford any mistakes in this period of time," Soderberg said. "We couldn't have any important payments slip through the cracks."

But Pennsylvania isn't the only state streamlining what seems like basic and fundamental processes involving money, how it's collected and how it's tracked. Here's a look at how other states are getting smart about doing more with less and making sure the state is getting all the funds it deserves.

ILLINOIS CATCHES GAS TAX EVADERS

In Illinois, officials beefed up auditing functions and hired additional investigators to crack down on businesses that evade the gas tax, costing the state millions in lost revenue.

By beefing up audits, the state found some gas stations were underreporting their overall total sales and therefore the sales tax was underreported.

"We were thinking it was going to be several million dollars but by Aug. 19, we had actually recouped $12.7 million," said John Chambers, chief of the bureau of criminal investigations for the Illinois Department of Revenue.

Since then, the efforts have continued and the state has collected more than $25 million in gas taxes, according to Chambers.

"We've recouped millions of dollars, but more importantly, hopefully we'll deter that from happening again," Chambers said. "That's going to be additional monies coming into the state every month."

And more money is important because, "it's no secret the state of Illinois has some budget issues," Chambers said.

TENNESSEE SHIFTS BUSINESS TAX COLLECTION

In 2009, the Tennessee legislature passed a law to shift the collection of business taxes from the county to the state department of revenue. Collecting the taxes through the revenue department meant greater efficiencies for the state.

"With this change, the Department of Revenue has used its resources and experience in tax administration to provide greater efficiency in the collection process and increased revenue for the state and for local governments," said Sara Jo Houghland, director of communications for the revenue department.

"We decided to administer this tax as we do all of the other taxes we cover with our expertise and our databases," she said. "Also, generally, people are more compliant at the federal level than the state, and it goes the same with people being more compliant on the state level than the local level."

Through the state's ability to leverage streamlined processes, the department of revenue was able to identify nonfilers by making use of existing data sources including other state tax registration information and data from other state and federal agencies.

Because of more efficient efforts, the department has assessed in excess of $1.7 million in business taxes and collected more than $1.2 million of that amount, according to Houghland.

NEW TAX SYSTEM IN MARYLAND NETS BIG BUCKS

Maryland's new Modernized Integrated Tax System has snagged the state nearly $65 million in back taxes, just by upgrading to the latest technologies. Using other strategies, the agency collected more than $1.4 billion in late taxes over the last four years, according to the comptroller's office.

The centerpiece of that effort is a state-of-the-art data warehousing and tax collection system that brings the office processes to a whole new level of efficiency.

That's allowed the office to take on more data-matching projects to determine where taxes were being underreported and "these were new projects that we were able to automate," said Daniel Riley, deputy director of compliance division in Maryland.

That's important because without an automated, efficient system, big data-matching projects would have to be done by hand, involving more staff to do all the legwork. Sure, the office could run all kinds of projects to make sure folks are paying their taxes, but that's the kind of effort that takes massive manpower.

"If everyone had all the staff that they wanted, this wouldn't be an issue," Riley said. "The reality is that government agencies are being asked to work with less all the time."

PART

X

Policy Challenges

Different chapter, same story. The central policy challenge for most state and local governments is the same as it was last year and the year before that. That challenge was basically the subject of Part IX, and Part IX in last year's edition, and Part IX in . . . well, you get the idea. The central policy challenge is crystal clear, has been around for a few years, and is not going anywhere soon. That challenge, of course, is simply balancing the books. Fighting to keep expenditures from devouring all the revenue and then asking for seconds, however, is not the central purpose of government. The aim of governance is not balanced accounts; revenues and expenditures are means, not ends, for state and local governments. These governments exist to provide public services and programs, respond to citizen demands, and address social problems. The demand for all of those things has not slowed while policy makers frantically try to build dikes to hold back red ink.

The real issue is not simply balancing the books, but trying to figure out how to keep conducting the business of governance on a severely tightened belt. State and local governments have always been expected to tackle a breathtaking array of enormous policy responsibilities. Education, law enforcement, infrastructure, public transportation . . . the list goes on and on. Increasingly added to this list are high-profile issues like health care and illegal immigration. Governments cannot simply beg off of dealing with the ever-growing list of expectations piled on them because they are basically broke. Not doing anything really is not an option. The real challenge, then, is not wrestling revenues into some sort of balance with expenditures. It is figuring out how to address all those policy responsibilities

175

without more cash. Governments very literally are being asked to do a whole lot more with a whole lot less.

The readings in this chapter lay out some of those big challenges and how subnational governments plan on addressing them in tough times. Some of this involves not just what to do and how to pay for it, but a reexamination of relations among governments and how government does business. First, Lauren Stewart summarizes 35 State of the State speeches, detailing the top challenges and policy proposals identified by the states' governors. Though cuts, consolidations, and efficiencies are commonplace, state leaders still recognize the need to continue investment, innovation, and increased services in several policy areas.

Following the budgetary crisis theme of this book, a report by Norman Ornstein warns that state and local governments should no longer expect to be bailed out by federal dollars. With a newly elected Congress, more conservative than ever, fiscal conservatism is the wave of the immediate future and does not bode well for local help from Washington. With these challenges in mind, three state and local government experts weigh in on how the Great Recession has illuminated the necessity for rethinking business as usual, in Bruce Perlman's article. Services have long outpaced revenue, and politics have won over pragmatism. States need new leaders, new government structures, and overall better governance.

Finally, there are some issues that cannot be ignored, even in a time of budgetary cuts and reduced government. As the federal government stalls on immigration reform, Alan Greenblatt reports that more and more state and local governments are taking matters into their own hands. Utah and Arizona have taken opposite approaches to the problem of increases in undocumented workers, and their success or failure may influence other states' and national policy.

36

Interim Analysis: 2011 State of the State Addresses

Lauren Stewart

Summaries of 35 State of the State governors' speeches indicate the budgetary crisis is in the forefront with calls for efficiencies, cuts and consolidations; yet, governors still outline plans for innovation, investment and increases in service in several policy areas.

From *NGA Center for Best Practices*, February 2011.

EXECUTIVE SUMMARY

The governors' 2011 State of the State addresses are being delivered in a time of continuing fiscal stress for states and high unemployment. As a result, the 2011 speeches are rich with references to tough budget choices, smaller government, and strategies to create jobs. The governors' 2011 State of the State addresses signal that government redesign is not a temporary issue; it is part a new reality that will bring about fundamental change in the nature and volume of state services.

The following analysis is based on the 35 speeches available at the time of this publication's release.[1]

REDESIGN

State budget cuts in reaction to the recession are not temporary; they are part of a larger effort to permanently redesign state government. More than 20 governors referenced redesigning state government as a priority in their 2011 State of the State address. The word "budget" is mentioned 340 times in the 31 speeches. As Governor Andrew Cuomo of New York said, "You can't make up these kinds of savings over this long of period of time through a budget cutting or trimming exercise. We are going to have to reinvent government."

A major component of government redesign is organizational streamlining. Governors are focusing on consolidation, streamlining bureaucratic processes, and controlling employee and pension costs.

Consolidation

Thirteen governors from Alaska, California, Colorado, Connecticut, Kansas, Missouri, Nevada, New York, South Carolina, South Dakota, Virginia, Washington, and Wyoming announced intentions to shrink the size of state government through eliminating or consolidating targeted agencies, boards, and commissions. California Governor Jerry Brown, for example, is proposing to eliminate the state's redevelopment agencies and put the funding toward public schools and other core services instead.

Similarly, Nevada Governor Brian Sandoval's budget recommends the consolidation, elimination, or centralization of 20 departments and agencies. The governor also announced plans to introduce legislation that sunsets every existing licensing and advisory board. Washington Governor Chris Gregoire announced her intention to reduce the number of natural resource agencies from 11 to five and the number of state central service agencies from five to two, among other proposals to consolidate government functions.

Some governors are redesigning their own offices to save money. For example, South Dakota cut the governor's office budget by 10 percent overall. New Mexico Governor Susana Martinez cut costs at the governor's residence by 55 percent.

Streamlining

Twenty governors from Alaska, Colorado, Connecticut, Delaware, Idaho, Kansas, Maryland, Michigan, Nevada, New Hampshire, New Mexico, New Jersey, New York, South Carolina, South Dakota, Utah, Virgin Islands, Vermont, Wisconsin, and Wyoming voiced their commitment to streamlining processes and regulations to make government more business-friendly and efficient. For example, Colorado Governor John Hickenlooper proposed requiring a regulatory impact statement to estimate the cost to businesses of any new regulations.

Other governors are focused on streamlining existing regulations. New York Governor Andrew Cuomo will create the Mandate Relief Task Force to eliminate any unnecessary state mandates by April 1, 2011. Similarly, Kansas Governor Sam Brownback will establish an Office of the Repealer to identify regulations or statutes for repeal that are costly, outdated, and ineffective.

New Mexico Governor Susana Martinez proposed the Red Tape Reduction Act to standardize multi-agency administrative practices and address regulatory problems in the current system. Governor John P. de Jongh, Jr. of the Virgin Islands called for a making the state's permitting processes 30 percent faster during this fiscal year.

Employee Costs

Governors are concerned with the size of the state workforce and the scope of employee salaries and benefits. Twelve governors from Delaware, Georgia, Hawaii, Indiana, Kansas, Nevada, New Jersey, South Dakota, Virginia, West Virginia, Wisconsin, and Wyoming mention downsizing the state workforce as part of state redesign efforts.

Nevada Governor Brian Sandoval announced that state employee salaries will be reduced by 5 percent this year to avoid layoffs and furloughs. Many other governors are ordering hiring freezes or reducing state positions. New Mexico Governor Susana Martinez plans to cut her own salary by 15 percent, and every member of her cabinet has agreed to cut his or her salary by at least 10 percent. Similarly, Kentucky Governor Steve Beshear and his cabinet cut their own salaries by 10 percent this year.

Georgia Governor Nathan Deal is reducing the state workforce by 10 percent by adjusting the authorized position count downward and eliminating about 14,000 positions, effectively freezing state employment at current levels. Kansas Governor Sam Brownback plans to eliminate more than 2,000 unfilled employee positions.

Pensions and Benefits

Lowering state employee costs will require restructuring state pension systems. The word "pension" is mentioned as many as 60 times by 14 governors. It is mentioned 21 times by New Jersey Governor Chris Christie, who said, "Without [pension] reform, the problem we face is simple: Benefits are too rich, and contributions are too small, and the system is on a path to bankruptcy."

Hawaii Governor Neil Abercrombie is proposing to end state funded reimbursement for federal Medicare Part B benefits for Hawaii government employees. The governor said, "It is a bonus paid for by taxpayers that can no longer be justified in light of our current fiscal and social crisis."

Governors are raising the retirement age, reducing benefits, and increasing employee contributions. Virginia Governor Bob McDonnell proposed to increase employee contributions.

Some governors are improving cost effectiveness by closing loopholes in their current pension systems. For example, Indiana Governor Mitch Daniels said, "The conflict of interest when double-dipping government workers simultaneously sit on city or county councils, interrogating their own supervisors and deciding their own salaries, must end."

HEALTH CARE

Virtually every state mentions health as a priority. Governors' speeches focus on health policy, including preparing for health care reform implementation. Medicaid was also mentioned as an important issue for governors' 2011 agendas.

Health Policy

Governors are planning for major changes in health policy in 2011. Nevada Governor Brian Sandoval included funding to plan for a Health Insurance Exchange, and submitted legislation to address the operation and oversight of a Nevada Health Insurance Exchange. Colorado Governor John Hickenlooper said the state is well-positioned to develop architecture for a health care exchange.

Governors are seeking to increase access, affordability, and quality of health care, while still lowering costs, through strategies like encouraging preventative care and using electronic medical records. Michigan Governor Rick Snyder, for example, called for vigorous improvements in the state's health care system in terms of cost, quality and access, with an emphasis on wellness and preventative care from primary care providers for all citizens. Vermont Governor Peter Shumlin called for the creation of a single payer health plan before spring; a move the governor said will save $500 million in the first year alone. Virginia Governor Bob McDonnell pledged to lead in innovation in delivery of health care services and improve training for our health care workforce by expanding the use of technology and electronic medical records to reduce costs improve quality and safety.

Some governors are moving toward new models of delivery to reach these goals. Idaho Governor C.L.

"Butch" Otter is convening a Medical Home Collaborative to pilot a coordinated managed-care initiative aimed at controlling health care costs. Similarly, New Hampshire Governor John Lynch highlighted the state's nine medical home pilots and an additional pilot project for Accountable Care Organizations in an effort to change the financial incentives of the health care system.

Some governors are proposing to redesign state health departments in an effort to increase efficiency. South Carolina Governor Nikki Haley expressed support for consolidating similar health and human service agencies into the governor's cabinet. Similarly, Wyoming Governor Matt Mead suggested reorganizing the Department of Health. He proposed allowing the governor to appoint the head of the Health Care Financing Unit and having that person report directly to the governor.

Medicaid

Medicaid is mentioned 68 times by at least 10 governors (Arkansas, Delaware, Georgia, Kansas, Kentucky, Mississippi, New York, South Dakota, Virginia, and Wisconsin). Governor Nathan Deal of Georgia said addressing Medicaid is a top priority of this administration. Kansas Governor Sam Brownback: "Next year, Medicaid will command over 18% of the state general fund, and the program is growing faster than the economy."

New York Governor Andrew Cuomo has created a Medicaid Redesign team to find efficiencies in the program in order to provide a better service for less money. Virginia Governor Bob McDonnell proposed managed care and other new incentives to control costs for the Commonwealth's entire Medicaid population. Mississippi Governor Haley Barbour announced plans to place 7,800 Medicaid beneficiaries into community care.

Arkansas Governor Mike Beebe is looking at ways to move from a fee-for-service model toward one that rewards results and not just treatment in Medicaid services. Governor Beebe proposed a self-imposed tax for Medicaid providers to ensure that more funding will be available and to capture more Medicaid matching funds from the federal government.

EDUCATION

Virtually every state mentions education as a priority. Governors recognize that education has implications for states' future prosperity. Nebraska Governor Dave Heineman said, "The University of Nebraska is a critical component to our state's economic future." South Dakota Governor Dennis Daugaard said, "The foundation of our economy is an educated workforce." Georgia and New Jersey's governors say education is their state's top priority.

Some governors are looking at redesigning their education systems with the goal of maximizing efficiency and performance. Washington Governor Chris Gregoire presented a sweeping proposal to enact legislation creating one agency, the Department of Education, to comprise one seamless education system from pre-school to Ph.D. South Carolina Governor Nikki Haley proposed allowing voters to decide if future governors should be given the authority to appoint cabinet heads like the Superintendent of Education. Similarly, Nevada Governor Brian Sandoval is proposing changes to the K-12 governance model to one in which the governor appoints the state board of education and the superintendent of public instruction.

Early Childhood Education

Despite budget shortfalls, several governors from states including Georgia, Hawaii, Kansas, Kentucky, Missouri, Michigan, New Hampshire, and Utah emphasized the need for early childhood education. Michigan Governor Rick Snyder announced it is now, "Time to view educational system as running prenatal through lifelong learning. It is really B-20, not just K-12." Utah Governor Gary Herbert proposed optional all-day kindergarten. Vermont Governor Peter Shumlin proposed expanding the state's pre-kindergarten program for ages three, four, and five by lifting the cap on the number of students counted in Pre-K funding.

Kansas Governor Sam Brownback proposed $6 million this year from the Children's Initiative Fund to the development of early childhood education centers in the state's most needy school districts. Missouri Governor Jay Nixon's budget for 2012 provides funding for early childhood programs such as First Steps, Head Start, and Early Childhood Special Education.

Hawaii Governor Neil Abercrombie announced efforts to develop a leadership position in the governor's office for early education to coordinate efforts across departments and in the private sector as the state lays the groundwork for the eventual establishment of a Department of Early Childhood.

K-12

The predominant topics among governors for K-12 education are maximizing state resources in the classroom; teacher pay; and school choice, with a heavy emphasis on charter schools. Several governors also mention STEM education as a key aspect of their education agendas.

Maximizing State Resources in the Classroom

A number of strategies are being proposed to improve school performance and efficiency. Governors are working to move funding from administrative costs to classrooms. New York Governor Andrew Cuomo, for example, proposed to introduce a $250 million competition for administration efficiency to reward districts that can find administrative savings through methods such as efficiencies and shared services. Nevada Governor Brian Sandoval proposed the creation of a Block Grant Program that encourages districts to be innovative and results-oriented.

Governors are working to stretch the value of education dollars by modernizing classrooms with an increase in virtual learning opportunities. Governors from Idaho, Nbraska, and New Hampshire mentioned virtual learning as a way to modernize learning opportunities and maximize efficiency. Nebraska Governor Dave Heineman voiced support for the state's $8.5 million initiative to develop a virtual high school using lottery funds. Delaware Governor Jack Markell announced the state will offer Chinese language courses online as part of Delaware's new requirement that high school graduates complete a foreign language requirement.

Teacher pay

Governors from Delaware, Indiana, Nevada, New Jersey, and Wyoming stressed changing the way teachers are paid so that effective teachers can be rewarded and ineffective teachers can be removed. New Jersey Governor Chris Christie stated, "The time to eliminate teacher tenure is now." Governor Christie proposed rewarding teachers based on merit, at the individual level, rather than seniority. He has established an expert task force of teachers, principals, and administrators to address the issue.

Nevada Governor Brian Sandoval also called for ending teacher tenure and proposed $20 million in performance pay for the state's most effective teachers. Delaware Governor Jack Markell proposed measuring student growth in every subject area so that teacher evaluations can be linked with how much their students learn in their classroom.

HIGHER EDUCATION

Governors view their higher education systems as a critical foundation for future prosperity. Nebraska Governor Dave Heineman said, "Economic success and education success are linked together. We need both." Gov. Heineman announced he will not reduce higher education funding this year, and proposed a one-time $25 million investment in the University of Nebraska to jump start and accelerate the development of Innovation Campus.

Several governors from states including Alaska, Arkansas, Hawaii, Missouri, Nevada, Utah, Virginia and Washington have set goals to increase degree completion. To increase college completion rates, governors are using two main strategies: performance-based funding for public colleges and universities and increasing access for students.

Performance-Based Funding

Governors are stretching higher education funding by moving to performance-based funding models. Arkansas Governor Mike Beebe said, "We can and must double the number of college graduates in Arkansas by 2025 if we are to stay competitive." The governor proposed tying funding for higher education institutions to completion and graduation rates instead of enrollment. Virginia Governor Bob McDonnell highlighted his goal for the state to issue 100,000 more degrees in the Commonwealth over the next 15 years; part of the governor's Top Jobs for the 21st Century initiative, which includes an enrollment-based funding model.

North Dakota Governor Jack Dalrymple will ask the board of higher education to develop a funding methodology that is based on the outcomes that education leaders and citizens would like to see from their college campuses. Similarly, Nevada Governor Brian Sandoval called on universities and community colleges to develop

a more strategic focus that connects degree programs and the state's economic development efforts.

Washington Governor Chris Gregoire encouraged "complete to compete" for increasing degree completion. The governor also called for tuition flexibility, greater accountability, and improved access through a $1 billion Washington Pledge Scholarship Program.

Increasing Access

Governors recognize that access to higher education is critical to increasing degree attainment and building an educated workforce. Vermont Governor Peter Shumlin said, "Ensuring that young Vermonters pursue post-secondary education is critical to our economic future." The governor proposed a sustainable higher education income tax credit that will enable Vermont students who live and work in the state to reduce their college debt. Maryland Governor Martin O'Malley will freeze in-state tuition for the fourth year in a row.

Governors from Alaska and Missouri are using scholarship programs to help increase access to higher education. Missouri Governor Jay Nixon's budget for 2012 includes funding for Missouri's most successful college scholarship programs, including programs to help keep top students at Missouri institutions and programs designed to improve students' preparation for careers in science and technology. The governor set a goal to increase degree completion from 35 percent of Missouri adults up to 60 percent. Hawaii Governor Neil Abercrombie also announced a goal for the University of Hawaii to increase the number of college graduates by 25 percent by 2015.

Several governors, including Georgia, Mississippi, Missouri, Nebraska, New Hampshire, and West Virginia emphasized support for community and technical colleges. Mississippi Governor Haley Barbour said, "Our community colleges have been and remain critical in the enormous and continuing improvement of skills in our workforce."

South Dakota Governor Dennis Daugaard announced that he will be sponsoring a bill to increase the bonding capacity of post-secondary tech schools to allow them to continue expanding their campuses and adding new programs. Similarly, West Virginia Governor Earl Ray Tomblin called for $28 million in new bond funding for upgrades at technical colleges.

ECONOMIC DEVELOPMENT

Economic development is a major challenge for states this year. Governors are talking about growing state economies and creating jobs, but have limited capacity to do so. The main strategies discussed in the State of the State addresses are investing in public universities; changing the state governance structure to better support private sector growth; and assisting small businesses through tax credits and regulatory reform, among other ideas.

Investing in Universities for Job Creation

Governors from Georgia, Hawaii, Kansas, Nebraska, and Virginia are pledging new state investment despite budget shortfalls. Kansas Governor Sam Brownback, for example, is proposing a three-year, $105 million University Economic Growth initiative to enhance job growth in key economic sectors such as aviation, cancer research, animal health, and engineering. Each university will be required to provide, through private sector or reprogrammed funds, 50 percent of the cost of the program initiative.

Nebraska Governor Dave Heineman proposed a one-time, $25 million investment to jump start and accelerate the development of the University of Nebraska's Innovation Campus. The governor also announced the Nebraska Internship Program to increase the number of college and university students interning with Nebraska businesses. This $1.5 million training program will be funded with redirected resources from the Nebraska Job Training Cash Fund and matched by funds from the private sector.

Creating Business-Friendly State Governance

Another way that governors are approaching economic development is through developing a business-friendly governance structure at the state level. Governors from Delaware, Kansas, Michigan, Missouri, Nebraska, New Hampshire, New York, Oregon, and South Dakota are creating councils or other one-stop shops designed to engage with the private sector and support economic growth.

Michigan Governor Rick Snyder proposed to offer statewide job posting services to every company that expands, relocates, or starts a business in the state. Similarly, New Hampshire Governor John Lynch's budget will include funding to create an online Business One-Stop Center, which will provide a central place for businesses to interact with state government.

Some governors are positioning to engage more directly with the private sector in economic development efforts. Nevada Governor Brian Sandoval, for example, is proposing to redesign the Commission on Economic Development and replace it with a cabinet-level private-public partnership, Nevada Jobs Unlimited. The governor is also recommending a 50 percent increase in General Fund dollars to run it.

Supporting Small business

At least 19 governors from states including Colorado, Delaware, Hawaii, Indiana, Kentucky, Maryland, Michigan, Mississippi, Missouri, Nebraska, New Mexico, North Dakota, South Carolina, South Dakota, Virginia, Utah, Washington, Wisconsin, and Wyoming specifically mentioned supporting small businesses as an economic development strategy.

Colorado Governor John Hickenlooper proposed establishing a venture capital fund for small businesses. South Dakota Governor Dennis Daugaard pledged to revamp the state's MicroLOAN program to prioritize loans to aid in the sale of small businesses and streamline approval and permitting processes.

Virginia Governor Bob McDonnell pledged $5 million in funding for Virginia Small Business Financing Authority to help small businesses gain access to capital. Nebraska Governor Dave Heineman is proposing a $7 million program, the Business Innovation Act, in part to expand small business outreach efforts.

New Mexico Governor Susana Martinez proposed encouraging small businesses to hire unemployed workers by covering part of their salaries for the first six months through the unemployment fund. Washington Governor Chris Gregoire proposed cutting the unemployment insurance and workers compensation rates by more than $1 billion to help businesses and the unemployed get back to work.

CORRECTIONS AND PUBLIC SAFETY

Seventeen governors discussed public safety and corrections systems. Governors from Arkansas, Idaho, and New Hampshire said that public safety is the top priority for 2011. For many governors, goals in this area are related to one thing: cutting costs while protecting public safety. South Carolina Governor Nikki Haley said one of the state's key challenges will be "reforming our adult corrections system and pulling us out of that deficit." Governors are focusing on reducing prison populations to reach this goal.

Reducing Prison Populations

Recognizing that housing prisoners poses significant costs to state budgets and is increasing in many states such as Arkansas, Delaware, New Hampshire, New York, Vermont, and Virginia, governors' discussion of corrections was largely focused on safely reducing prison populations and reducing recidivism. Several governors, including Delaware Governor Jack Markell called for using evidence-based practices to make targeted reforms in corrections.

Vermont Governor Peter Shumlin proposed several reforms to better use prison space, estimated to save the state $2 million. The governor also proposed investing $1 million in prevention and alternative justice in community-based programs across Vermont to help keep non-violent offenders out of jail.

Many governors focused on reducing recidivism rates in juvenile systems. Arkansas Governor Mike Beebe said, 'We will protect our people and not use up a bed that some kid who, given a second chance, could turn his life around, but still needs to undergo the consequences of criminal behavior in a different way."

ENVIRONMENT AND ENERGY

More than 20 governors talked about environment and energy priorities for 2011. Governors are focusing on energy, water, and leading by example through making government more energy efficient. Vermont Governor Peter Shumlin, for example, said, "Increasing investments in energy efficiency is a top priority of my administration."

Energy

Many governors, including Alaska, Nevada, North Dakota, and Virginia, mentioned energy as part of their economic development strategies. Virginia Governor Bob McDonnell referenced his goal to make Virginia the "Energy Capital of the East Coast."

Governors outlined a broad range of energy priorities, with a main focus on renewables such as wind, solar, and energy efficiency, to meet the energy needs of the future. Kansas Governor Sam Brownback said, "I want Kansas to be known as the not only as the Wheat State - but as

the Renewable State." Maryland Governor Martin O'Malley called for passage of the Maryland Offshore Wind Energy Act, which would require power companies in the state to purchase offshore wind power.

Nevada Governor Brian Sandoval called for strengthening the state's leadership role in the renewable energy and energy efficiency industries through ongoing efforts, such as the Nevada Retrofit Initiative partnership with higher education, nonprofits, and local banks for the construction and financing of residential energy efficiency retrofits, and Renewable Energy Loan Fund. The governor called for the development of business models this year that will allow for the export of renewable energy to California.

Alaska Governor Sean Parnell stated that he has set out to derive 50 percent of the state's electrical power from renewable sources by 2025 through several significant state investments, including $25 million for renewable energy grants; $10 million for a Southeast Energy Grant Fund; and $25 million for weatherization.

Water

Several governors cited water as a major state priority. Colorado Governor John Hickenlooper said water is his top priority. Similarly, Georgia Governor Nathan Deal said, "One of the biggest threats to that future is water." The governor is recommending a new state investment of $300 million, spread over the next four years, for reservoir creation and expansion.

New Hampshire Governor John Lynch will establish by Executive Order a commission to create a 20-year Water Sustainability plan for evaluating the infrastructure, investments, and other measures the state must make to ensure that New Hampshire families, businesses, and communities have the clean water they will need in the future. Wyoming Governor Matt Mead also voiced support for funding new water development projects.

Lead by Example

States continue to lead by example in promoting energy efficiency and other best practices for the environment. States such as Missouri, New Mexico, New Hampshire, and South Dakota have downsized state vehicle fleets and state travel to realize emissions reductions and cost savings. Missouri Governor Matt Mead estimates the savings from these reductions at close to $7 million in the next two years. New Mexico Governor Susana

Martinez ordered a one-year moratorium on all new state car purchases, except for law enforcement.

New Hampshire Governor John Lynch estimated $3 million in savings realized through reducing energy use across all state agencies.

TRANSPORTATION AND INFRASTRUCTURE

At least 10 governors highlighted transportation as a state priority. Some governors have even proposed new investments during these tough economic times. For example, Virginia Governor Bob McDonnell presented a plan to invest $4 billion in transportation over the next three years. He does not plan to increase taxes and will create a new $1 billion Virginia Transportation Infrastructure Bank through $1.1 billion in direct Grant Anticipation Revenue Vehicle (GARVEE) bonds and leveraging as much as $6 billion in bonds for public-private partnerships.

Vermont Governor Peter Shumlin is proposing to spend $106 million on improvements to more than 65 bridges and culverts and preventive maintenance work on dozens of other structures. The governor said that expanding passenger and freight rail is also a top priority.

The governors of Delaware, Nevada, and New Hampshire also voiced support for new revolving loan funds for infrastructure investment. Wyoming Governor Matt Mead proposed diverting revenue from the state's statutory severance tax on minerals to fund roads and bridges.

Michigan Governor Rick Snyder created a new executive group to bridge gaps between state government's investments in economic development, transportation, and housing and better position the state to revitalize communities by linking the state's departments of economic development, transportation, housing, and energy.

TAXES

The word "tax" is mentioned more than 370 times in the 35 State of the State addresses surveyed for this brief. Governors are focusing on two things: lowering taxes and examining tax expenditures.

A number of governors express the desire to lower taxes in their speeches. Governors from Delaware, Indiana, New Jersey, South Dakota, and West Virginia pledged no new taxes this year.

Many governors are reconsidering tax expenditures to recoup revenue where they are not producing desired results. Missouri Governor Jay Nixon asked the members of the legislature to consider implementing the recommendations of the governor's bipartisan tax credit commission, which spent four months reviewing Missouri's 61 tax credit programs.

Some governors are acting to repeal tax expenditures that are not producing desired results. New Mexico Governor Susana Martinez proposed reducing the state's film subsidy from 25 percent to 15 percent, which is where it first started. Kansas Governor Sam Brownback intends to fund job creation programs by eliminating corporate tax subsidies.

Hawaii Governor Neil Abercrombie proposed a repeal of the state tax deduction for state taxes and to begin treating pension income like all other income for tax purposes in an effort to increase state revenues. The governor announced proposals to increase the alcohol tax and will also propose a fee on soda and similar drinks. Revenues from these fees will be used to repair the public health infrastructure and fund prevention and education programs.

Governors from New Hampshire, Wisconsin, and Wyoming voiced support for extending tax credit programs targeting job creation.

CONCLUSION

Government redesign efforts are coloring virtually every aspect of state policy in 2011 as governors adjust to the new normal in the wake of the great recession. The State of the State addresses reflect the top issues for governors this year: the budget, the size of state government, and jobs.

NOTES

1. The 35 states included in this analysis are: Alaska, Arizona, Arkansas, California, Colorado, Connecticut, Delaware, Georgia, Hawaii, Idaho, Indiana, Kansas, Kentucky, Maryland, Michigan, Mississippi, Missouri, Nebraska, Nevada, New Hampshire, New Jersey, New Mexico, New York, North Dakota, Oregon, South Carolina, South Dakota, Utah, Vermont, Virginia, Virgin Islands, Washington, West Virginia, Wisconsin, and Wyoming.

37

Right Turn: A New Congress Intent on Fiscal Discipline Means States Can Expect Little Budget Help from Washington

Norman J. Ornstein

With Republicans taking over the majority in the House after the 2010 mid-term elections, fiscal conservatism may preclude future federal-to-state funding sources.

From *State Legislatures,* February 2011.

A few weeks after the November elections, a news story triggered a national controversy: In Arizona, state officials decided summarily to deny organ transplants to Medicaid patients, including snatching a new liver away from a dying recipient.

Shortly thereafter, another flap arose in Indiana, with a decision by the state government to deny a 6-month-old on Medicaid a life-saving treatment that works in more than 90 percent of such cases, calling it experimental.

These decisions—made in Arizona by the administration of newly elected Governor Jan Brewer and in Indiana by that of Governor Mitch Daniels—were caused by the excruciating budget pressures hitting every state. The need to balance budgets in a sagging economy, coupled with ballooning Medicaid costs driven in part by stubbornly high unemployment, are precipitating unpleasant, even embarrassing, administrative decisions and actions for well-regarded and less-well-regarded state governments alike.

These Medicaid controversies had nothing to do with the Affordable Care Act, the health care reform Republicans like to call "Obamacare." And they were unrelated to the election results. Their implications, however, are very much affected by the midterm elections and the political alignments they will produce.

They may be a harbinger of the problems states will face as a cadre of Republican fiscal hawks take power in Congress; challenges to federal health care reform work their way through the courts; and state lawmakers—many of them new to office—try to close deep budget gaps. Even in the face of high unemployment and increasing demand for state services, legislators can expect little in the way of a fiscal helping hand from Washington.

HISTORIC GAINS

The 2010 midterm elections were by every standard an historic partisan sweep. The GOP gained the most seats by either party in the U.S. House of Representatives since 1948 (the most in a midterm since 1938), a victory that also included handsome gains in the U.S. Senate, governorships, state legislatures and further down the ballot. To be sure, Republicans fell short of their standard set in 1994, when they captured not just the House after 40 years of wandering in the desert of the minority, but the Senate as well. This time the Senate proved elusive. But the huge gains across the board were more impressive since they came only two years after the Republican Party had been declared nearly dead by a coterie of pundits.

There also were dramatic changes at the state level, suggesting something more profound than just a short-term, spasmodic rejection of the status quo and the party in power. Republicans ended up with the largest number of state legislative seats since the Great Depression, with big gains especially striking in both the Midwest and the South. The Midwest had been a bastion for Democrats, who now are reduced to fewer than 40 percent of the legislative seats there, the lowest number in more than 50 years. The Minnesota Senate has a Republican majority for the first time in nearly a century.

Republicans captured both houses in the Alabama Legislature for the first time since Reconstruction and the North Carolina Senate for the first time since 1870.

In 1990, Republicans held no state legislative majorities in the South and only 26 percent of the seats. Today, they control 18 legislative chambers and have 54 percent of the seats. Moreover, a slew of Democrats in Southern legislatures have switched parties since the election, suggesting a deeper cultural shift and a sign, from ambitious politicians, that the future is brighter on the red side than the blue in states such as Georgia and Louisiana. Republicans now have a firm grip on power in more states than at any time in modern memory, with 29 governors, 25 state legislatures—another eight split—and full control in 20 states, compared to only 11 for Democrats.

THE NEW WAVE

This was the third straight wave election, an extraordinarily unusual phenomenon.

The first two waves moved in the same direction, producing big gains for Democrats in 2006 and the recapture of both houses of Congress, and an across-the-board landslide for Democrats in 2008. Both of those elections were characterized by unhappiness over two wars and the economy. There also was anger at Washington, driven by a sense that the parties were more interested in their insular, partisan battles and protecting their special interests than in getting together to solve our collective problems. The focus of ire was the Republicans.

That same anger erupted in 2010, but this time, the agents of change in 2006 and 2008 became the enemies of change, and the Democratic president and his majority Democrats took the hit. Perhaps ironically, this wave of anger actually began before Barack Obama was elected. The vote in September 2008 for the Bush administration's Troubled Assets Relief Program or TARP was seen by voters as emblematic of a Washington out of control—rewarding the miscreants who had triggered the economic collapse using the tax dollars of those who had suffered.

TARP was followed by the bailout of the auto industry, a stimulus package passed without a single Republican vote in the House that seemed to have little direct impact on the sagging economy, and then a focus more on health reform and less on jobs. All that led to the giant public backlash against the Democrats.

The results left Republicans at all levels ebullient. But GOP congressional leaders and many governors cautioned their legislative colleagues and acolytes in the media not to overreach or overreact. The election, they said, was much less an embrace of Republicans than a rejection of Democrats and the status quo. The lesson was to focus on jobs and growing the economy, and on the core issues where Republicans were in sync with a majority of voters: cutting the size and scope of government, including rolling back the health care plan; continuing the push to cut taxes; and focusing on the emerging problems of ballooning deficits and debt.

Leaderly caution notwithstanding, rebellious new members, many of them boosted by the Tea Party movement, are much more inclined to move quickly and dramatically to fulfill what they see as their mandate: taking a meat ax to Washington and to government, slashing and burning existing programs and ways of doing business.

Post-election surveys showed that voters, by nearly 2-to-1 margins, want to see cooperation and compromise in Washington. They overwhelmingly approved the first sign of cooperation, the bipartisan deal on taxes achieved by the White House and congressional Republicans in December. But there were few signs that the deal would herald more bipartisan action. It adds substantially to deficits, making the pivot to deficit and debt reduction even more challenging.

In the U.S. House, nearly all of the members of the freshman class, numbering more than one-third of the Republican majority, made clear that they will not vote in the spring of 2011 to increase the federal debt limit unless deep spending cuts were already achieved or voted for. There was near-unanimity on the desirability of banning earmarks, and incoming House Budget Committee Chairman Paul Ryan suggested that the House budget would begin by freezing discretionary domestic spending at 2008 levels.

NEW POWER, NEW CHALLENGES

For incoming governors and state lawmakers, the new positions of power brought challenges in some ways greater than those of their predecessors, many of whom lost in the wave. For those predecessors, the difficulties of balancing state budgets in a deep recession were ameliorated by stimulus money. That money will run out, however, by the time the new leadership teams take over, and will not be supplemented by the new stimulus programs in the bipartisan tax deal. Nearly all those tax breaks go directly to individuals. At the same time, state governments have been through wave after wave of budget cutbacks, including all the fat and much of the muscle, leaving few easy choices. Continuing stubborn

> *Republican governors will turn to ... Congress for help when times get especially tough. Those Republican allies in Congress, however, will be going through their own agony as they search to find more acceptable budget cuts to fulfill their promise to reduce deficits and debt.*

unemployment levels, along with sagging home prices and high foreclosure rates, have made the demand for state services, especially Medicaid, soar.

One side benefit of the tax deal for states and localities is the continuation for a year of unemployment benefits. If those benefits had ended, the pressure on Medicaid and on hospitals hit with surges in emergency room calls by those with no other health care option would have been greater yet, as would the demand on other social services.

But heavy demands will remain. No doubt, many Republican governors will turn to their friends, colleagues and supporters in Congress for help when times get especially tough. Those Republican allies in Congress, however, will be going through their own agony as they search to find more acceptable budget cuts to fulfill their promise to reduce deficits and debt. They face a landscape in which tax increases are off the table and voters want to reduce deficits without painful cuts to Social Security, Medicare, defense or programs other than foreign aid. In the face of their own headaches, the willingness of Republicans in Congress, much less Democrats, to help out Republican governors and state legislators will be nearly nonexistent.

These aren't the only challenges for governors and state legislatures. Passage of the health reform act puts a series of requirements on states, including the need to create the insurance exchanges that are a core part of the bill. That is complicated by a combination of legal challenges to the constitutionality of the bill and especially to another core element, the individual mandate to purchase insurance. Couple that with the vow by incoming House Speaker John Boehner and his leadership team to try to delay or deter implementation of the health reform act, and states face deep uncertainty in their efforts to comply with a complex and moving target.

There is one potential bright side to the nasty and brutish governing times ahead. Senators Ron Wyden, an

Oregon Democrat, and Scott Brown, a Massachusetts Republican, have introduced a bill to accelerate from 2017 to 2013 the date at which states can offer their own alternative plans for health reform and delivery to replace the system under the Affordable Care Act, so long as they meet the same standards of coverage and affordability.

Their idea has met with a positive response from many liberals and conservatives alike. That suggests there may be a broader coalition willing to move more in the direction of freedom for states to innovate. There may be room to create tradeoffs where, if states are not going to get federal subsidies at rates they have been promised or received in the past, they will have more freedom to experiment with their own efficiencies and different delivery systems.

At a time of even more belt-tightening and fiscal austerity, that may be scant comfort. But it may be all states have for at least the next two years.

38

Governance Challenges and Options for State and Local Governments

Bruce J. Periman

Three experts weigh in on how local and state governments can and should respond to the daunting challenges exacerbated by the Great Recession, agreeing that a few things must change for future viability—new leaders, new structures, and better governance.

INTRODUCTION

There is little new in a view that State and Local Governments are having a difficult time during what has come to be called the Great Recession. What is new is the endeavor to understand the dimensions and key factors in what is a global crisis for State and Local Governments in the United States. An innovative approach would be to attempt to explain the dynamics of this crisis facing State and Local governments and look for ways to address it. Accordingly, we decided to take up the effort and examine the challenges for Governance at the State and Local levels in our current situation of sustained economic downturn and look at how they might be addressed. This is an undertaking that is likely to provoke thought in those interested in how we govern the non-Federal parts of our government in the United States and that, ultimately, may raise as many questions as it answers.

Because this is the final issue of Volume 42 of the State and Local Government Review, the first volume done completely under the auspices of its new publisher, Sage Publications, Inc., we wanted to do something that was both provocative and innovative for the Governance Matters section. In keeping with our desire to innovate, we decided to try something we had not done before in the Review: ask experts for their opinions. Fortunately for us, we were able to convince three experts who have their fingers on the pulse of policy and practice in state and local governments across the United States and who have within arm's reach the latest data and research on what is transpiring in them, Jacqueline Byers, Director of Research for the National Association of Counties, Chris Hoene, Director of the Center for Research and Innovation of the National League of Cities, and John

From *State and Local Government Review,* 2010.

Thomasian, Director of the Center for Best Practices of the National Governors' Association. We cannot thank them enough and are sure that readers will feel the same.

They were consulted in a two-hour "roundtable discussion" phone conference on September 9, 2010, moderated by the editor of the Governance Matters section, who is also the author of this piece, though not the author of the ideas in it: those ideas belong to our experts. Each of the three experts took five minutes to give their views about challenges. Then they discussed their views in a follow-up conversation. The follow-up was far ranging, but all three continued to come back to certain issues that constitute the themes presented here.

Not surprisingly, these themes comprise the fundamental issues and problems that state and local governments face in the current climate. The ideas of our experts concerning them are outlined below. These ideas include such things as demand for and the organization of services, existing debt—whether financial or structural— and the Intergovernmental system as well as political will and leadership. What might be done about these issues and problems is discussed below in a conclusion that draws on the ideas and views of our experts.

GOVERNANCE CHALLENGES AT THE STATE AND LOCAL LEVELS IN THE UNITED STATES: VIEWS OF RESEARCH DIRECTORS

As might be expected, our experts all touch on a recurring theme that has been the topic of several iterations of the GM section: the impact of the "Great Recession" on State and Local governments. However, unlike many commentators, they did not focus on the event as either a, unique, "one off" occurrence or without opportunity for State and Local governments. Rather, they agreed that from the perspective of State and Local Governments, though abrupt and sudden, the economic crisis was an exacerbation of historical conditions for them and not a trajectory shifting event.

Spending, and the Recession: Paying for State and Local Government

The problem for State and Local Governments is not just that they have too little now, but that they have had too much in the past. Economic growth and therefore

revenues from sources as diverse as building permits to local property taxes, outpaced demand in most local jurisdictions and thus masked the structural problem that levels and types of service demand in local jurisdictions was growing at an unsustainable rate.

Services. From this vantage point, the recession was not so much an event as a wakeup call. It has led to recognition of service demands that may need to be rethought, at the very least. As Chris Hoene from National League of Cities (NLC) put it

> The current pressures are not new, really. Local governments have had a structural imbalance problem going back to at least the mid or late 1970's. A key problem is that the public is not willing to pay for the full range of expected services. But sustained growth in the 1990's masked the underlying structural problems; it exacerbated problems by giving cities the opportunity to keep spending by expanding services without worrying how to pay for them in the longer term. Today's discussions about whether taxes or spending are too high or too low lose the battle to reconfigure services before it has begun. We need a new social compact of what people expect from government and we need to do a better job in government of asking and challenging what the public wants. There are all sorts of assumptions about what people want that are out of line. For example, public safety is often viewed as a core service that has to be provided first. This may not be true for all places.

Although in agreement with the notion that Chris expressed about structural problems in the mismatch between the expectations of citizens, their willingness to pay, and the rising costs of local government, Jackie Byers from National Association of Counties (NACO) saw the problem as having an even earlier origin:

> The problem goes back to the 60's and 70's maybe even the 50's. We were in a false reality; living on false money. I agree that the boom masked problems. NACo tried to conduct a survey in the late 90s to see how much revenue counties were

receiving from the growth they were experiencing and officials couldn't say because they were busy expanding services to meet this new growth. Local officials are going to have to learn how to adjust citizen expectations of service delivery. Originally counties were created as administrative districts of the state in order to carry out service delivery at a level that is closer to people; that is their job. They are going to have to start looking for new ways to deliver services that includes regionalism, functional consolidation or consolidation of governmental entities, outsourcing and privatization.

John Thomasian from the National Governors Association (NGA) agreed that the problems were similar, though not identical as we will see, at the State level. He focused more on the notion of core services and how difficult getting citizen involvement in this area can be. Like Jackie Byers, he saw a need to reinvent government:

We have a big problem. State revenues will not return to a 2008, pre-recession level until 2013 by many estimates. At the same time, the cost of government services continues to rise. We have to addresses things like reinvention in government: what will it do, what will it not do, and how can it do it better? One of the biggest challenges is how to get citizens to take ownership of these decisions. How do we make citizens part of those decisions about what the core services of government should be? But this is not just making sure that they are part of that decision, but that they understand the ramifications of those decisions on the services they expect.

Debt. While the changing economy affects operating budgets negatively, it may present an opportunity for capital budgets. Moves by the central bank to stimulate lending have kept interest rates low. This may make this the right time to attend to interest rate needs, provided that the debt can be serviced. Two of our experts saw this as a possibility. Chris Hoene thought that

Local governments should be looking at their overall debt, their needs, and at the interest rates. Local governments have huge infrastructure needs. If debt levels are reasonable, it may be a good time for more investment. A lot of recent popular media

has focused on the prospect of municipal defaults, but the outliers are driving the attention when it comes to government debt. Most local governments are in relatively good shape. The debt problem is mostly at the Federal level.

And John Thomasian agreed that the problems of only a few states affected perceptions:

When people talk about big State bond debt they are talking about New York, Illinois, and California. Also worries about using this debt for operating budgets is over played. Ninety-nine percent of states have limits on this in law.

All three agreed that the situation in which we find ourselves today in State and Local Governments is a result of the tide of rising expectations for government services finally swamping budgets as the recession hit and growth and development declined. "We are all on the same page on this," concurred John Thomasian of NGA. However, the three saw clearly that the impact was somewhat different at the County and City level than it was at the State because of the different responsibilities for delivering public services and the different revenue sources.

On one hand Cities and Counties are hardest hit by the reduction in growth and development and the subsequent reduction in property and ad valorem taxes and thus their ability to pay for services and service debt. On the other hand, States are hardest hit by the rising demand for services as declining State and Local economies stress the social safety net and require more individual economic support for citizens such as work searches, assistance to needy families, and Medicaid matches or support for local education. Additionally, States find themselves in the same situation of maintaining current service levels while revenue shrinks as do local jurisdictions.

One interesting agreement among our three experts on the impact of this structural problem is the political impact of the situation with regard to polarization of publics. Calls for cutting government are not really about cutting the delivery of core services, but rather about scaling back this growth of expectations from citizens. Likewise, attempts to protect these service levels are not really about essential core services but about protecting political constituencies. In addition they agreed that, getting this done will take both leadership and political will.

Leadership and Political Will

One result of the demand for change that our panelists saw was the increased need for leadership to lead the change and the political will to make it. The sort of polarized politics that are seen on the national level will not support either. John Thomasian strongly made the point that, although enormously challenging, at the State and Local level, the current economic crisis presents opportunity as well as challenge:

> The current environment is creating political will for change. What kind of services we deliver is no longer sacrosanct. Even the way government provides education is no longer sacrosanct. There are risks in trying to solve these problems, but also opportunities. Looking at everything government does must be on the table.

In agreement with him about the need and possibility of leadership, but also its difficulty was Chris Hoene:

> The organizations that are leading best adapt. Leadership is hard but it means using the bully pulpit. It means telling people how the world is changing and what needs to be done. Leaders have to manage relationships and deliver outcomes that cross the lines of agencies, sectors, and publics. Leaders pull people together and ask "what do we need to get things done?

Nevertheless, although clear about the need for a change in service levels and hopeful about achieving it, Jackie Byers had a somewhat narrower idea of its scope at the local level. She saw governance problems involved in local mandates and limited discretion given by the United States Intergovernmental and Constitutional system. In short, our system does not give local jurisdictions the sort of control needed to cut back some essential services and this presents a twofold challenge. First, changing these services may require changes in legal structures—whether Constitutional or statutory—that are difficult to achieve without the cooperation of legislatures or wide ranging

referenda. Second, often these services are the ones most affected by the economic downturn. As she sees it:

> 80-90% of services that are provided are mandated by state or federal law not by the counties themselves. It is difficult for counties to cut back some things. Most counties have a constitutionally elected sheriff who runs a mandated jail. They cannot privatize him. It is very difficult for counties to figure out how to get out of this on their own. Many have to go back to state legislatures or to a referendum to get the authorization they need to make these governance and service delivery changes. They really have little discretion over what they can or cannot deliver.

All three of our experts were emphatic about one thing: to lead in the situation in which we find ourselves now in State and Local Governments will take not only leadership but the political will to use it: it will take courage. This new leadership will come from people who were working on national campaigns and who will arrive to statehouses with some clout at the national level, from individuals who have held executive office before and either know the challenges that await them and the levers to pull to get things done, or from some, at the Gubernatorial level especially, who do not care about ruffling feathers but understand what must be done and are not afraid to do it. In Thomasian's words:

> What is the thing we will need over the next couple of years above all else? Strong leadership. Governors are going to have to burn political capital shrinking government. It will take an extraordinary type of leader who can do this and can make the tough choices.

If new leaders are elected who know how to and actually do cut the size of their government, the effect may be large and long lasting. Certainly, it will change the style of Governance almost immediately. The impact of this sort of leadership and cutting Government or shifting responsibilities on our structure and system of Governance cannot be underestimated. Strong, intelligent, focused leadership, especially at the State level, will change our system of Governance: some things done by

States will be done by localities; some services delivered by localities will be delivered by the private sector; some services will not be delivered at all and the resources devoted to them in both sectors will be into other enterprises or needs (the financial sector comes to mind). All three experts agree that the new brand of leadership will need to help State and Local Governments decide on core services. This has a good chance at the Local level as Chris and then Jackie point out:

> We worry less about party differences at the local level. Party lines are not very clean at local levels. Most local systems routinely have people from both parties working together. Local staff in particular is usually made up of highly professionalized people who cope with the reality of governing and delivering services day to day. If someone takes up a national issue, the local officials may politicize the debate, but they rarely have the levers to make the change.
>
> People do not pay attention locally to what can be done at the national level. There are very few things that translate from national political issues to the local level. County officials need to figure out how to get the roads fixed and snow removed and other activities that are far removed from national politics.

Nevertheless, it is easy to talk of core services, but it is difficult to build a legislative and citizen consensus on what they are exactly. There is no way of knowing what agreements strong leaders can craft for cutbacks and what they will be. Will it be reductions in State support for social services or education that might be shifted to the third sector and which some think are too broadly supported today? Or will it be a further scaling back of Services that are squeezed already like public defenders or district attorneys? Could it be the erosion of openness and transparency in State and Local Governments through such moves as changes in the time limits involved in or the way costs are born in seeking public records and inspecting public information? One citizen's discretionary government service is another's essential government obligation. Ahead of time, there is no way to know if the baby will be sliding down the drain with the bath water.

In addition, the impact of strong leadership that results in effectively cutting back government on Governability is not to be discounted. If strong leadership results in effective legislative and public consensus about what we can and should pay for at different levels of government, we could see a less polarized and more positive, participative, and hopeful electorate. If these changes take place in a climate of difference and thin political margins, they may result in greater disaffection with, less affection for, and stronger resistance to the political process.

Federalism and Intergovernmental Relations

Of course, even with strong and enlightened leadership, change will not come easily. Some of the structures and processes to which states and localities are subject as well as those they use are formal, others are informal or customary. The relations of State and Local Governments among themselves and with the Federal Government are the most notable of these. Some of the conditions for working with the Federal government are set by law and others are influenced by the style of the Federal Government. Relations among cities and counties can be formal arrangements set by the Feds or a State, while others, for example interjurisdictional service contracts, are completely determined bilaterally. Change will have to come within the framework of Federalism and in Intergovernmental Relations (IGR). This is one of the most important areas of Governance for states and localities.

According to our experts, the state of IGR could be better. Unfortunately, they do not believe that it is getting better. Moreover, due to the strains of the recession and reconfigured federal programs, it may be getting worse. All of them see this as an accelerated but not new phenomenon and crucial for State and Local, as well as Federal policies to work. Moreover, the fault is mostly the Federal Government's in their view. As Chris Hoene said commenting on the view from municipalities:

> The federal government has spent twenty to thirty years breaking the IGR system. It's now at the point where officials at the different levels of government do not know how to talk to each other anymore.

Whether a governor and mayor can talk depends on their relationship and their political parties some times. The success of the Obama stimulus package was largely based on a functioning IGR system, but that system had been undermined by previous administrations on both sides of the aisle. Rather than focusing on getting money to where it was needed the most, the stimulus package emphasized transparency above everything. The result was that the federal government was blaming local and state governments for not adequately spending funding that hadn't been delivered efficiently via federal agencies.

From the State perspective, it is not any better. Yet, another problem is the illogical interdependence that has built up in the IGR system because of the pressures to get things done. John Thomasian summarized his view from the States as:

There are lots of interconnections that function well but they can make problems, too. There are some IGR connections that are getting in the way of things. Our system has semi-sovereign entities within semi-sovereign entities. Even at the state level, there are many local jurisdictions that maintain independent but similar functions as their neighboring jurisdictions. This requires states to spread local aid across redundant services that could be delivered more cheaply through consolidation. Some of this is forced by state laws and constitutions. We really have to unravel these things. But it will take some time and cause problems.

From the county level, there is a need for strengthening or creating other IGR structures. These ought to help to fix the system and get it working. Jackie Byers sees the greatest opportunity in IGR as occurring between the States and localities and the greatest need for mediating structures that integrate regions more closely:

We need more metro governments like Kansas City, Indianapolis, Metro-Dade, and others. The question is how do you have an intervening level? That is the only way to manage transportation; through things like MPO's. We had lots of these regional planning groups in 1976: every state drew

up regional plans but we missed the boat on continuing to use them effectively in the long term. It is difficult to do transportation or economic development on the single local level. Several states have established planning regions and they work. However, the ability to do regional planning for service delivery and comprehensive land use continues to be a missed opportunity and a challenge for many governments.

Federalism and the federal government. Clearly, the three see the Federal government's interference, attempt to strongly guide and dictate what happens at the local level, and the Federal government's move to deliver services, when they try, as not only usurping the functions of local government, but badly done. All three agreed that the Federal government needs to reduce its role in States and Localities but provide more resources. The attempt by the Federal Government to get involved in lots of things at the local level transfers Federal paralysis and inability to execute to the local level, where much innovation has gone in American government. Jackie Byers saw direct effects in current controversies

The Federal Government has been polarized for so long that they are not tackling the issues that are most important, like immigration, to localities. Border counties are being crushed by the services demanded of them due to the Federal Government's dominance of certain issues and their failure to act. That's why we have Arizona and Prince William County in the headlines. No one at the local level has over arching authority to solve these problems themselves.

On a more philosophical level, this was echoed by John Thomasian from NGA:

There is a pathetic lack of understanding of the Federalist system at the Federal level. They are not schooled in how that system works. The assets to do things are at the State and Local level, and it is a big mistake to try and run things from Washington. The federal government plays its role best when it sets performance standards. But when the Federal Government gets into delivering services they mess up badly.

In response, Jackie Byers focused on the way the Federal Government has created a necessity to act first in order for local governments to get things done:

This is like the Federalism of the sixties. If we want it done the Feds have to do it. To get anything done, first you have to go to the Feds and say, 'you have to make a law.'

All three were clear on what the Federal government can do well, cannot do well, and how they should do it:

Outside of civil rights, human rights, the federal government is best equipped to redistribute money and that should be its principal role in the IGR system. Service delivery should be tailored at the local level and the federal government should help redistribute dollars to meet local needs. (Chris Hoene)

John Thomasian agreed:

We need block grants, with broad aims and structures. Environmental laws are a good example. The federal government sets broad performance goals, but most of the standard setting, enforcement, and compliance strategies are done by states and localities with federal financial support. The federal government can provide funding and performance targets, and they can use cooperative agreements with states to carry out programs. But Washington does not have the assets to deliver services.

Federal mandates and regulation. Similarly, they concurred that the weight of Federal government decisions and mandates stressed States and Localities as much as the Federal Government's failure to act. The lack of funding to get things done was a clear problem for them. As Thomasian saw it

Most of the fights have been about regulations that have no money behind them. Take the 'Real ID' legislation, for example. This created a massive burden for States that they did not want with little money to do it.

And Jackie Byers saw not only the same problem, but an irony:

There is always something at the Federal level that is not funded: they have training grants but no dollars to put behind them. Take the new regs for the Americans with Disabilities Act (ADA). Counties are scrambling to implement these but don't have the money, especially now and the Feds demand but don't finance compliance. Renovations to older facilities can cost them three times as much today as when they should have done them. Counties would be in a better position today, if they had complied 12 years ago. Now, they are opened to lawsuit, if they have not complied to any degree.

State and local relations. Our experts could agree on the need for the problems in and the need for changing IGR between the Federal Government and the States and Localities. Nevertheless, when it came to IGR between the States and Localities, there was not complete agreement. In discussing things like money coming from the Federal Government to States and localities or from States to Local Government, there were some differences on how to handle this. The biggest disagreement was not over the appropriate level of administrative costs kept at the State level—something that does come up in City Hall's and County Governments—but rather the appropriate control of the distribution of the dollars. As might be expected, John Thomasian saw the largest role for the States

All money should flow through States. The big problem is Federal money that goes directly to Cities because it may be out of whack with the political goals of the State. It is the State that has responsibility to make sure that monies are distributed between the urban and rural areas to achieve broader goals.

However, both Jackie and Chris thought this was too pat and disagreed. They did not believe Governors or State Governments are the best arbiters of local needs in a State. Nor did they think this was done on the basis of need. Jackie Byers was clear on the latter point:

Much of the distribution of federal pass through funding is not done rationally on need. States make political decisions about where they distribute money and who gets it. Dollars go into transit in urban areas and not bridges and roads in rural areas because of where the votes are. Even state CDBG pass through agencies often make political decisions about where the money will go.

Chris Hoene agreed emphatically. He also echoed an earlier theme about regional structures:

For example, it comes down to whether to fund bridges in Northern Michigan or rapid transit in Detroit and which of these choices serves more people? The states had too many lower-priority projects that were designed to never actually be taken off the shelf, but were technically "shovel-ready," and were funded as a result. Many of the projects served relatively few people and produced relatively few jobs. Plus, local governments are not structured to cooperate, which is a role that the States can play. ARRA would have been better off structured around economic regions.

Benefit Costs and the Meaning of Work in the Public Sector

Each of the panelists did have a take on costs to State and Local Governments with respect to things other than direct service delivery. They did agree across the board that the cost of benefits was a key issue. However, they differed somewhat on the importance of Health Care costs in the benefit package. For example, Jackie Byers had this to say about Health Care costs:

Our big challenge is getting a handle on the costs of health care. This is not a result of the health reform law but is exacerbated by it. States will have to help people get insurance or provide it through Medicaid. To do this, States will have to cut costs. It is an albatross around the neck of states. Here at NACO we think that health and pension benefits will take counties down. GASB has forced us to look at this quite extensively. The reality is that the only way that the public sector could compete

with the private sector in the past for top employees was through good benefits, like in Health Care. If we change this, how will counties get good people?"

Chris Hoene agreed on the importance of Health Care, but had more to say about other benefits as well:

I would have to include pensions along with Health Care—these two liabilities are on an unsustainable track. Pensions are a local policy issue: we can only get a handle on them by restructuring contracts and their benefits. Health care is the opposite. Most Health Care cost issues are driven by costs that are system-wide and that are the same for the private and public sectors.

John Thomasian agreed about benefits but did not see Health Care costs for retirees as the same problem for State or Local Governments as pension benefits.

We are all on the same page about benefits. But the health care benefits for retirees are different from pension benefits. Most states are able to alter how much they pay for retiree health care because these benefits are not embedded in contracts or state constitutional requirements. Pension benefits are different. They are harder to alter—and should be—for current retirees. That is why most of the pension changes are directed at new employees.

The importance of benefits is tied up with the importance of work and the attractiveness of employment. On this topic our experts agreed on one thing: that the meaning and structure of work in the public sector was changing and would change even more. However, they differed on whether labor market factors or demographic changes were the largest influence on this area. Chris Hoene came down as much on the latter area as the former:

One of the biggest challenges for the future will be restructuring what work means in the public sector. The whole sector is out of kilter in terms of attracting and retaining the best people, most of whom are looking for careers that bridge sectors. There used to be this assumption that the public sector was a lifetime career and that has changed. Today, the best people want to float between NGOS and the private and public sectors.

To a degree, Jackie Byers agreed:

Counties are laying off people. They have to do the same work without as many workers which makes the job more difficult. Attracting people and getting them to stay will be difficult. It is generational: a lot of young people won't devote ten to fifteen years to any job. Maybe they will give five years. Counties need to experiment. How do they recruit good people, train them and get them to bring in the knowledge and new ideas that they have?

However, there was not unanimity on the importance of this issue. For one, John Thomasian did not share the views of the other two:

This issue is at the bottom of my list. Government is and will be downsizing and shedding jobs. However, even without big benefit and pension packages, government jobs remain good jobs. Government won't have any problems attracting people in the foreseeable future.

Yet Chris Hoene thought that not only was recruitment of good people a problem but highlighted the affects of Local public pension systems on the retention and promotion of good people.

We need to worry about both ends of the career spectrum: new people and experienced people. There are problems at both ends. Young people wanting to make change in the world often look at government as a life sentence, so we need to restructure salaries, benefits, and incentives to make public service less bureaucratic. At the other end we have all these incentives in place so that a really good local manager at the peak of his or her profession has every incentive, due to pension and benefit systems, to retire with a nearly full pension and take the same job in a community down the road at the same salary level.

FINAL THOUGHTS: CHANGE IN STATE AND LOCAL GOVERNMENT

Our focus group of three experts in State and Local Government did not agree on everything. However, they did agree on a surprising number of things. The thing on which they agreed most emphatically was the desirability and likelihood of change. Maybe this was because of the shared circumstance of the financial crisis. Jackie Byers pointed out:

We all provide services. If I could make one change it would be to encourage all local officials to play nice in the sandbox. Local government officials have to do this, but they don't want to give up any of their power or authority. They need to be able to divide up the work and reinforce each other across jurisdictional boundaries. It is reinvention of government: every single government does not have to do everything.

Chris Hoene thought there was a possibility of change due the current conditions:

Crisis makes for strange bedfellows. Certainly we are not blaming each other for the situation. If we had this conversation five years ago it would not have had such unanimity.

John Thomasian was emphatic that de facto change is on the way in leadership in the form of elections. He also saw a need for change and believes that, although it was occurring already and that it would continue, he did not think it would be radical in nature unless citizens supported fewer services:

We are looking at a sea change in the executive branch of States. We will see twenty-seven to thirty new administrations in January. That said, we are not going to see radical changes of agenda at the State and Local level unless citizens stand behind those changes. Throughout the last few decades, the public continues to demand the same core services from government. Elected officials need to do a better job explaining the true implications of smaller government to these core services.

CONCLUSION

Our experts paint a transfixing, if not a pretty picture of the challenges for effective governance at the State and Local level in the United States. In some respects, it is like the proverbial train wreck: impossible to look at for long but impossible to look away as well. Just how we got in this mess is not completely clear and how to get out of it is not obvious at all. However, two themes run through the remarks of the commentators as suggestions for how to start to address the challenges we face and these two themes should be explored in conclusion: the need for new leadership and the need for new structures.

New Leadership: Political and Managerial

Political leadership is not an easy theme to explore; leadership in the American political system can often look like "followership." Clearly, that is not what our three experts are advocating. They advocate leadership in decision making about the mix of, responsibility for, and resources devoted to public services expected by citizens at the State and Local levels of government.

The current crisis presents an opportunity for reconditioning the publics' expectations about service levels, who will deliver them, and how much they will cost. All are in agreement that this moment is unique because for the first time in perhaps forty years, the tide of rising expectations may be falling. So, the crisis presents not only challenge but an opportunity.

Nevertheless, it is apparent from what our experts say that a certain sort of leadership must be achieved to help us benefit from the moment, make these important decisions, and thus lead us out of the problems that we face today. This is a sort of leadership that has two characteristics. First, this leadership is *political* because it aims at accomplishing things and getting them done, investing political capital when needed, using the bully pulpit if necessary, or power sharing when that is what will get results. Second, this leadership is *managerial because* it must embrace a technical understanding of what is required to formulate and implement policy and the role that government organizations and government management play in achieving an efficacy in service delivery that gives government a good name.

Where successful, the new leadership will take its cues less from the party and the electorate and be more concerned about giving them their cues. The new style of leadership necessary to help guide us through the new era of reduced national power, reduced economic growth, and reduced expectations and inspire the necessary transformations in our State and Local governance structures will not aim at adopting policies because they are popular and translate into votes. Rather, it will aspire to win votes through accomplishment and proven change rather than pandering to voters.

What this may mean in practice for new leaders who are elected officials is that fewer of them will be reelected and that fewer may decide to stand for reelection. For public officials who are not elected, it may mean taking more risks and perhaps leaving public service earlier than expected. Also, it may mean that more experienced people will seek to reenter the world of public service who are sufficiently experienced to get the job done and yet are sufficiently senior that they have little to prove or no aspiration beyond doing the right thing. In any event, it will take someone with all of these qualities to get us through the wilderness of the great recession to the promised land of rising resources.

In addition, the new leadership will need to focus not only on presenting the right thing to the public but on making sure the option presented is technically solid and feasible. Accordingly, our political leaders must have a renewed respect for and understanding of the importance that sound management of public entities plays in getting us where we need to go at the State and Local level. This is nothing short of having public officials— both elected and appointed— who are technically adept, data-driven, and take managerial decisions.

In practice what this means for elected officials is that they will have to understand that there is a distinct advantage of good management and deep technical knowledge for their broader political and legislative agendas. Just as decoupling political leadership from votes makes genuine leadership possible and changes the political game from giving the public what they want to convincing the public that the technical decisions taken are what they need, coupling political leadership with an interest in managerial efficiency makes it possible for leaders to move their broader agenda. It does so by reducing resources needed for policy out-put—that is what efficiency does—and either lessening pressure on leaders when trying to distribute or, in the best of cases, giving them slack resources.

It is worth mentioning that this element of public management in leadership is present to a large degree at the local level in the figure of the City Manager. This may be a good model for the kind of leadership we need at the State and Local levels across the board: loosely coupled to politics and more closely coupled to management and technique. Nevertheless, the technical orientation does not predominate always, even for City Managers, so further structural change will be necessary to make this a reality and the notion of a public management component in leadership for public officials reaches to elected officials as well as appointed ones like City Managers.

New Structures and Better Governance

Our experts spoke both passionately and profoundly for our need to think through a little more our structures of governance at the State and Local levels. As they pointed out, it is not necessary for all State and Local governments to do everything they do now and do it using the same mechanisms and organizational configurations that they have currently.

Simply put, Governance is how a society's or polity's government is carried out; that is, the mix of institutions, processes, and mechanisms whether public or private. Governability, a related but separate concept, is the capacity of a society or polity to govern or be governed. Therefore, the discussion about structures of government in this essay is mostly about Governance yet to a lesser degree it has implications for Governability.

Our experts do recommend, though not directly, a way of addressing these issues. This recommendation consists in making greater use of underworked governance structures that group existing governments together. These are the mediating, mid level, and regional structures like Councils of Governments, Regional Authorities, or contracting relationships that State and Local governments can use to plan, pay for, and deliver services especially those that are cross-jurisdictional and require a stewardship of capital infrastructure that endures beyond electoral terms. Such structures can be used for two key ends. First, they can be employed to shore up the weak and nearly dysfunctional relations between the federal government and other governments. Second, they can be employed to locate services more effectively and to support the delivery of services more efficiently rather than leaving everything in the current default position of local delivery.

It is the nonconstitutional and non-foundational existence of such structures that recommends them. Not being pegged to a constitutionally mandated figure like a sheriff or tied to a function like health or public welfare specifically granted to a government by a constitution or other charter, these structures can link governments together when it makes sense for them to coordinate activity, pool resources where economies of scale obtain, and keep large scale, capital intensive efforts (e.g., trains) going through long-term planning and ensure their ability to collect revenue and finance growth and improvement in these efforts. They can be the glue that holds governments together and makes them more governable for the public officials that have to run them.

One caveat is important to note here: just how these changes can be incentivized or can come about on their own is not immediately obvious. Just who will steward them or if they can be developed is not an easy question to answer. The fomentation of changes in and the addition of governance structures, even if only temporary, perhaps through the efforts of the Federal government or through the offices of other bodies like NGA, NLC, or NACO could provide support for needed change. There is a lot to gain by moving in this direction. Strengthening governance at the State and Local level might improve the govern-ability of these jurisdictions as well and thus promote a downward spiral in their costs of doing business. Too, these changes would provide a context for the new leadership outlined here to grow and to nurture success in the way we govern ourselves. We just have to remain convinced, as are our experts, that Governance Matters.

39

Seeking Solutions

Alan Greenblatt

As the federal government stalls on immigration reform, more and more state and local governments are taking matters into their own hands. Utah and Arizona have taken opposite approaches to the problem of increases in undocumented workers, and their success or failure may influence other states' and national policy.

Utah legislators are crafting a compromise on immigration law that could end up being a model for across-the-aisle cooperation for other states. Last year, Republican Governor Gary Herbert signed a bill requiring employers to check the citizenship status of their new hires through the federal E-Verify system. He said he would sign it only if legislators agreed to come back later in special session to soften the law, making the verification requirement voluntary for the first year.

Before the governor could call legislators back to Salt Lake City, however, Arizona had passed its controversial immigration law.

Arizona's Senate Bill 1070 required local police to check the immigration status of individuals they had reason to suspect were in the country illegally. Many lawmakers there believed the estimated 500,000 illegal immigrants in the state contributed to an atmosphere of violence and they had lost faith in the federal government to take meaningful action.

It now seemed to Herbert that if he asked the Utah Legislature to reopen its immigration bill, lawmakers might emulate Arizona's tough new approach instead of softening it.

"The mood had changed," says Utah Representative Stephen Sandstrom.

Even though the number of illegal immigrants in the country had dropped from more than 12 million in 2006 to about 11.2 million in 2010, according to the Pew Hispanic Center, many people support tougher laws. National polls following passage of the Arizona law showed a majority of Americans supported the legislation, and even larger majorities supported individual aspects of the

From *State Legislatures,* March 2011.

law, such as making it a crime to support someone who is an illegal immigrant.

Although much of the law was struck down by a federal judge a day before it took effect, Sandstrom still thinks Utah should follow Arizona's lead.

Nonetheless, Sandstrom has been working with legislators from both parties for months on a version of the bill that would not only impose tougher penalties on illegal immigrants and their employers, but also would allow new immigrants into the country to meet specific workforce needs. Sandstrom insists this hybrid approach is "not a compromise."

> *"We're going to crack down on the illegals who are here in the country, but at the same time there's a need for migrant workers."*
>
> —Utah Representative Stephen Sandstrom

"It's kind of the carrot and the stick," he says. "We're going to crack down on the illegals who are here in the country, but at the same time there's a need for migrant workers."

If the bill passes, it may provide a model for other states that are still looking for the best ways to address illegal immigration.

MIXED HISTORY

Congress has been unable for years to come up with any sort of approach that can satisfy those concerned with the public safety and costs associated with illegal immigration, while also satisfying those who believe removing more

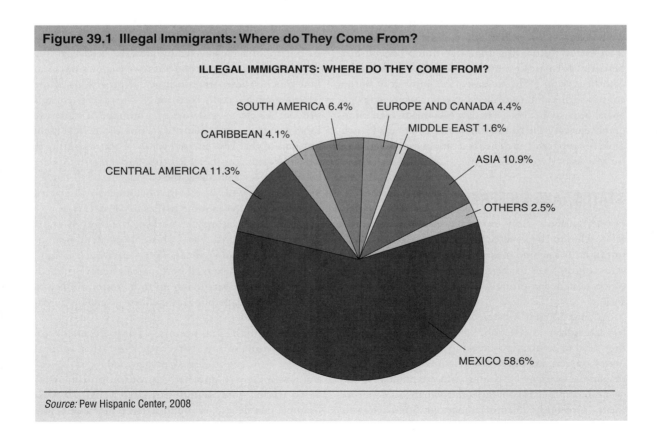

Figure 39.1 Illegal Immigrants: Where do They Come From?

ILLEGAL IMMIGRANTS: WHERE DO THEY COME FROM?

SOUTH AMERICA 6.4%
EUROPE AND CANADA 4.4%
CARIBBEAN 4.1%
MIDDLE EAST 1.6%
CENTRAL AMERICA 11.3%
ASIA 10.9%
OTHERS 2.5%
MEXICO 58.6%

Source: Pew Hispanic Center, 2008

than 11 million illegal immigrants from the country would cause economic chaos and human rights abuses. A Congress now under divided control will likely make little progress at all.

"Continuing political stalemate is the most likely scenario. Congress is not going to act," says Stephen Camarota, director of research at the Center for Immigration Studies, which favors a tough approach on immigration.

There have been laws restricting immigrants since the late 19th century. More recently, the federal Immigration and Nationality Act of 1965 eliminated country-specific quotas and nearly doubled the number of legal immigrants who could enter the country.

The 1986 Immigration Reform and Control Act granted legal status to 2.7 million illegal immigrants and tried to curb future illegal immigration by establishing penalties for employers who knowingly hired them. Another law in 1996 increased the number of border control agents and made illegal immigrants ineligible for Social Security benefits. The law even made legal immigrants entering the country after 1996 were made ineligible for programs such as food stamps and Medic-aid for five years.

STATES TAKE DIFFERENT PATHS

For several years now, states have adopted different approaches to the issue. Some have tried to help illegal immigrants become more productive by offering in-state tuition rates to their children or setting up state offices designed to promote a smoother integration into society.

Arizona Senator Kyrsten Sinema says that although legislators have to give police and prosecutors the tools they need to combat law-breaking, it's incumbent upon both Congress and the states to figure out a more "comprehensive" strategy for coping with the millions of illegal immigrants already in the country than just deporting them. "Obviously, an enforcement-only approach is not going to work," Sinema says. "That is what we've been

> *"Obviously, an enforcement-only approach is not going to work. That is what we've been doing for the last several decades, and it's been a failure."*
> —Arizona Senator Kyrsten Sinema

doing for the last several decades and it's been a failure."

Suman Raghunathan, an immigration policy specialist for the Progressive States Network, says that "contrary to popular belief, not all state-level legislation is restrictive and anti-immigrant."

State lawmakers have passed numerous bills addressing worker shortages in different sectors, and helping legal immigrants with housing, employment, education and other things.

Most attention, however, continues to focus on laws that make life more difficult for illegal immigrants and those who hire or house them. It's been a big shift from the trends that were prevalent a decade ago.

"It does seem that the people who want enforcement are somewhat better organized at the state level," Camarota says.

But after having enacted hundreds of laws regarding illegal immigration over the last few years, it's not clear how much stricter states can get. If provisions of the Arizona law are restored through the federal appeals process, it's clear legislators in a number of states are interested in copying many of its provisions. The main portions of that law have not survived court scrutiny as yet, however. Another idea that some legislators are considering—challenging the citizenship of all native-born children under the 14th Amendment—is guaranteed to provoke even more battles in the courts.

Although states may be pushing the limit by crafting policy in an area that is primarily a federal responsibility, that doesn't mean they won't keep trying. Many state lawmakers of both parties believe the federal government isn't living up to its responsibility to address the issue, despite recent efforts to step up border enforcement.

"The fundamental premise of any discussion on immigration policy rests with the failed federal poli-cies—the abject, dismal, pathetic failure of the federal government to do what it is constitutionally mandated to do," said Republican Utah Senator Curtis Bramble in a debate on immigration policy just before the Legislature convened.

His Democratic colleague, Utah Senator Luz Robles, could hardly agree more: "Regardless of where you stand on immigration," she says, "Congress has failed to address this problem."

It's clear legislators want to find ways to address illegal immigration. The issue was one of the few to command widespread attention in last year's election season, amid the dominant concern about the economy. Many state lawmakers believe the costs associated with illegal immigrants far exceed any benefit they bring into state and local coffers through tax revenue.

STEPPING UP ENFORCEMENT

Although state lawmakers may be running short of truly innovative ideas in this area, they won't stop seeking ways to better enforce existing laws or borrowing ideas from one another. The many new Republican governors and legislative majorities will likely help spread so-called pro-enforcement legislation to more states.

"Even if there isn't anything radically new, there's an increase in the number of states saying, 'We're going to protect ourselves,' " says Ira Mehlman, a spokesman for the Federation for American Immigration Reform, an anti-immigrant group.

Some ideas that seemed cutting-edge or even radical when they were first introduced have gained widespread acceptance. The E-Verify program, for example, which requires employers to check on the eligibility of employees to work in the United States, has survived most court challenges. Arizona's law imposing penalties on companies that knowingly hire illegal immigrants is currently before the U.S. Supreme Court. If it is upheld, other states are expected to join the few that already have passed similar legislation.

The federal 287(g) program, which allows trained police officers to carry out federal law enforcement functions, was approved in 1997, and the Florida Department of Law Enforcement signed on in 2002. Although most participants are city and county law enforcement agencies, additional states are looking into signing up. The Secure Communities strategy, which calls for sharing information—such as fingerprint records—between federal agencies and local law enforcement, is becoming even more entrenched.

"You're certainly going to see a lot more cooperation between local law enforcement and the feds," says Tamar Jacoby, president of ImmigrationWorks USA, a coalition of employers. "They've widened an avenue that more states are going to go down."

Oklahoma Representative Randy Terrill says his state will be looking for ways to provide local police and sheriff departments more incentive to vigorously enforce the laws that are on the books. He has introduced legislation that would allow the seizure of property in crimes involving illegal immigrants.

"Basically, [my bill] will take the latest Arizona legislation and add to it," he says, "creating enhanced criminal penalties for illegal immigrants who are involved in drug crimes and human trafficking, and who have guns."

COLLABORATIVE APPROACH

In taking Arizona to court over issues raised by SB 1070, the Obama administration may have sought to ward off efforts in other states to pass copycat legislation. Despite the court ruling in the administration's favor, however, lawmakers in several other states have introduced their own versions of the legislation. The court decision, some say, provided only a road map for avoiding potential legal pitfalls.

"Of course, the decision has zero bearing in Utah, but it was prudent to look at it," says Sandstrom. "I made changes to my enforcement bill that makes it better, so that it will pass the scrutiny of the courts."

The biggest change from when Sandstrom first considered such legislation, however, is his willingness to pair it with ideas for training and hiring new immigrants. Businesses and church groups—including the Mormons—have supported a "compact" to promote legislation that would show respect for illegal immigrants and keep their families intact.

"We've been working on creating a coalition of both progressives and conservatives," says Utah's Robles. "We're becoming the laboratory state for both a comprehensive approach and accountability."

Robles compares the potential for finding legislation that works for people across the spectrum of opinions on illegal immigration to earlier breakthroughs in the states, such as Wisconsin's approach to welfare in the 1990s. It remains to be seen whether a deal can be reached in

Figure 39.2 Types Of Legal Immigration

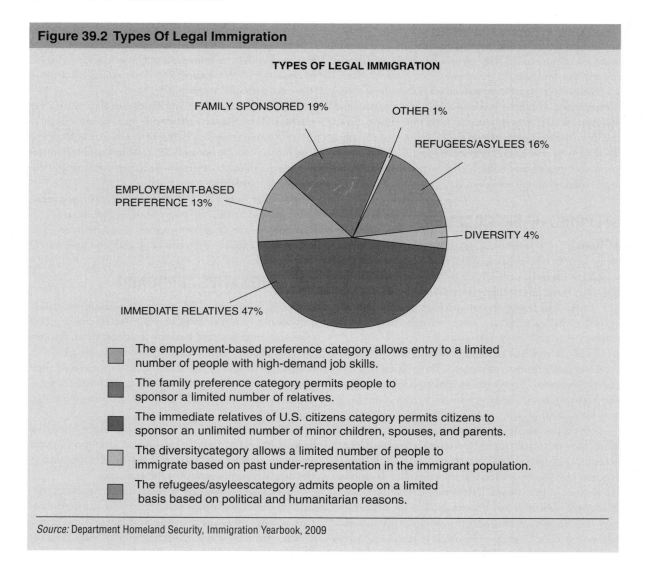

TYPES OF LEGAL IMMIGRATION

FAMILY SPONSORED 19%

OTHER 1%

REFUGEES/ASYLEES 16%

EMPLOYEMENT-BASED PREFERENCE 13%

DIVERSITY 4%

IMMEDIATE RELATIVES 47%

The employment-based preference category allows entry to a limited number of people with high-demand job skills.

The family preference category permits people to sponsor a limited number of relatives.

The immediate relatives of U.S. citizens category permits citizens to sponsor an unlimited number of minor children, spouses, and parents.

The diversitycategory allows a limited number of people to immigrate based on past under-representation in the immigrant population.

The refugees/asyleescategory admits people on a limited basis based on political and humanitarian reasons.

Source: Department Homeland Security, Immigration Yearbook, 2009

Utah, and whether such a bipartisan approach will travel as rapidly across state borders.

Advocates nationwide are watching.

"An extremely conservative, overwhelmingly Republican state is considering saying that 'enforcement only' is not the way to go on immigration," says Jacoby. "It's quite exciting. Everyone in the state wants to come together and find a consensual answer. I haven't been in a state legislature where you find that kind of enthusiasm in a long time."

Text Credits

Chapter	Credit
1.	© National Conference of State Legislatures. Alan Greenblatt. 2010. "Federalism in the Age of Obama." State Legislatures. July/August: 26-28.
2.	John R. Lombard and John C. Morris, State and Local Government Review, Vol. 42, No. 1, pp. 73-81. Copyright © 2010 by John R. Lombard and John C. Morris. Reprinted by permission of SAGE Publications Inc.
3.	Donald Kettl. 2010. "What Really Matters in Health-Care Reform." Governing. http://www.governing.com/columns/potomac-chronicle/What-Really-Matters-in-Health-Care-Reform.html#. Accessed January 28, 2011.
4.	By Emily Badger, Miller-McCune.com. Emily Badger. August 3, 2010. "An End Run on the Electoral College." Miller-McCune. Http://www.miller-mccune.com/politics/an-end-run-on-the-electoral-college-20276/#. Accessed January 24, 2011.
5.	© National Conference of State Legislatures. Karen Hansen. 2010. "Red Tide." State Legislatures. December: 14-17.
6.	By Emily Badger, Miller-McCune.com. Emily Badger. June 3, 2010. "Prison-Based Gerrymandering Dilutes Blacks' Voting Power." Miller-McCune. Http://www.miller-mccune.com/politics/prison-based-gerrymandering-dilutes-blacks-voting-power-16880. Accessed Nov. 29, 2010.

7.   Josh Goodman. 2010. "The Future of Redistricting and Rural America." Governing. Http://www.governing.com/topics/politics/Future-redistricting-rural-america.html. Accessed November 29, 2010.

8.   Material used courtesy of Campaigns & Elections. Micah Altman and Michael McDonald. January 20, 2011. "The Dawn of Do-It-Yourself Redistricting? Online Software Puts Redistricting Tools in the Hands of the Public." Campaigns & Elections. Http://www.politicsmagazine.com/magazine-issues/January-2011/The-Dawn-of-Do-It-Yourself-Redistricting. Accessed January 31, 2011.

9.   Material used courtesy of Campaigns & Elections. Lara Brown. October 27, 2010. "Restlessness Unleashed: The Tea Partiers and the Lessons of History." Campaigns & Elections. http://www.politicsmagazine.com/magazine-issues/October_2010/Relentlessness-Unleashed-The-Tea-Partiers-and-the-Lessons-of-History. Accessed February 10, 2011.

10.   Pamela Prah. March 12, 2010. "Tempest in a Tea Party." Stateline.org. Http://www.stateline.org/live/printable/story?contentId=468058. Accessed October 12, 2010. Stateline is a nonpartisan, nonprofit news service of the Pew Center on the States that reports and analyzes trends in state policy.

11.   © National Conference of State Legislatures. Garry Boulard. 2011. "The Great Divide." State Legislatures. February: 22-24.

12.   Louis Jacobson. 2011. "State Political Parties Stand the Risk of Losing Major Party Status in Future Elections." Governing. http://www.governing.com/blogs/politics/State-Political-Parties-Stand-the-Risk-of-Losing-Major-Party-Status-in-Future-Elections.html#.

13.   © National Conference of State Legislatures. Alan Greenblatt. 2011. "Newly in Charge." State Legislatures. April: 17-21.

14.   Russell Nichols. 2011. "Dealing With Term-Limited Legislators." Governing. http://www.governing.com/topics/politics/dealing-with-term-limited-legislators.html#. Accessed January 10, 2011.

15.   © National Conference of State Legislatures. Karl Kurtz and Brian Weberg. 2010. "What Legislatures Need Now." State Legislatures. July/August: 47-50.

16.   Melissa Maynard. December 20, 2010. "Legislatures Expand Training for New Members." Stateline.org. http://www.stateline.org/live/printable/story?contentId=536402. Accessed February 7, 2011. Stateline is a nonpartisan, nonprofit news service of the Pew Center on the States that reports and analyzes trends in state policy.

17.   Josh Goodman. 2010. "Goodbye Moderate Governors, Hello Partisans." Governing. http://www.governing.com/topics/politics/goodbye-moderate-governors-hello-partisans.html. Accessed November 29, 2010.

18.   Stateline Staff. February 17, 2011. "Governors Set the Agenda for a Lean 2011." Stateline.org. http://www.stateline.org/live/details/story?contentId=551280. Accessed April 4, 2011. Stateline is a nonpartisan, nonprofit news service of the Pew Center on the States that reports and analyzes trends in state policy.

19.   Josh Goodman. 2010. "The Rise of Attorneys General." Governing. http://www.governing.com/topics/politics/The-Rise-of-Attorneys-General.html#. Accessed November 30, 2010.

20.   John Buntin. 2011. "The Nation's Only Health Insurance Commissioner Takes on the Health-Care System." Governing. http://www.governing.com/topics/health-human-services/Nations-Only-Health-Insurance-Commissioner-Takes-Health-Care-System.html. Accessed February 14, 2011.

21.   Emily Rock and Lawrence Baum. 2010. "The Impact of High-Visibility Contests

for U.S. State Court Judgeships: Partisan Voting in Nonpartisan Elections." State Politics and Policy Quarterly 10 (4): 368-396. From State Politics and Policy Quarterly. Copyright 2010 by the Board of Trustees of the University of Illinois. Used with permission of the University of Illinois Press.

22. Sample, James, Adam Skaggs, Jonathan Blitzer, Linda Casey. 2010. "Executive Summary." In The New Politics of Judicial Elections, 2000-2009: Decade of Change. Charles Hall, ed. Brennan Center for Justice, NYU Law School; Justice at Stake Campaign; National Institute of Money in State Politics. http://www.brennancenter. org/content/resource/the_new_politics_of_ judicial_elections/. Accessed April 13, 2011.

23. Brennan Center for Justice, NYU Law School; Justice at Stake Campaign Brennan Center for Justice. Nov. 3, 2010. "2010 Judicial Elections Increase Pressure on Courts, Reform Groups Say." http://www .justiceatstake.org/state/judicial_elections_ 2010/election_2010_news_releases.cfm/ 2010_judicial_elections_increase_pressure_ on_courts_reform_groups_ say?show=news&newsID=9129. Accessed April 13, 2011.

24. Harkness, Peter. March 2011. "Public Servants as Public Enemy #1." Governing. http://www.governing.com/columns/ potomac-chronicle/Public-Servants-Public-Enemy-1.html. Accessed April 13, 2011.

25. Fehr, Stephen C. Nov. 4, 2010. "Election Adds Pressure to Change Public Pensions." Stateline.org. http://www.stateline.org/live/ details/story?contentId=526037. Accessed April 14, 2011. Stateline is a nonpartisan, nonprofit news service of the Pew Center on the States that reports and analyzes trends in state policy.

26. Hoene, Christopher W., and Jacqueline J. Byers. July 2010. "Local Governments Cutting Jobs and Services." Research Brief. The United States Conference of Mayors, National League of Cities, and National Association of Counties. www.usmayors. org/pressreleases/uploads/LJAreport.pdf. Accessed April 14, 2011.

27. Buntin, John. April 2011. "Does Government Work Require Government Employees?" Governing. http://www.governing. com/topics/public-justice-safety/Does-Government-Work-Require-Government-Employees-.html. Accessed April 14, 2011.

28. Greenblatt, Alan. April 2011. "States Handing Off More Responsibilities to Cities." Governing. http://www.governing .com/topics/mgmt/States-Handing-Off-More-to-Cities.html. Accessed April 18, 2011.

29. Benedict S. Jimenez and Rebecca Hendrick, State and Local Government Review, Vol. 42, No. 3, pp. 258-270. Copyright © 2010 by Benedict S. Jimenez and Rebecca Hendrick. Reprinted by permission of SAGE Publications Inc.

30. Patton, Zach. September 2010. "Colorado Springs' Do-It-Yourself Government." Governing. http://www.governing.com/ topics/mgmt/Colorado-Springs-DIY-government.html#. Accessed April 18, 2011.

31. Greenblatt, Alan. July 10, 2010. "The Big Apple: Urban Incubator." National Journal. National journal by GOVERNMENT RESEARCH CORPORATION. Copyright 2010 Reproduced with permission of NATIONAL JOURNAL GROUP, INC. in the format Textbook via Copyright Clearance Center.

32. © National Conference of State Legislatures. Eckl, Corina. February 2011. "Deep Holes, Few Options." State Legislatures. http://www.ncsl.org/?tabid=22080. Accessed April 19, 2011.

33. Weldon, Tim. January/February 2011. "Bringing State Tax Systems into the 21st Century." Capitol Ideas. http://www.csg .org/pubs/capitolideas/Jan_Feb_2011/ TaxCommissions.aspx. Accessed April 19,

2011. Reprinted with permission from The Council of State Governments.

34. Patton, Zach. April 2011. "Lottery Revenues Not a Sure Bet." Governing. http://www.governing.com/topics/finance/lottery-revenues-not-sure-bet.html. Accessed April 19, 2011.

35. Chavers, Mikel. January/February 2011. "Efficiency in State Government." Capitol Ideas.http://www.csg.org/pubs/capitolideas/Jan_Feb_2011/EfficiencyinState Government.aspx. Accessed April 19, 2011. Reprinted with permission from The Council of State Governments.

36. © National Governors Association. Reproduced by permission of the National Governors Association. Further reproduction prohibited. Stewart, Lauren. February 7, 2011. "Interim Analysis: 2011 State of the State Addresses." NGA Center for Best Practices. www.nga.org/Files/pdf/ SOTSINTERIMANALYSIS2011.PDF. Accessed April 22, 2011.

37. © National Conference of State Legislatures. Ornstein, Norman J. February 2011. "Right Turn: A New Congress Intent on Fiscal Discipline Means States Can Expect Little Budget Help from Washington." State Legislatures. http://www.ncsl.org/?tabid=22068. Accessed April 22, 2011.

38. Bruce J. Perlman, State and Local Government Review, Vol. 42, No. 3, pp. 246-257. Copyright © 2010 by Bruce J. Perlman. Reprinted by permission of SAGE Publications Inc.

39. © National Conference of State Legislatures. Greenblatt, Alan. March 2011. "A Special Report: Immigration and the States." State Legislatures. http://www.ncsl.org/?tabid=22261. Accessed April 25, 2011.